5⁰⁰

INCENDIARY
CIRCUMSTANCES

INCENDIARY CIRCUMSTANCES

A Chronicle of the
Turmoil of Our Times

AMITAV GHOSH

HOUGHTON MIFFLIN COMPANY

Boston · New York · 2005

For information about permission to reproduce selections
from this book, write Permissions, Houghton Mifflin Company,
215 Park Avenue South, New York, NY 10003.

Visit our Web site: www.houghtonmifflinbooks.com.

Library of Congress Cataloging-in-Publication Data
Ghosh, Amitav.
Incendiary circumstances : a chronicle of the turmoil
of our times / Amitav Ghosh.
p. cm.
Includes bibliographical references.
ISBN-13: 978-0-618-37806-7
ISBN-10: 0-618-37806-5
1. Ghosh, Amitav. 2. Authors, India — 20th century — Biography.
3. Journalists — India — Biography. 4. History, Modern — 1945– I. Title.
PR9499.3.G536Z466 2005
823'.914 — dc22 2005012175

Book design by Melissa Lotfy

Printed in the United State of America

MP 10 9 8 7 6 5 4 3 2 1

For details of previous publication and permissions, see page 305.

To Barbara and Jeffrey J. W. Baker

Acknowledgments

For believing in this collection and bringing about its publication, I would like to thank Barney Karpfinger, my agent, and Janet Silver, publisher, of Houghton Mifflin. However, this volume would not have found its present form but for Meg Lemke, who edited and oversaw it, and even suggested the title. I owe her a great debt of gratitude.

My thanks are due also to the editors who first published these pieces: Leon Wiesletier at the *New Republic,* Katrina Vanden Heuvel at *The Nation,* N. Ram at the *Hindu,* Michael Neumann at *Die Zeit,* and most of all, Bill Buford, who as the editor of *Granta* and then as the fiction editor of *The New Yorker* was responsible for seeing many of these pieces into print.

My wife, Deborah Baker, assisted at the birth of many of these essays, and my gratitude to her, is, as always, beyond measure. I am grateful also to my children, Lila and Nayan, not least for providing me with the hours of wakefulness in which many of these pieces were written. Finally, I am glad to be afforded this opportunity to thank Barbara and Jeffrey Baker, not just for being the most welcoming of in-laws, but also for personifying the openness and generosity of America at its best.

CONTENTS

PREFACE

Although these essays were written over a period of twenty years, some issues, themes, and concerns echo through all of them. The most important of these is stated, if only obliquely, in the passage from which the collection takes its title: "The deadly logic of terrorism is precisely to invite repression: it is thus that it brings into being the social gulf on which its existence is predicated. To write carelessly can all too easily add to the problem by appearing to endorse either terrorism or violent repression. In such incendiary circumstances words can cost lives, and it is only appropriate that those who deal in them should pay scrupulous attention to what they say."

These words were written not today or yesterday but ten years ago, as a meditation on an event that had occurred even earlier, in 1984: they are from "The Ghosts of Mrs. Gandhi," which was published in *The New Yorker* in 1995. But the passage owes its origins to a Gandhi other than that of the title: the Mahatma, who was for my generation of Indians what Freud had once been to Central Europeans — that is to say, a ghost who was proof against all attempts at exorcism. His ideas had to be contended with, precisely because they were so strangely at variance with the disorder and violence of the world we lived in. For me, the aspect of Gandhi's thought that has been most productive perhaps is his insistence on the identity of means and ends. There is no such thing, Gandhi tells us, as a means to an end: means *are* ends.

André Breton once wrote that a ghost is "the finite representation of a torment." It is in this sense that Gandhi's ideas shaped the question that haunts these essays: is it possible to write about situations of violence without allowing your work to become complicit with the subject?

No doubt the reason that this question had a special urgency for me was because the "incendiary circumstances" of the title have been a part of the background of my everyday life since my childhood. Until recently it was possible to believe that there was something unusual or exceptional about those circumstances — that they were merely an aspect of what V. S. Naipaul has called "half-made worlds." But not the least of the many momentous changes that have followed upon the tragedy of September 11, 2001, is the realization that the half-made world has become, as I write elsewhere in this collection, "the diviner of the fully formed."

It affords me no satisfaction that the "incendiary circumstances" of these essays are no longer exceptional anywhere in the world. But their contemporary relevance lies, I hope, not merely in the circumstances they address but also in the renewed urgency of the question of means and ends. For if there is anything instructive in the present turmoil of the world, it is surely that few ideas are as dangerous as the belief that all possible means are permissible in the service of a desirable end.

AMITAV GHOSH
Brooklyn, New York
February 14, 2005

INCENDIARY
CIRCUMSTANCES

THE TOWN BY THE SEA

2005

THE ANDAMAN AND NICOBAR ISLANDS are one of those quadrants of the globe where political and geological fault lines run on parallel courses. Politically the islands have been administered from the Indian mainland ever since their annexation by the British; today they are Indian "Union Territories," ruled directly by New Delhi. But geologically the chain stands just beyond the edge of the Indian tectonic plate. Stretching through 435 miles of the Bay of Bengal, the islands are held aloft by a range of undersea mountains that stand guard over the abyssal deep of the Sunda Trench. Of the 572 islands, only 36 are inhabited: the Andamans is the name given to the northern part of the archipelago, while the Nicobars lie to the south. At their uppermost point, the Andamans are just a few dozen miles from Burma's Coco Islands, infamous for their prisons, while the southernmost edge of the Nicobars is only 125 miles from the ever-restless region of Aceh. This part of the chain is so positioned that the tsunami of December 26, 2004, hit it just minutes after it hit the coastline of northern Sumatra.

Despite the hundreds of miles of water that separate the Andamans from the Indian mainland, many of the relief camps in Port Blair, the islands' capital city, have the appearance of miniaturized portraits of the nation. Only a small percentage of their inmates are indigenous to the islands; the others are settlers from dif-

I

ferent parts of the mainland: Bengal, Orissa, Punjab, Andhra Pradesh, and Uttar Pradesh. If this comes as a surprise, it is because the identity of the islands — and indeed the alibi for the present form of their rule — lies in an administrative conception of the "primitive" that dates back to the British Raj. The idea that these islands are somehow synonymous with backwardness is energetically promoted in today's Port Blair. Hoardings depicting naked "primitives" line the streets, and I heard of a sign that instructs onlookers to "Love Your Primitive Tribe." In most parts of the mainland, these images would long since have been defaced or torn down, for the sheer offensiveness of their depictions; not so on these islands, which are more a projection of India than a part of its body politic. As with many colonies, they represent a distended and compressed version of the mother country, in its weaknesses and strengths, its aspirations and failings. Over the past two weeks, both the fault lines that underlie the islands seem suddenly to have been set in motion: it is as if the hurried history of an emergent nation had collided here with the deep time of geology.

The mainland settlers in the camps are almost unanimous in describing themselves as having come to the islands in search of land and opportunity. Listening to their stories, it is easy to believe that most of them found what they were looking for: here, in this far-flung chain of islands, tens of thousands of settlers were able to make their way out of poverty, into the ranks of the country's expanding middle class. But on the morning of December 26, this hard-won betterment became a potent source of vulnerability, for to be middle-class, in India or anywhere else, is to be kept afloat on a life raft of paper: identity cards, licenses, ration cards, school certificates, checkbooks, certificates of life insurance, and receipts for fixed deposits. It was the particular nature of this disaster that it targeted not just the physical being of the victims but also the proof of the survivors' identities. An earthquake would have left remnants to rummage through; floods and hurricanes would have allowed time for survivors to safeguard their essential documents on their persons. The tsunami, in the suddenness of its onslaught, allowed for no preparations. Not only did it destroy the survivors' homes and decimate their families; it also robbed them of all the evidentiary traces of their place in the world.

On January 1, 2005, I went to visit the Nirmala School Camp in Port Blair. The camp, like the school in which it is housed, is run by the Catholic Church, and it is presided over by a mild-mannered young priest by the name of Father Johnson. On the morning of my visit, Father Johnson was at the center of an angry altercation. The refugees had spent the past three days waiting anxiously in the camp, and in that time no one had asked them where they wanted to go or when; none of them had any idea of what was to become of them, and the sense of being adrift had brought them to the end of their tether. The issue was neither deprivation nor hardship—there was enough food, and they had all the clothes they needed. It was the uncertainty that was intolerable. In the absence of any other figure of authority, they had laid siege to Father Johnson: When would they be allowed to move on? Where would they be going?

Father Johnson could give them no answers, for he was, in his own way, just as helpless as they were. The officials in charge of the relief effort had told him nothing about their plans for the refugees. Now time was running out: the schools in which the camps were located were to reopen on January 3. Father Johnson had no idea how his school was to function with more than 1600 refugees camping on the grounds.

Realizing at last that Father Johnson knew no more than they did, the inmates reduced their demands to a single modest query: could they be provided with some paper and a few pens? No sooner had this request been met than another uproar broke out; those who'd been given possession of pens and paper now became the center of the siege. Crowding together, people began to push and jostle, clamoring to have their names written down. Identity was now no more than a matter of assertion, and nothing seemed to matter more than to create a trail of paper. On this depended the eventual reclamation of a life.

Standing on the edges of the crowd was a stocky thirty-year-old man by the name of Obed Tara. He was, he told me, from the island of Car Nicobar and a member of an indigenous group whose affiliations, in language and ethnicity, lie with the Malay peoples to the east. But he himself was a *naik* (corporal) in the Tenth Madras Regiment of the Indian Army and was fluent in Hindi. On December 10 he had set off from Calcutta, where his unit was currently stationed, to travel to Car Nicobar. Like most Nicobarese people, he was a Christian, a member of the Anglican Church of North India, and he'd been looking forward to celebrating Christmas at home. But this year there was something else to look forward to as well: he was to be married on the first day of the New Year—the very day of our conversation.

On December 26, despite the celebrations and merrymaking of the night before, Obed Tara, like most members of his extended family, rose early in order to attend a Boxing Day service at their church. Their house was in the seafront settlement of Malacca, just a few hundred yards from the water. Their neighborhood was the commercial heart of the township, and their house was surrounded by shops and godowns. They were themselves a part of the market's bustle; they owned a Maruti Omni and operated a long-distance phone booth in their house. In other words, theirs was a family that had been swept into the middle class by the commercial opportunities of the past decade.

That morning, as the family was gathering outside the house, the earth began to heave with a violence that none of them had ever experienced before; it shook so hard that it was impossible to stand still, and they were forced to throw themselves on the ground. Then the ground cracked and fountains of mud-brown water came geysering out of these fissures. Like all the islanders, Obed Tara was accustomed to tremors in the earth, but neither he nor anyone else there had seen anything like this before. It took a while before the ground was still enough for them to regain their footing, and no sooner had he risen to his feet than he heard a wild, roaring sound. Looking seaward, he saw a wall of water advancing toward his house. Gathering his relatives, he began to run. By the time he looked back, his house, and the neighborhood in which it stood, had vanished under the waves. Two elderly members of the family were lost, and everything they possessed was gone — the car, the phone booth, the house. The family spent a couple of nights in the island's interior, and then the elders deputed Obed Tara to go to Port Blair to see what he could secure for them by way of relief and supplies.

By the time he finished telling me this story, there was a catch in his voice, and he was swallowing convulsively to keep from sobbing. I asked him, "Why don't you go to the army offices and tell them who you are? I am sure they will do what they can to help you."

He shook his head, as if to indicate that he had considered and dismissed this thought many times over. "The sea took my uniform, my ration card, my service card, my tribal papers — it took everything," he said. "I can't prove who I am. Why should they believe me?"

He led me to the far side of the camp, where another group of islanders was sitting patiently under a tent. They too had lost everything; their entire village had disappeared under the sea; saltwater had invaded their fields and taken away their orchards. They could not contemplate going back, they said; the stench of death was everywhere, and the water sources had been contaminated and would not be usable for years.

The leader of the group was a man by the name of Sylvester Solomon. A one-time serviceman in the navy, he had retired some years ago. He too had lost all his papers; he had no idea how he would claim his pension again. Worse still, the bank that had custody of his family's money had also been swept away, along with all its records.

I told him that by law the bank was obliged to return his money, and he smiled, as if at a child. I wanted to persuade him of the truth of what I'd said, but when I looked into his eyes, I knew that in his place, I too would not have the energy or the courage to take on the struggles that would be required to reclaim my life's savings from that bank.

In the same camp I encountered a Sikh woman by the name of Paramjeet Kaur. Noticing my notebook, she said, "Are you taking names too? Here, write mine down." She was a woman of determined aspect, dressed in a dun-colored *salwar kameez*. She had come to the islands some thirty years before, by dint of marriage. Her husband was a Sikh from Campbell Bay, a settlement on the southernmost tip of the Nicobar island chain, less than 125 miles from northern Sumatra. Like many others in the settlement, her husband belonged to a family that had been given a grant of land in recognition of service to the army (to distribute land in this way is a tradition that goes back to the British Indian Army and its efforts to engage the loyalties of Indian sepoys). But Paramjeet Kaur's in-laws came to the Nicobar Islands well after independence, in 1969, at a time when agricultural land had become scarce on the mainland. They were given 15 *bighas* of land and a plot to build a residence. The settlement that grew up around them was as varied as the regiments of the Indian army: there were Marathis, Malayalis, Jharkhandis, and people from Uttar Pradesh and Bihar.

"There was nothing there but jungle then," said Paramjeet Kaur. "We cleared it with our own hands, and we laid out orchards of areca and coconut. With God's blessing we prospered, and built a cement house with three rooms and a veranda."

The strip of land that was zoned for residential plots lay right on the seafront, providing the settlers with fine views of the beach. It was no mere accident, then, that placed Paramjeet Kaur's house in the path of the tsunami of December 26: its location was determined by an ordering of space that owed more to Europe than to its immediate surroundings. The sea poses little danger to the smiling corniches of the French Riviera or the coastline of Italy; the land-encircled Mediterranean is not subject to the play of tides, and it does not give birth to tropical storms. The Indian Ocean and especially the Bay of Bengal, however, are fecund in the breeding of cyclones. This may be the reason that a certain wariness of the sea can be seen in the lineaments of the ancient harbor cities of southern Asia. They are often situated in upriver locations, at a cautious distance from open water. In recent times the pattern seems to have been reversed, so that it could almost be stated as a rule that the more modern and prosperous a settlement, the more likely it is to hug the water. On Car Nicobar, for example, the Indian Air Force base was built a few dozen yards from the water's edge, and it was laid out so that the more senior the servicemen were, the closer they were to the sea. Although it is true that no one could have anticipated the tsunami, the choice of location is still surprising. Cyclones, frequent in this region, are associated with surges of water that rise to heights of 40 or 50 feet, and their effect would have been similar. Surely the planners were not unaware of this? But of course it is all too easy to be wise after the event: given the choice between a view of the beach and a plot in the mosquito-infested interior, what would anyone have chosen before December 26, 2004?

On the morning of that day, Paramjeet Kaur and her family were inside their sea-facing house when the earthquake struck. The ground rippled under their feet like a sheet waving in the wind, and no sooner had the shaking stopped than they heard a noise "like the sound of a helicopter." Paramjeet Kaur's husband, Pavitter Singh, looked outside and saw a wall of water speeding toward them. "The sea has split apart [*Samundar phat gaya*]," he shouted. "Run, run!" There was no time to pick up documents or jewelry; everyone who stopped to do so was killed. Paramjeet Kaur and her family ran for more than a mile without looking back, and were just able to save themselves.

"But for what?" Thirty years of labor had been washed away in an instant; everything they had accumulated was gone, and their land was sown with salt. "When we were young, we had the energy to cut the jungle and reclaim the land. We laid out fields and orchards and we did well. But at my age, how can I start again? Where will I begin?"

"What will you do, then?" I asked.

"We will go back to Punjab, where we have family. The government must give us land there; that is our demand."

In other camps I met office workers from Uttar Pradesh, fishermen from coastal Andhra Pradesh, and construction laborers from Bengal. They had all built good lives for themselves in the islands, but now, having lost their homes, their relatives, and even their identities, they were intent on returning to the mainland, no matter what.

"If nothing else," one of them said to me, "we will live in slums beside the rail tracks. But never again by the sea."

How do we quantify the help needed to rebuild these ruined lives? The question is answered easily enough if we pose it not in the abstract but in relation to ourselves. To put ourselves in the place of these victims is to know that all the help in the world would not be enough. Sufficiency is not a concept that is applicable here; potentially there is no limit to the amount of relief that can be used. This is the assumption that motivates ordinary people to open their purses, even though they know that governments and big companies have already contributed a great deal. This is why no disaster assistance group has ever been known to say, "We have to raise exactly this much and no more." But when it comes to the disbursement of these funds, the assumptions seem to undergo a drastic change, and nowhere more than in out-of-the-way places.

In the Andaman and Nicobar Islands, although the manpower and machinery for the relief effort are supplied largely by the armed forces, overall authority is concentrated in the hands of a small clutch of senior civil servants in Port Blair. No matter the sense of crisis elsewhere; the attitude of the officials of Port Blair is one of disdainful self-sufficiency. On more than one occasion I heard them dismissing offers of help as unnecessary and misdirected. Supplies were available aplenty, they said; in fact, they had more on their hands than they could distribute, and there was a danger that perishable materials would rot on the runways.

This argument is of course entirely circular: logically speaking, bottlenecks of distribution imply a need for *more* help, not less. But for the mandarins of Port Blair, the relief effort is a zero-sum game in which they are the referees. What conceivable help could their subjects need other than the amount that they, the providers, decide is appropriate to their various stations?

Are supplies really available aplenty, throughout the islands? The tale told in the relief camps is of course exactly the opposite of that which echoes out of the lairs of officialdom. Most of the refugees had to wait several days before they were evacuated. Forgotten in their far-remote islands, they listened to radio broadcasts that told them their nation was rushing aid to Sri Lanka and had refused all outside help as unnecessary. For the thirsty and hungry, there was little consolation in the thought that these measures might help their country establish itself as a superpower. In Campbell Bay, according to several reports, refugees were moved to such fury by the indifference of the local officials that they assaulted an officer who was found ushering in the New Year with a feast. Accounts of this incident, confirmed by several sources in the coast guard and police, were, characteristically, denied by the civil authorities.

In Port Blair, relief camps are the main sources of aid and sustenance for the refugees. These are all sustained by private initiatives: they are staffed by volunteers from local youth groups, religious foundations, and so on, and their supplies are provided by local shopkeepers, businessmen, and citizens' organizations. I met with the organizers of several relief camps, and they were unanimous in stating that they had received no aid whatsoever from the government, apart from some water. They knew that people on the mainland were eager to help and that a great deal of money had been raised. None of these funds had reached them; presumably the money had met the same bottlenecks of distribution as the supplies that were lying piled on the runways. That it should be possible for the people of a small town like Port Blair to provide relief to so many refugees is the bright side of this dismal story: it is proof, if any were needed, that the development of civil society in India has far outpaced the institutions of state and the personnel who staff them.

The attitude of the armed forces is not the same as that of the civilian authorities. At all levels of the chain of command, from Lieutenant General B. S. Thakur, the commanding officer in Port Blair, to the *jawans* (privates) who are combing through the ruins of Car Nicobar, there is an urgency, a diligence, and an openness that are in striking contrast to the stance of the civilian personnel. Indeed, the feats performed by some units speak of an exemplary dedication to duty. Consider, for example, the case of Wing Commander B.S.K. Kumar, a helicopter pilot at the Car Nicobar airbase. On December 26, he was asleep when the earthquake made itself felt. His quarters were a mere hundred feet from the sea. Not only did he manage to outrun the tsunami, with his wife and child; he was airborne within ten minutes of the first wave. In the course of the day he winched up some sixty stranded people and evacuated another two hundred and forty. His colleague, Wing Commander Maheshwari, woke too late to escape the wave. As the waters rose, he was forced to retreat to the roof of his building with his wife and daughter. Along with twenty-nine other people, he fought for his footing on the roof until all were swept off. He managed to make his way to land but was separated from his family; two hours passed before they were found, clinging to the trunk of a tree. Of the twenty-nine people on that roof, only six survived. And yet, despite the ordeal, Wing Commander Maheshwari flew several sorties that day.

Considering the diligence of the armed forces and the enthusiasm and generosity of ordinary citizens, how is the attitude of the island's civilian administration to be accounted for? The answer is simple: a lack of democracy and popular empowerment. As a Union Territory, the Andaman and Nicobar Islands have no legislature and thus no elected representatives with any clout, apart from a single member of Parliament. Elsewhere in India, in any crisis, officials have to answer to legislators at every level, and a failure to act would result in their being hounded by legislators and harried by trade unions, student groups, and the like. As Amartya Sen has shown in his work on famines, these mechanisms are essential to the proper distribution of resources in any situation of extreme scarcity. In effect, the political system serves as a means by which demands are articulated. The media similarly serve to create flows of information. These are precisely the mechanisms that are absent in the Andaman and Nicobar Islands. There are no elected representatives to speak for the people, and the media have been excluded from large swaths of territory. It is not for no reason that on the mainland, where these mechanisms do exist, the attitude of administrators in the affected districts has been more sensitive to the needs of the victims and substantially more open to the oversight of the press and to offers of help from other parts of the country.

It is common for civil servants to complain of the perils of political interference. The situation on the islands is proof that in the absence of vigorous oversight, many (although certainly not all) officials will revert to the indifference and inertia that are the natural condition of any bureaucracy.

Clearly the central government is aware that there is a problem, for the relief operation was restructured on January 2, reportedly at the personal intervention of Sonia Gandhi. What is more, several senior members of the ruling party have been dispatched to the outlying islands, not just for token visits but to make sure that supplies are properly distributed. These are welcome first steps, but it is essential for the central government to move quickly to create a more responsive and efficient disaster relief operation in this region, not just for the management of this disaster but for the long term. If anything can be said with any certainty, it is that the tsunami will not be the last seismic upheaval to shake the Andaman and Nicobar Islands.

In 1991, after lying dormant for two hundred years, the volcano of Barren Island became active again, and there are reports that it erupted around the time of the earthquake of December 26. On

September 14, 2002, a 6.5 magnitude earthquake occurred near Diglipur in North Andaman Island; now there are unconfirmed reports of a minor eruption in the same area. The signs are clear: no one can say the earth has not provided warnings of its intent.

In Port Blair I found that the tsunami's effects on the outlying islands could only be guessed at. The refugees in the camps spoke of apocalyptic devastation and tens of thousands dead; the authorities' estimates were much more modest. There were few, if any, reliable independent assessments, for the civil authorities had decided that no journalists or other "outsiders" were to be allowed to travel to the outlying islands. The reason given was that of the battlefield: too many resources would be spent on their protection. But no battle was under way in the islands, and the dangers of the tsunami were long past. Public ferry and steamer services linking Port Blair to the outer islands were in operation and had plenty of room for paying passengers. And yet journalists, Indian and foreign, who attempted to board these ships were forcibly dragged off.

On January 1 there was an unexpected parting in this curtain of exclusion. A couple of senior members of the ruling party came to Port Blair with the intent of traveling farther afield. It was quickly made known that an air force plane would be provided to take the ministers, and a retinue of journalists, to Car Nicobar the next day. This island, which is positioned halfway between the Andaman and Nicobar chains, is home to some 30,000 people, and it houses an air base that makes it something of a hub in relation to the more southerly islands.

Hoping to get on this plane, I duly presented myself at the airport, only to find that a great many others had arrived with the same expectation. As always in such situations, there was considerable confusion about who would get on. After the ministers had boarded, a minor melee ensued at the foot of the ramp that led to the plane's capacious belly. Knowing that I stood little chance of prevailing in this contest, I had almost resigned myself to being left behind when a young man in a blue uniform tapped my elbow and pointed across the airfield. "You want to go to Car Nicobar? That plane over there is carrying relief supplies. Just go and sit down. No one will say anything."

I sought no explanation for this unsolicited act of consideration; it seemed typical of the general goodwill of the military personnel I had encountered on the islands. As if on tiptoe, I walked across the tarmac and up the ramp. The plane was a twin-engine Soviet-era AN-26, rusty but dependable, and its capacious fuselage was lined with folding benches. The round portholes that pierced its sides were like eyes that had grown rheumy with age; time had sandpapered the panes of glass so that they were almost opaque. The cargo area was packed with mattresses, folding beds, cases of mineral water, and sacks of food, all covered with a net of webbing. Some half-dozen men were inside, sitting on the benches with their feet planted askew beside the mass of supplies. I seated myself in the only available space, beside a short, portly man with thick glasses and well-oiled, curly hair. He was dressed in a stiffly ironed brown safari suit, and he had an air of irascibility that spoke of a surfeit of time spent in filing papers and running offices. He was muttering angrily when I came aboard: "What do those people care? What have they ever done to help anyone . . . ?" Of all the people on that plane, he was perhaps the last I would have chosen to sit beside. I was keen to make myself as inconspicuous as possible, while he seemed determined to draw attention to himself. It could be only a matter of minutes, I thought, before the airmen evicted him. Inexplicably, they did not.

When the engines started up, my neighbor turned his attention to me. "These big people think they are so great, but what help have they given?" I assumed this to be a general expression of disgust, of the kind that is to be heard on every train and bus in the country. But then he added suddenly, "Let them go through what I have gone through. Let them suffer — then they would see . . ."

This hit me with the force of a shock. His well-laundered safari suit, his air of almost comical self-importance, his irascibility —

there was nothing about him that bespoke the victim. But I understood now why the airmen had ignored his rants; they knew something about him that I did not, and this was their way of showing
compassion.

In the meanwhile the tirade continued: "If those politicians had
suffered as I have, what would they do? This is the question I want
to ask."

I winced to think of my first response to his mutterings. "What
exactly has happened?" I asked. "Tell me."

He did not want his name published, so I shall call him "the Director." This indeed was his official title: he had been posted to Car
Nicobar in 1991, as the director of the island's Malaria Research
Centre and had lived there ever since. He was originally from Puri,
in Orissa, and had been trained at the University of Berhampore.
During his tenure in Car Nicobar, he had married and had two
children, a son, who was now thirteen, and a daughter, who was
ten. His home was in Malacca — the seafront township I'd heard
about in the camps — and his office was just a few minutes' walk
from where he lived. In this office he had accumulated a great
wealth of epidemiological knowledge. Car Nicobar had once been
rife with malaria, he told me. In an island with a population of
just 30,000, the annual incidence had been as high as 3810, even as
recently as 1989. But during his time there he had succeeded in
bringing the rate down to a fraction of this number. It was clear,
from the readiness with which he quoted the figures, that he was
immensely — and justly — proud of what he had achieved during
his stay on the island.

On December 25, 2004, the Director was in Port Blair, on his
way to New Delhi. Since he was traveling for official reasons, he
had left his family in Malacca. He spent the night of December 25
in a government guesthouse — the Haddo Circuit House, which
stands close to the water. On the morning of the twenty-sixth he
was woken by the shaking of his bed. He stepped down to find the
floor heaving and realized that an earthquake had hit the town. As

he was running out of the building, his mobile phone rang. Glancing quickly at the screen, he saw that his wife was calling from Malacca. He guessed that the earthquake had struck Car Nicobar too, but he was not unduly alarmed. Tremors were frequently felt on the island, and he thought his wife would be able to cope. The guesthouse, meanwhile, was still shaking, and there was no time to talk. He cut off the call and ran outside; he would phone back later, he decided, once the tremors stopped.

He waited out the earthquake outside, and when the ground was still at last, he hit the call button on his phone. There was no answer, and he wondered if the network was down. But he had little time to think about the matter, because a strange phenomenon had suddenly begun to take place before him: the water in the harbor had begun to rise, very rapidly, and the anchored ships seemed to be swirling about in the grip of an unseen hand. Along with everyone else, he ran to higher ground.

The islands of the Andaman chain rise steeply out of the sea, and the harbor and waterfront of Port Blair are sheltered by a network of winding fjords and inlets. Such is the lay of the land that the turbulence that radiated outward from the earthquake's epicenter manifested itself here not as an onrushing wall of water but as a surge in the water level. Although this caused a good deal of alarm, the damage was not severe.

It was not long, however, before it occurred to the Director that the incoming swell in Port Blair's harbor might have taken a different form elsewhere. The Nicobar Islands do not have the high elevations of their northern neighbors, the Andamans. They are low-lying, for the most part, and some, like Car Nicobar, stand no more than a few yards above sea level at their highest point. Already anxious, the Director became frantic when word of the tsunami trickled down to the waterfront from the naval offices farther up the slope.

The Director knew of a government office in Car Nicobar that had a satellite phone. He dialed the number again and again; it was either busy or there was no answer. When at last he got through, the voice at the other end told him, with some reluctance, that Malacca had been badly hit. It was known that there were some survivors, but as for his family, there was no word.

The Director kept calling, and in the afternoon he learned that his thirteen-year-old son had been found clinging to the rafters of a church some 200 yards behind their house. Arrangements were made to bring the boy to the phone, and the Director was able to speak to him directly later that night. He learned from his son that the family had been in the bedroom when the earthquake started. A short while later, a terrifying sound from the direction of the sea had driven the three of them into the drawing room. The boy had kept running, right into the kitchen. The house was built of wood, on a cement foundation. When the wave hit, the house dissolved into splinters and the boy was carried away as if on a wind. Flailing his arms, he succeeded in taking hold of something that seemed to be fixed to the earth. Through wave after wave he managed to keep his grip. When the water receded, he saw that he was holding on to the only upright structure within a radius of several hundred yards. Of the township, nothing was left but a deep crust of wreckage.

"And your mother and sister?" the Director had asked.

"Baba, they just disappeared . . ." And now for the first time the boy began to cry, and the Director's heart broke, for he knew his son was crying because he thought he would be scolded and blamed for what had happened.

"I was strict with him, sir," the Director told me, his voice trailing off. "I am a strict man — that is my nature. But I must say he is a brave boy, a very brave boy."

Having spent thirteen years on the island, the Director was well acquainted with the local administration and the officers on the air base. Through their intervention he was able to get on a flight the very next day. He spent the day searching through the rubble; he found many possessions, but no trace of his daughter or his wife. He returned to Port Blair with his son the same evening, and the two of them moved in with some friends. Every day since then he'd been trying to go back, to find out what had become of his wife and daughter, but the flights had been closed—until this one.

"Tell me," he said, his voice becoming uncharacteristically soft. "What do you think—is there any hope?"

It took me a moment to collect my wits. "Of course there is hope," I said. "There is always hope. They could have been swept ashore on another part of the island."

He nodded. "We will see. I hope I will find out today, in Malacca."

With some hesitation I asked if it would be all right if I came with him. He answered with a prompt nod. "You can come."

I had the impression that he had been dreading the lonely search that lay ahead and would be glad of some company. "All right then," I said. "I will."

At the airfield in Car Nicobar, the Director arranged a ride for us on a yellow construction truck that had been set to the task of distributing relief supplies. The truck went bouncing down the runway before turning off into a narrow road that led into a forest. Once the airstrip was behind us, it was as though we had been transported to some long-ago land, unspoiled and untouched. The road wound through a dense tropical jungle, dotted at intervals with groves of slender areca palms and huts mounted on stilts. Some of these had metamorphosed into makeshift camps, sprouting awnings of plastic and tarpaulin. It was clear that the island's interior was sparsely inhabited, with the population being concentrated along the seafront.

Earlier, while the plane was making its descent, I had had a panoramic, if blurred, view of the island in the crisp morning sunlight. No more than a few miles across, it was flat and low, and its interior was covered by a dense canopy of greenery. A turquoise halo surrounded its shores, where a fringe of sand had once formed an almost continuous length of beach; this was now still mainly underwater. I saw to my surprise that many coconut palms were still standing, even on the edge of the water. Relatively few palms had been flattened; most remained upright and in full possession of their greenery. As for the forest, the canopy seemed almost undisturbed. All trace of habitation, in contrast, had been obliterated. The foundations of many buildings could be clearly seen on the ground, but of the structures they had once supported, nothing remained.

It was evident from above that the tsunami had been peculiarly selective in the manner of its destruction. Had the island been hit by a major cyclone, not a frond would have survived on the coconut palms and the forest canopy would have been denuded. Most human dwellings, on the other hand, would have retained their walls, even if they lost their roofs. Not so in this instance. The villages along the shore were not merely damaged; they were erased. It was as if the island had been hit by a weapon devised to cause the maximum possible damage to life and property while leaving nature largely unharmed.

We came to an intersection that was flanked by low whitewashed buildings. This was the administrative center of the island, the Director explained; the settlement of Malacca lay a good distance away, and we would have to walk. After getting off the truck, we came to the district library, a building of surprising size and solidity. Like the surrounding offices, it was unharmed, but a medical camp, manned by the Indo-Tibetan Border Force, had sprung up on its grounds, under the shade of a spreading, moss-twined padauk tree.

The Director spotted a doctor sitting in a tent. He darted away and slipped under the tent's blue flap. "Doctor, have you heard anything about my family?" he said. "I've come because I heard some survivors had been found . . ."

The doctor's face froze, and after a moment's silence he said, in a tone that was noncommittal and yet not discouraging, "No news has reached me — I've not heard anything."

We continued on our way, walking past the airy bungalows of the island's top officials, with their well-tended gardens. Soon we came upon two men who were sitting by the road, beside an odd assortment of salvaged goods. "That's mine," said the Director, pointing to a lampstand of turned wood. "I paid a lot for it — it's made of padauk wood." There was no rancor in his voice, and nor did he seem to want to reclaim the object. We walked on.

A few steps ahead the road dipped toward a large clearing fringed by thick stands of coconut palm. It was a *maidan,* a space for people to promenade and forgather, and as with many small town maidans, there was a plaster bust of Mahatma Gandhi standing in its center. So far on our journey from the airport we had seen no outward sign of the damage caused by the tsunami, but now we had arrived at the periphery of the band of destruction. Mounds of splintered planks and other building materials lay scattered across the clearing, and the red, white, and green fence that surrounded the bust of Mahatma Gandhi was swathed in refuse and dead coconut fronds. Everywhere, evidence of the tsunami's incursion could be seen in pools of water that had turned rank over the past few days.

At the far end of the maidan, a fire was blazing among the coconut palms. The warehouse that supplied the island with cooking gas had stood at that spot. The tsunami had swept the warehouse away, leaving the canisters exposed to the sun, and a fire had ensued. Every few minutes the ground shook with the blast of exploding canisters.

Oblivious of the fire, the Director stepped away to accost a passerby who was wheeling a loaded bicycle. Over his shoulder, he said to me, "This is Michael. He worked in my office." Michael was a sturdy, grizzled Nicobarese dressed in green shorts and a gray shirt. Laying his hands on the bicycle's handlebars, the Director said in Hindi, "Michael, listen — has there been any news of madam? You know what she looks like. Have you seen any trace of her?"

Michael dropped his eyes, as if in embarrassment, and answered with a tiny shake of his head.

Lowering his voice, the Director continued: "And have you heard anyone speak of a girl roaming in the jungle?" When this too failed to elicit an answer, he went on. "Michael, I need your help. Bring some men and come. I need to dig through the rubble to see if I can find anything." Even as he was speaking, his attention shifted to the contents of the plastic bags that were hanging from Michael's handlebars. Flinching, he let go of the handlebar. "Michael!" he cried. "What is all this stuff you've picked up? You should know better than to take things from over there — they may be contaminated."

Michael hung his head and wheeled his bicycle silently away.

"They're all looting," said the Director, shaking his head. "I've heard the bazaar in Port Blair has received three sackfuls of gold from the islands . . ."

In the clump of burning palm trees, yet another gas canister exploded. It was close enough that we could feel the rattle of the blast in the debris under our feet; a shard of metal struck an onlooker, fortunately without injury. Oblivious of the flames, the Director hurried toward a spot where a mound of mangled household objects lay piled, having been pushed through the screen of coconut palms like dough through a sieve.

"Look, that's mine," he said, pointing to a blue Aristocrat suitcase made of molded plastic. It had been hacked open with a sharp-bladed instrument and its contents were gone. The Director picked it up and shook it. "I saw it the last time I was here," he said. "It was already empty. Everything had been looted." His eyes moved over to a steel trunk lying nearby. "That's mine too. Go and look." Stepping over, I saw that the trunk's lock had been forced open. On the side, written in large black letters, was the Director's name and designation. "You see," the Director said, as if in vindication. "Everything I've been telling you is true. These things were all mine."

A short distance away a wooden cabinet lay overturned, and heaps of paper could be seen spilling out of its belly. The Director beckoned to me. "See — there are all the records from my office. Thirteen years of research, all gone." We went to kneel beside the cabinet, and I saw that the papers were mimeographed data sheets, with the letterhead of the Malaria Research Centre printed on top.

Somewhere among the papers I spotted a few old photographs. Somehow it was a matter of great relief to me to come upon a retrievable memento, and I was quick to draw the Director's attention to the pictures. On examination it turned out that most of them had been defaced by the water, but I found one where he, the Director, could be seen standing among a group of people. I held it out to him, and he took it with an indifferent shrug. "That photo was taken at the air base, I remember." He let go, and it fluttered into a puddle of stinking water.

"Don't you want to keep it?" I said in astonishment.

"No," he said simply. "It means nothing. These are just work pictures."

Then suddenly his eyes lit up. "Look," he said, "my slides . . ." A drawer had come open, shaking loose several decks of white-rimmed photographic slides. Most were sodden, but some were dry and had preserved their images. To my untrained eyes, the pictures appeared to be of bacteria, hugely magnified by the lens of a microscope. The Director sorted quickly through the slides and chose a dozen or so. Close at hand there lay a roll of unused plastic bags that had been washed out of a drowned shop and dried by the sun. Peeling off one of these bags, he placed the slides carefully inside before fastening his fingers on them.

"Your home must have been nearby?" I said.

"No," came the answer. "The wave carried these things right out of the town. My house is still a half a mile away, over there."

I had imagined that his possessions were bunched together because his house had stood nearby. This was an indication of how little I understood of the power of the surge. Its strength was such that it had tossed the Director's house aside, picked up his belongings, and punched them through a half-mile-wide expanse of dense habitation.

The place the Director had pointed to was on the far side of the burning coconut palms, and it was evident that to get there we would have to pass quite close to the fire, which was now spreading rapidly. We set off almost at a run and soon came to a point where our path was blocked by a fallen tree. He clambered over, hanging on to his slides, and I followed. The fire was now about a hundred yards to our right, and as I was climbing over, there was another detonation, followed by a crackling, whooshing sound. I fell quickly to the ground and shut my eyes. When I looked up, the Director was still standing, gazing down at me with puzzled impatience. "Come on, come on — that's where we have to go, over there."

When I rose to my feet, I had my first glimpse of the seafront where the town of Malacca had once stood; till now it had been largely screened from view by the coconut palms. On a stretch of land about a mile long, there were now only five structures still standing: the staring, skull-like shell of a school that had lost all its doors and windows; a single neatly whitewashed bungalow in the distance; an arched gateway that had the words "Rajiv Gandhi Memorial Park" painted on it; a small, miraculously unharmed Murugan temple, right beside the sea; and, last, the skeleton of a church, with a row of parallel arches rising from the rubble like the bleached ribs of a dead animal. This was the structure that had saved the life of the Director's son. The palms along the seafront were undamaged and upright, their fronds intact, but the other trees on the site had lost all their leaves, and a couple had buses, cars, and sheets of corrugated iron wrapped around their trunks. If not for the tree trunks and the waving palms, the first visual analogy to suggest itself would have been Hiroshima after the bomb: the resemblance lay not just in the destruction but also in the discernible directionality of the blast. But there the parallel ended, for the sky here was a cloudless blue and there were no wisps of smoke rising from the ruins.

The Director led the way across the debris as if he were following a route imprinted in memory, a familiar map of streets and lanes. Despite a stiff breeze blowing in from the sea, an odor of death flowed over the site, not evenly, but in whirls and eddies, sometimes growing so powerful as to indicate the presence of a yet undiscovered body. Stray dogs rooting in the ruins looked up as if amazed at the sight of human beings who were still on their feet.

We came to a point where a rectangular platform of cement shone brightly under the sun. The Director stepped up to it and placed his feet in the middle. "This was my house," he said. "Only the foundation was concrete. The rest was wood. My wife used to say that she had moved from a white house to a log cabin. You see, she was from an affluent family — she grew up in a bungalow with an air conditioner. She used to teach English in a school here, but she always wanted to leave. I applied many times, but the transfer never came." He paused, thinking back. For much of the time that we had been together his voice had carried a note of sharp but undirected annoyance; now it softened. "There was so much she could have achieved," he said. "I was never able to give her the opportunity."

I reached out to touch his arm, but he shook my hand brusquely away; he was not the kind of man who takes kindly to expressions of sympathy. I could tell from his demeanor that he was accustomed to adversity and had invented many rules for dealing with it. The emotion he felt for his family he had rarely expressed; he had hoarded it inside himself, in the way a squirrel gathers food for the winter. Loath to spend it in his hectic middle years, he had put it away to be savored when there was a greater sense of ease in his life, at a time when his battles were past and he could give his hoarded love his full attention. He had never dreamed — and who could? — that one bright December day, soon after dawn, it would be stolen, unsavored, by the sea.

I began to walk toward the gently lapping waves, no more than a hundred yards away. The Director took fright at this and called me back: "Don't go that way, the tide is coming in. It's time to leave."

I turned to follow him, and we were heading back toward the blazing palms when he stopped to point to a yellow paint box peeping out of the rubble. "That belonged to Vineeta, my daughter," he said, and the flatness of his voice was harder to listen to than an outburst would have been. "She loved to paint; she was very good at it. She was even given a prize, from Hyderabad."

I had expected that he would stoop to pick up the box, but instead he turned away and walked on, gripping his bag of slides. "Wait!" I cried. "Don't you want to take the box?"

"No," he said vehemently, shaking his head. "What good will it do? What will it give back?" He stopped to look at me over the rim of his glasses. "Do you know what happened the last time I was here? Someone had found my daughter's schoolbag and saved it for me. It was handed to me, like a card. It was the worst thing I could have seen. It was unbearable."

He started to walk off again. Unable to restrain myself, I called out after him, "Are you sure you don't want it — the paint box?"

Without looking around, he said, "Yes, I am sure."

I stood amazed as he walked toward the blazing fire with his slides still folded in his grip. How was it possible that the only memento he had chosen to retrieve was those magnified images? As a husband, a father, a human being, it was impossible not to wonder, What would I have done? What would I have felt? What would I have chosen to keep of the past? The truth is, nobody can know, except in the extremity of that moment, and then the choice is not a choice at all but an expression of the innermost sovereignty of the self, which decides because nothing now remains to cloud its vision. In the manner of the Director's choosing there was not a particle of hesitation, not the faintest glimmer of a doubt. Was it perhaps that in this moment of utter desolation, there was some comfort in the knowledge of an impersonal effort? Could it be that he was seeking refuge in the one aspect of his existence that could not be erased by an act of nature? Or was there some consolation in the very lack of immediacy — did the value of those slides lie precisely in their exclusion from the unendurable pain of his loss? Whatever the reason, it was plain his mind had fixed on a set of objects that derived their meaning from the part of his life that was lived in thought and contemplation.

There are times when words seem futile, and to no one more so than a writer. At these moments it seems that nothing is of value other than to act and to intervene in the course of events. To think, to reflect, to write, seems trivial and wasteful. But the life of the mind takes many forms, and after the day had passed I understood that in the manner of his choosing, the Director had mounted the most singular, the most powerful defense of it that I would ever witness.

IMPERIAL TEMPTATIONS

2003

THE IDEA OF EMPIRE, once so effectively used by Ronald Reagan to discredit the Soviet Union, has recently undergone a strange rehabilitation in the United States. This process, which started some years ago, has accelerated markedly since September 11. References to empire are no longer deployed ironically or in a tone of warning; the idea has become respectable enough that the *New York Times* ran an article describing the enthusiasm it now evokes in certain circles.

It is of some significance that these circles are not easily identified as being located either on the right or on the left. If there are some on the right who celebrate the projection of U.S. power, there are others on the left who believe that the world can only benefit from an ever-increasing U.S. engagement and intervention abroad—for example, in ethnic and religious conflicts (such as those in Rwanda and Bosnia) or in states run by despotic regimes or "rogue" leaders (such as Iraq). It is on grounds like these that the idea of a new imperialism has recently been embraced by Britain's Labour Party.

That elements of the left and the right should discover common ground on the matter of empire should come as no surprise. Contrary to popular belief, empire is by no means a strictly conservative project; historically it has always held just as much appeal for liberals. Conversely, the single greatest critic of the British Empire, Edmund Burke, was an archconservative who saw imperialism as an essentially radical project, not unlike that of the French Revolution.

The idea of empire may seem too antiquated to be worth combating. But it is always the ideas that appeal to both ends of the spectrum that stand the best chance of precipitating an unspoken consensus, especially when they bear the imprimatur of such figures as the British prime minister. That is why this may be a good time to remind ourselves of some of the reasons that imperialism fell into discredit in the first place.

To begin with, empire cannot be the object of universal human aspirations. In a world run by empires, some people are rulers and some are the ruled; it is impossible to think of a situation in which all peoples possess an empire. In contrast, the idea of the nation-state, for all its failings, holds the great advantage that it can indeed be generalized to all peoples everywhere. The proposition that every human being should belong to a nation and that all nations should be equal is not a contradiction in terms, although it may well be utterly unfounded as a description of the real world.

It is precisely the exclusivism of empire that makes it a program for ever-increasing conflict. If the mark of success for a nation consists of the possession of an empire, then it follows that every nation that wants to achieve success must aspire to one. That is why the twentieth century was a period of such cataclysmic conflict: emergent powers like Germany and Japan wanted empires as proof of their success. Those who embrace the idea frequently cite the advantages of an imperial peace over the disorder of the current world situation, but this disregards the fact that the peace of the British, French, and Austro-Hungarian empires was purchased at the cost of a destabilization so radical as to generate the two greatest conflicts in human history, the world wars. Because of the proliferation of weapons of mass destruction, there can be no doubt that a twenty-first-century empire would have consequences that are graver still.

An imperium also generates an unstoppable push toward over-reach, which is one of the reasons it is a charter for destabilization. This is not only because of an empire's inherent tendency to expand; there is another reason, so simple as often to go unnoticed. The knowledge that an imperial center can be induced to intervene in local disputes, at a certain price, is itself an incentive for lesser players to provoke intervention. I remember an occasion a few years ago when one of the leaders of a minor and utterly hopeless insurgency asked me, What kind of death toll do you think we need to get the United States to intervene here?

There can be no doubt that political catastrophes can often be prevented by multilateral intervention, and clearly such actions are sometimes necessary. But it is also true that in certain circumstances the very prospect of intervention can become an incentive, as it were, for the escalation of violence. The reason the idea of empire appeals to many liberals is that it appears to offer a means of bettering the world's predicament. History shows us, unfortunately, that the road to empire is all too often thickly paved with good intentions.

During the past few months, much has been said and written on the subject of a "new American empire." I believe this term to be a misnomer. If the Iraq war is to be seen as an imperial venture, then the project is neither new nor purely American. What President Bush likes to call the "coalition of the willing" is dominated, after all, by America, Britain, and Australia — three English-speaking countries whose allegiances are rooted not just in a shared culture and common institutions but in a shared history of territorial expansion. Seen in this light, the alignment is only the newest phase in the evolution of the most potent political force of the past two centuries: the anglophone empire.

I am an Indian, and my history has been shaped as much by the institutions of this empire as by a long tradition of struggle against them. Now I live in New York; for me, the September 11 attacks and their aftermath were filled with disquieting historical resonances. I was vividly reminded, for example, of the Indian uprising of 1857, an event known to the British as the Great Indian Mutiny. That year in Kanpur, a busy trading junction beside the Ganges, several hundred defenseless British civilians, including women and children, were cut down in an orgy of blood lust by Indians loyal to a local potentate, Nana Sahib. Many of the Indians involved in the rebellion were erstwhile soldiers of the empire who had been seized by nihilistic ideas. The rebels' methods were so extreme that Indian moderates were torn between sympathy, revulsion, and fear. Many Indians chose to distance themselves from the uprising. Others went so far as to join hands with the British. A similar process is clearly under way in today's Middle East, where Islamist fundamentalism has inflamed some Arabs while alienating others.

The phrase "shock and awe," used by the U.S. military to describe the initial air attack on Baghdad, provided another reminder of the 1857 uprising. In the aftermath of the mutiny, the British too mounted a campaign to create terror and awe among the rebels' supporters. The road from Kanpur to Allahabad was lined with the corpses of Indian soldiers who had been hanged; there were public displays of rebels being shot from cannons. British soldiers sacked cities across northern India. The instruments of state were deployed in such a way as to reward allies and to punish areas and populations that had supported the rebels. The effects of these policies were felt for generations and arguably can still be observed in the disparities that divide, say, the relatively affluent region of Punjab and the impoverished state of Bihar.

The rights and wrongs of the British actions are not at issue here. I want, rather, to pose a question that is not articulated often enough: Do such exercises of power work? Many believe that displays of military might are always erased or offset by countervailing forces of resistance. But those who are accustomed to the exercise of power know otherwise. They know that power can sometimes be used to redirect the forces of resistance.

In the case of the 1857 uprising, the truth is that the reigning power's brutal response resulted in some significant changes in Indian political life. Britain's overwhelming victory was instrumental in persuading a majority of Indians that it was futile to oppose the empire by force of arms. This consensus caused many in the next generation of anticolonialists to turn in a more parliamentary and constitutionalist direction, and was thus a necessary backdrop to Mahatma Gandhi's tactics of nonviolent resistance.

Some of today's imperial enthusiasts have pointed to Indian democracy as proof that a colonial presence can be reconstructive, helping to create a stable civil society. To counter this argument, however, we need only look at a list of cities where al Qaeda's fugitive leaders are said to have taken refuge: Aden, Rawalpindi, Peshawar, Quetta, Lahore, Karachi. The British dominated these cities for centuries, and yet the antagonism to the West that simmers in them now is greater even than it was in 1857.

In the world of human beings, even defeat is a transaction. If there is any lesson to be drawn from the subcontinent's experience of empire, it is that defeat can be negotiated in many different ways. In India democracy thrives, while in Pakistan democracy has consistently devolved into authoritarianism. For Iraq to go the way of India, the current avatar of the anglophone empire will have to succeed in creating, in the span of a few years, what earlier incarnations failed to do over decades.

The chances of success are close to nil. The strongest counterindications are to be seen, paradoxically, in the very imbalance in military power that led to the toppling of Saddam Hussein's regime. The military power of the United States is so overwhelming that it has caused American advocates of empire to forget that the imperial project rests on two pillars. Weaponry is only the first and most obvious of these; the other is persuasion. When empire was in British hands, its rulers paid almost as much attention to this second pillar as to the first. Its armies were often accompanied by an enormously energetic apparatus of persuasion, which included educational institutions, workshops, media outlets, printing houses, and so on.

Many hawks in the United States now openly admit to a veneration of past empires, yet they seem to have absorbed the military lessons of imperialism to the exclusion of all else. I suspect that this is the reason that many in the British political establishment were so dismayed by the buildup to the Iraq war. They know all too well that an aura of legitimacy and consent is essential in matters of empire.

Legitimacy and the tactics of persuasion are obviously not high priorities for the Bush administration. But the task would be difficult anyway. In the nineteenth century, the apparatus of persuasion was effective partly because the colonizing force could exercise close control over the flow of information. In Iraq, every effort at persuasion will be offset by daily doses of dissuasion, delivered through the Internet and satellite television channels. The persuasive effectiveness of nineteenth-century empires also rested in large part on the talismanic role of science. Today high technology is too widespread to astonish. Although smart bombs are terrifying, they do not have the mystique that the Gatling gun once held.

The modern connotations of the word "empire" also show how the context of imperialism has changed. For many, especially in America, it is a reminder of an image that played a significant part in discrediting the Soviet Union: the "evil empire." This is not a purely rhetorical anxiety; the unease goes deeper than that. A substantial proportion of America's population remains unconvinced of the need to undertake a new version of a "civilizing mission." This is what distinguishes America from the imperial nations of the past.

As George Orwell and many other observers of imperialism have pointed out, empires imprison their rulers as well as their subjects. In today's United States, where people are increasingly disinclined to venture beyond their borders, this has already come to pass. But perhaps, in these accelerated times, it won't be long before most Americans begin to dream of an escape from the imprisonment of absolute power.

SEPTEMBER 11

2001

In 1999, SOON AFTER MOVING to Fort Greene, in Brooklyn, my wife and I were befriended by Frank and Nicole De Martini, two architects. As construction manager of the World Trade Center, Frank worked in an office on the eighty-eighth floor of the north tower. Nicole is an employee of the engineering firm that built the World Trade Center, Leslie E. Robertson Associates. Hired as a "surveillance engineer," she was a member of a team that conducted year-round structural-integrity inspections of the Twin Towers. Her offices were on the thirty-fifth floor of the south tower.

Frank is forty-nine, sturdily built, with wavy salt-and-pepper hair and deeply etched laugh lines around his eyes. His manner is expansively avuncular. The Twin Towers were both a livelihood and a passion for him: he would speak of them with the absorbed fascination with which poets sometimes speak of Dante's canzones. Nicole is forty-two, blond and blue-eyed, with a gaze that is at once brisk and friendly. She was born in Basel, Switzerland, and met Frank while studying design in New York. They have two children—Sabrina, ten, and Dominic, eight. It was through our children that we first met.

Shortly after the basement bomb explosion of 1993, Frank was hired to do bomb-damage assessment at the World Trade Center.

An assignment that he thought would last only a few months quickly turned into a consuming passion. "He fell in love with the buildings," Nicole told me. "For him, they represented an incredible human feat. He was awed by their scale and magnitude, by their design, and by the efficiency of the use of materials. One of his most repeated sayings about the towers is that they were built to take the impact of a light airplane."

On Tuesday morning, Frank and Nicole dropped their children off at school, in Brooklyn Heights, and then drove on to the World Trade Center. Traffic was light, and they arrived unexpectedly early, so Nicole decided to go up to Frank's office for a cup of coffee. It was about a quarter past eight when they got upstairs. A half-hour later, she stood up to go. She was on her way out when the walls and the floor suddenly heaved under the shock of a massive impact. Through the window, she saw a wave of flame bursting out overhead, like a torrent spewing from the floodgates of a dam. The blast was clearly centered on the floor directly above; she assumed that it was a bomb. Neither she nor Frank was unduly alarmed: few people knew the building's strength and resilience better than they. They assumed that the worst was over and that the structure had absorbed the impact. Sure enough, within seconds of the initial tumult, a sense of calm descended on their floor. Frank herded Nicole and a group of some two dozen other people into a room that was relatively free of smoke. Then he went off to scout the escape routes and stairways. Minutes later, he returned to announce that he had found a stairway that was intact. They could reach it fairly easily, by climbing over a pile of rubble.

The bank of rubble that barred the entrance to the fire escape was almost knee-high. Just as Nicole was about to clamber over, she noticed that Frank was hanging back. She begged him to come with her. He shook his head and told her to go on without him. There were people on their floor who had been hurt by the blast, he said; he would follow her down as soon as he had helped the injured.

Frank must have gone back to his office shortly afterward, because he made a call from his desk at about nine o'clock. He called his sister Nina, on West Ninety-third Street in Manhattan, and said, "Nicole and I are fine. Don't worry."

Nicole remembers the descent as quiet and orderly. The evacuees went down in single file, leaving room for the firemen who were running in the opposite direction. On many floors, there were people to direct the evacuees, and in the lower reaches of the building there was even electricity. The descent took about half an hour, and on reaching the plaza, Nicole began to walk in the direction of the Brooklyn Bridge. She was within a few hundred feet of the bridge when the first tower collapsed. "It was like the onset of a nuclear winter," she said. "Suddenly everything went absolutely quiet and you were in the middle of a fog that was as blindingly bright as a snowstorm on a sunny day."

It was early evening by the time Nicole reached Fort Greene. She had received calls from several people who had seen Frank on their way down the fire escape, but he had not been heard from directly. Their children stayed with us that night while Nicole sat up with Frank's sister Nina, waiting by the telephone.

The next morning Nicole decided that her children had to be told that there was no word of their father. Both she and Nina were calm when they arrived at our door, even though they had not slept all night. Nicole's voice was grave but unwavering as she spoke to her children about what had happened the day before.

The children listened with wide-eyed interest, but soon afterward they went back to their interrupted games. A little later, my son came to me and whispered, "Guess what Dominic's doing?"

"What?" I said, steeling myself.

"He's learning to wiggle his ears."

This was, I realized, how my children — or any children, for that matter — would have responded: turning their attention elsewhere before the news could begin to gain purchase in their minds.

At about noon we took the children to the park. It was a bright, sunny day, and they were soon absorbed in riding their bicycles.

My wife, Deborah, and I sat on a shaded bench and spoke with Nicole. "Frank could easily have got out in the time that passed between the blast and the fall of the building," Nicole said. "The only thing I can think of is that he stayed back to help with the evacuation. Nobody knew the building like he did, and he must have thought he had to."

She paused. "I think it was only because Frank saw me leave that he decided he could stay," she said. "He knew that I would be safe and the kids would be looked after. That was why he felt he could go back to help the others. He loved the towers and had complete faith in them. Whatever happens, I know that what he did was his own choice."

THE GREATEST SORROW

Times of Joy Recalled in Wretchedness

2001

> *Nessun maggior dolore che ricordarsi del*
> *tempo felice ne la miseria.*
>
> There is no greater sorrow than to recall
> our times of joy in wretchedness.

ON JULY 27 this year, landing in Colombo's Katunayake
airport, I saw at first hand how fragile a machine an aircraft is.
My plane landed on a runway that was flanked with wreckage on
either side. Through the scarred glass of my window, I spotted a
blackened pile of debris that ended in the intact tail section of a
plane. The shape of the vanished fuselage was etched into the tarmac like the outline of a cigar that has burned itself slowly to extinction, leaving its ring standing in its ashes. Then there was another and still another, the charred remains lying scattered around
the apron like a boxful of half-smoked Havanas arranged around
the edges of an ebony table.

It was just four days since a small suicide squad of Tamil Tiger
guerrillas had succeeded in entering Colombo's carefully guarded
Katunayake airport. The strike was executed with meticulous pre-
cision, and the guerrillas had destroyed some fourteen aircraft, virtually disabling Sri Lanka's civilian and military air fleets. It was till
then perhaps the single most successful attack of its kind.

Thirty-six years had passed since I first landed at that airport, in a shuddering blunt-nosed Dakota. The aerodrome, as it was then spoken of, was a relic of an older war, in which Colombo had served as the nerve center of Lord Mountbatten's Southeast Asia Command. I was nine then, a fresh entrant into that moment of childhood when we first begin to truly inhabit the world, in the particular sense of committing it to memory. I remember Colombo's red-tiled roofs, like stacks of hardback books spread open on a desk; I remember my school, Royal College, and the stairway where I first tasted blood on my lip; I remember after-school cricket matches on Layard's Road and wickets knocked over by kabaragoyas; I remember marshmallow ice cream at Elephant House and the pearly insides of mangosteens; I remember the palm trees at Hikkaduwa leaning like dancers over the golden sands; I remember Elephant's Pass and the road to Jaffna, as narrow as the clasp between a necklace and its pendant; I remember at Pollonaruwa a cobra coiled on the floor of a rest house, looking up as though in surprise at my silhouette in the doorway; I remember a train on a slope, its smoke mingling with the mists of Nuwara Eliya.

Such was the paradise from which I was abruptly torn when I arrived upon the threshold of adolescence. In the summer of 1967, when I had reached the age of eleven, I was sent away to be educated at the other end of the subcontinent, in Dehradun, which was said to be one of the most picturesque places in India. But for me this sub-Himalayan valley proved to be anything but Arcadia: I found myself imprisoned in a walled city of woe, with five hundred adolescents who had been herded together to be instructed in the dark arts of harrowing their peers. That it was my parents who were the agents of my expulsion from paradise was not the least part of the bewildering pain of my banishment. It was in that sub-Himalayan purgatory that I learned what it was to recall a time of joy in wretchedness. Now, in the recollection of that emotion, I have come to recognize a commonality with many, perhaps most, Sri Lankans — indeed, with everyone who remembers what it was to live in Serendib before the Fall.

Michael Ondaatje writes:

> The last Sinhala word I lost
> was *vatura.*
> The word for water.
> Forest water. The water in a kiss. The tears
> I gave to my ayah Rosalin on leaving
> the first home of my life.
>
> More water for her than any other
> that fled my eyes again
> this year, remembering her,
> a lost almost-mother in those years
> of thirsty love
>
> No photograph of her, no meeting
> since the age of eleven,
> not even knowledge of her grave.
>
> Who abandoned who, I wonder now.

These lines look back — as do I when I think of Sri Lanka — to a childhood long past. But the poem was published recently, in New York, and I doubt that it would have sounded this exact note had it been written at any other time and in any other circumstances. This is not merely a eulogy for Rosalin; it is an elegy of homecoming spoken in a voice that has been orphaned not just by the loss of an almost-mother but by history itself. It is a lament that mourns the passing of the paradise that made Rosalin possible.

At the other end of the subcontinent lies another land devastated by the twin terrors of armed insurgency and state repression: Kashmir, of which an emperor famously said:

> If there is a paradise on earth,
> It is this, it is this, it is this.

In the mid-1990s, at about the same time that Michael Ondaatje was writing his elegy to Rosalin, the Kashmiri poet Agha Shahid Ali was writing his great poem "The Last Saffron." The poem begins:

I will die, in autumn, in Kashmir,
and the shadowed routine of each vein
will almost be news, the blood censored,
for the *Saffron Sun* and the *Times of Rain*

The poem ends with these verses:

Yes, I remember it,
the day I'll die, I broadcast the crimson,

so long ago of that sky, its spread air,
its rushing dyes, and a piece of earth

bleeding, apart from the shore, as we went
on the day I'll die, past the guards, and he,

keeper of the world's last saffron, rowed me
on an island the size of a grave. On

two yards he rowed me into the sunset,
past all pain. On everyone's lips was news

of my death but only that beloved couplet,
broken, on his:

"If there is a paradise on earth,
It is this, it is this, it is this."

If the twin terrors of insurgency and repression could be said
to have engendered any single literary leitmotif, it is surely the narrative of the loss of paradise. Nowhere is this story more precisely
chronicled than in Shyam Selvadurai's 1994 novel, *Funny Boy*. The
novel is set in Colombo, in the turmoil of the early 1980s, when
long-simmering tensions between Sri Lanka's Sinhala-dominated
government and the minority Tamil population exploded into a
savagely violent conflict. The narrator is a teenage boy from a
wealthy Tamil family, and the novel's final chapter recounts the
events of July 1983, when a terrorist attack on the Sri Lankan army
triggered massive reprisals against the Tamils of Colombo.

In *Funny Boy* the destruction of paradise is assigned precise dates and an exact span of time: it starts at 9:30 A.M. on July 25, 1983. It is only a few hours since the novel's teenage narrator and his family have learned that "there [is] trouble in Colombo": the night before, a mob has gone wild after a funeral for thirteen slain soldiers and many Tamil houses have been burned. At 9:30 A.M. the family begins to ready itself for a hasty departure from its own house. "We are supposed to bring a few clothes and one other thing that is important to us. I can't decide which thing to take." But the boy's mother has already decided; not the least of her provisions for the uncertainties of the future is the preparation for the coming age of sorrow: "Amma is taking all the family albums. She says that if anything happens they will remind us of happier days."

All through the day, the family waits in the once-beloved home that has now become a prison. As the hours pass, the narrator seeks consolation in his journal, recording rumors and reports. He hears that the government has distributed electoral lists to help the mobs locate Tamil homes; he is hugely relieved when he is told that a curfew has been declared, and is therefore doubly dismayed to learn that the announcement has made no difference, the mob is still on the rampage. He hears of the police and army watching in silent indifference as a Tamil family is burned alive in a car. At 11:30 P.M. the boy writes: "The waiting is terrible. I wish the mob would come so that this dreadful waiting would end."

The next entry is written a little more than half a day later, but in that brief span of time the world has become a different place. Nothing will ever be the same again; the boy's childhood has become a place apart. This is the moment when history, the connection between time past and time ahead, has ended and memory has become an island that is severed forever from the present and the future. "July 26, 12:30 P.M.: I have just read my last entry and it seems unbelievable that only thirteen hours ago I was sitting on my bed writing in this journal. A year seems to have passed since that time. Our lives have completely changed. I try and try to make sense of it, but it just won't work."

What has happened is this: the long wait has come to an end

soon after the writing of the penultimate journal entry. On hearing the chants of an approaching mob, the family has taken refuge in a Sinhala neighbor's house. Huddled in a storeroom, they have listened as their house is burned to the ground.

The morning after, they have looked over the remains of the house. The sight has made little impression; it is almost incomprehensible. The boy notes that his vinyl records have dissolved into black puddles, that the furniture has cracked open to reveal the whiteness of common wood. "I observed all this with not a trace of remorse, not a touch of sorrow for the loss and destruction around me. Even now I feel no sorrow. I try to remind myself that the house is destroyed, that we will never live in it again, but my heart refuses to understand this." It is only later, on being told of the destruction of his grandparents' home, that he is able to grieve: "I thought about childhood spend-the-days and all the good times we had there. These thoughts made me cry. I couldn't cry for my own house, but it was easy to grieve for my grandparents' house." A precocious prescience has led the boy to grasp the precise nature of his grief: he ascribes it not to the immediacy of his own experience but to the memory of better times — to that act of remembrance than which, as Dante's Francesca da Rimini tells us, there is "no greater sorrow": that is to say, in the recollection of better times.

This depiction of the violence of 1983 — and to my mind *Funny Boy* is one of the most powerful and moving accounts of those events — was published in 1994 in Canada, where Shyam Selvadurai's family had settled after leaving Sri Lanka. I draw attention to this only to underscore two facts: that *Funny Boy* was written by a recent immigrant to North America and that it is an act of recollection that tells the story of a departure. These facts appear unremarkable, yet there is to my mind a puzzle here, and it lies in this: an immigrant's story is usually a narrative of arrival, not departure. And nowhere is this more true than in North America.

North America is famously peopled by immigrants, and nowhere else on earth is the experience of immigration so richly figured as it is here: in popular culture, literature, film, and indeed every aspect of public life. In photography, the emblematic image of this experience is that of a family of immigrants standing on the deck of the ship that has brought them across the Atlantic. In these pictures the immigrants' eyes are always turned in the direction of the waiting shore, toward the Statue of Liberty and the towers of the shining city ahead. Many of these immigrants have suffered terrible hardships, yet we would search in vain for similarly powerful images taken at the hour when they boarded the ship: that moment holds only passing interest in this story. This is because, classically, narratives of immigration to North America are stories of arrival, not departure, stories of suffering but not sorrow or regret; they are stories of hope, founded on a belief in the redemptive power of the land ahead. The vitality of these stories derives in no small part from the obvious parallels with the Biblical story of the Promised Land, which is, of course, equally a story of hope and of arrival. Those who followed Moses out of Egypt did not linger to cast glances of melancholy longing upon the Nile. They looked only ahead; their memory of Egypt was of unmitigated suffering; there were no times of joy there to be recalled in wretchedness. The mark of an exodus lies in the direction of these eyes, looking ahead toward the far shore, confident in the belief that the bonds of community will not perish in the process of migration. But this is not the direction in which Selvadurai's narrator has turned his gaze. Here is the novel's penultimate sentence: "When I reached the top of the road, I couldn't prevent myself from turning back to look at the house one last time." And this is how he ends his story, with the narrator looking back, through the rain, at the charred remains of a home that was once filled with happiness.

It is the direction of the gaze that identifies this as a story not of an exodus but of a dispersal, the story of an irrevocable sundering of the dual bonds that tie members of a community to each other and to other like communities. In the experience of an exodus there is an unspoken ambiguity: the sufferings of displacement are tinged with the hope of arrival and the opening of new vistas in the future. A dispersal offers no such consolation: the pain that haunts it is not that of remembered oppression; it is rather that particular species of pain that comes from the knowledge that the oppressor and the oppressed were once brothers. It is this species of pain, exactly, that runs so poignantly through the literature that resulted from the partition of the Indian subcontinent in 1947. We know, from that line of Boethius which Dante was later to give to Francesca da Rimini, that among fortune's many adversities, the most unhappy kind is to nurture the memory of having once been happy.

This is where recollection turns its back on history, for it is the burden of history to make sense of the past, while the memory of dispersal is haunted always by the essential inexplicability of what has come to pass; by the knowledge that there was nothing inevitable, nothing predestined about what has happened; that far from being primordial, the enmities that have led to the sufferings of the present are new and unaccountable; that there was a time once when neither protagonist saw the other as an adversary — a time that will be irrevocably lost with the dissolution of the history that made it possible for many parts to be a whole.

That which I, in the fever of my pride, am struggling to put into words has been much better said in Agha Shahid Ali's poem "Farewell":

> At a certain point I lost track of you.
> You needed me. You needed to perfect me:
> In your absence you polished me into the Enemy.
> Your history gets in the way of my memory.
> I am everything you lost. You can't forgive me.
> I am everything you lost. Your perfect enemy.
> Your memory gets in the way of my memory . . .
>
> There is nothing to forgive. You won't forgive me.
> I hid my pain even from myself; I revealed my pain only to myself.
> There is everything to forgive. You can't forgive me.

If only somehow you could have been mine,
what would not have been possible in the world?

There is nothing arbitrary, then, about the ending of Selvadurai's novel—the story ends here because it must. To carry it any further would be to link it to the present and the future, to imply the possibility of a consolation. And this, of course, the writer could not do, for the reason that there is no greater sorrow than the recalling of times of joy is precisely that this is a grief beyond consolation.

In 1983, at the time of the Colombo riots, I was hard at work on my first novel, *The Circle of Reason*. I was living in New Delhi, where I had succeeded in finding a minor appointment at Delhi University. Some of my colleagues and mentors at the university —Veena Das and Ashish Nandy, for example—had close connections with human rights activists in Sri Lanka. They were thus able to acquire many of the documents, records, and testimonies that were produced by Sri Lankan researchers. Newspaper accounts of the riots were shocking enough, but the picture that emerged from these independent reports was more menacing still. They left no doubt that some parts of the machinery of state had been used to target a minority population. I don't remember whether we asked ourselves what would happen if this pattern were to spread through the subcontinent. The question was perhaps too grim to pose in an India that was beset by insurgency, calamity, and terror.

A year later, with Indira Gandhi's assassination, the tide crested on our own doorsteps. I remember that day graphically: I remember taking the bus across Delhi; I remember the eerie silence in the university, I remember the evil that gleamed in the eyes of the thugs who began to attack Sikhs wherever they could find them. I have written about these events in detail elsewhere (see "The Ghosts of Mrs. Gandhi," page 187) and will limit myself here to noting only the close parallels between the patterns of violence in Colombo in 1983 and in New Delhi in 1984. In both instances, inexcusable crimes were committed by insurgent groups in the name of freedom; in both cases, the information-gathering function of government was turned to the sinister purpose of targeting minority populations; in both there were clear instances of collusion between officials and criminals.

Through the riots and their aftermath, I, like many of my friends and colleagues, worked with a citizens' relief organization called the Nagarik Ekta Manch. After the immediate crisis was over I returned to the manuscript I was working on. This novel, *The Circle of Reason,* was the story of a journey, and its central section told the story of a group of immigrants — South Asian and Middle Eastern — living in a fictitious oil-rich sheikdom in the Gulf. Looking back today, it strikes me that *The Circle of Reason* could, within the parameters that I have used here, be identified as an exodus novel, a story of migration in the classic sense of having its gaze turned firmly toward the future. The book ended with the words "Hope is the beginning."

I was working on the last part of the book in 1984 when the riots broke out. After the violence it was a struggle to bring the manuscript to a conclusion: my attention had turned away from it. Unlike Shyam Selvadurai, unlike the Sikhs of New Delhi, I was not in the position of a victim during the riots of 1984. But the violence had the effect of bringing to the surface of my memory events from my own childhood when I had indeed been in a similar situation.

Somehow I did manage to finish *The Circle of Reason,* and soon afterward I started the novel that would eventually be published as *The Shadow Lines.* When I began to work on the manuscript, I found that the book was following a pattern of growth that was exactly the opposite of its predecessor's. *The Circle of Reason* had grown upward, like a sapling rising from the soil of my immediate experience; *The Shadow Lines* had its opening planted in the present, but it grew downward, into the soil, like a root system straining to find a source of nourishment.

It was in this process that I came to examine the ways in which

my own life had been affected by civil violence. I remembered stories my mother had told me about the great Calcutta killing of
1946; I remembered my uncles' stories of anti-Indian riots in Rangoon in 1930 and 1938. At the heart of the book, however, was an
event that had occurred in Dhaka in 1964, the year before my family moved to Colombo; in the unlit depths of my memory there
stirred a recollection of a night when our house, flooded with
refugees, was besieged by an angry mob. I had not thought of this
event in decades, but after 1984 it began to haunt me: I was astonished by how vivid my memories were and how fully I could ac-
cess them once I had given myself permission to do so. But my
memories had no context; I had no way of knowing what had happened, whether it was an isolated incident, particular to the neighborhood we were living in, or whether it had implications beyond.
I decided to find out what had happened. I went to libraries and
sifted through hundreds of newspapers, and in the end, through
perseverance, luck, and guesswork, I did find out what had happened. The riots of my memory were not a local affair: they had
engulfed much of the subcontinent. The violence had been set in
motion by the reported theft of a holy relic from the Hazratbal
mosque in Srinagar. Although Kashmir was unaffected, other parts
of the subcontinent had gone up in flames. The rioting had continued for the better part of a week, in India as well as the two wings
of Pakistan.

The process by which I came to learn of this was itself to become a pivotal part of the narrative of *The Shadow Lines*. While
searching for evidence of the riots, I came across dozens of books
about the Indo-Chinese war of 1962. This was an event that had
evidently created a torrent of public discourse. Yet the bare fact is
that this war was fought in a remote patch of terrain, far removed
from major population centers, and it had few repercussions outside the immediate area. The riots of 1964, in contrast, had affected
many major cities and had caused extensive civilian casualties. Yet
there was not a single book devoted to this event. A cursory glance
at a library's bookshelves was enough to establish that in histori-

cal memory, a small war counts for much more than a major out-
break of civil violence. While the riots were under way, they had
received extensive and detailed coverage. Yet once contained, they
had vanished instantly, both from public memory and from the
discourse of history. Why was this so? Why is it that civil violence
seems to occur in parallel time, as though it were outside history?
Why is it that we can look back on these events in sorrow and outrage and yet be incapable of divining any lasting solutions or any
portents for the future?

Inasmuch as I addressed these conundrums in *The Shadow
Lines,* it was in these words:

> Every word I write about those events of 1964 is the product of a
> struggle with silence. It is a struggle that I am destined to lose —
> have already lost — for even after all these years I do not know
> where within me, in which corner of my world, this silence lies.
> All I know of it is what it is not. It is not, for example, the silence
> of a ruthless state — nothing like that: no barbed wire, no check-
> points to tell me where its boundaries lie. I know nothing of this
> silence except that it lies outside the reach of my intelligence, be-
> yond words — that is why this silence must win, must inevitably
> defeat me, because it is not a presence at all; it is simply a gap, a
> hole, an emptiness in which there are not words.
>
> The enemy of silence is speech, but there can be no speech
> without words, and there can be no words without meanings — so
> it follows inexorably, in the manner of syllogisms, that when we
> try to speak of events of which we do not know the meaning, we
> must lose ourselves in the silence that lies in the gap between
> words and the world . . . where there is no meaning, there is ba-
> nality, and that is what this silence consists in, that is why it cannot
> be defeated — because it is the silence of an absolute, impenetra-
> ble banality.

I can still feel the sorrow and outrage that provoked these words
— emotions that owed much more to the events of 1984 than to my
memories of 1964. Just as terrible as the violence itself was the
thought that so many lives had been expended for nothing, that

this terrible weight of suffering had created no discernibly new trajectory in the history or politics of the region. When we grieve for the appalling loss of life in World War II, our sorrow is not compounded by the thought that the war has changed nothing: we know that it has changed the world in very significant ways, has created a new epoch. But in the violence of 1984 — to take just one example — it was impossible to see any such portents. It was hard to see how a further partitioning of the subcontinent could provide a solution; on the contrary, it would create only a new set of minorities and new oppressions. In effect, it would amount only to a recasting of the problem itself, in a different form. In the absence of such meanings, there seemed to be no means of representing these events except in outrage and in sorrow.

It follows then that the reason that I — and many others who have written of such events — are compelled to look back in sorrow is that we cannot look ahead. It is as though the events of the immediate past have made the future even more obscure than it is usually acknowledged to be. Now, close on two decades later, I find myself asking, Why is this so? Why was it that in the 1980s, history itself seemed to stumble and come to a standstill?

The past, as Faulkner famously said, is not over; in fact, the past is not even the past. One of the paradoxes of history is that it is impossible to draw a chart of the past without imagining a map of the present and the future. History, in other words, is never innocent of teleologies, implicit or otherwise. Ranajit Guha, in a recent lecture on Hegel and the writing of history in South Asia, says, "It is the state which first supplies a content, which not only lends itself to the prose of history but actually helps to produce it." In other words, the actions of the state provide that essential element of continuity that makes time, as a collective experience, thinkable, by linking the past, the present, and the future. The state as thus conceived is not merely an apparatus of rule but "a conscious, ethical institution," an instrument designed to conquer the "unhistorical power of time." That is, since the nineteenth century, and perhaps even earlier, it is the state that has provided the grid on which history is mapped.

It was perhaps this politically insignificant but epistemologically indispensable aspect of time's continuity that was most vitally damaged by the conflagrations of the 1980s. Even before then, it had often been suspected that elements of the state's machinery had been colluding in the production of communal violence; after the violence of the eighties, this became established as a fact. It became evident that certain parts of the state had been absorbed by —had indeed become sponsors of—criminal violence. No longer could the state be seen as a protagonist in its own right. It is for this reason that I have used the self-contradictory phrase "civil violence" here, in preference to other, more commonly used terms: because these events signaled the collapse of the familiar categories of "state" and "civil society."

The flames created by our recent past are so plentiful that only poets noticed the unsung death of a teleology. "Everything is finished, nothing remains," writes Agha Shahid Ali of a poet who returns to Kashmir in search of the keeper of a destroyed minaret.

> "Nothing will remain, everything's finished,"
> I see his voice again: "This is a shrine
> of words. You'll find your letters to me. And mine
> to you. Come soon and tear open these vanished
> envelopes." . . .
>
> This is an archive. I've found the remains
> of his voice, that map of longings with no limit.

Buried within the poet's "shrine of words" lies a map: a chart "of longings without limit." It is not the fall of the minaret but the loss of the map that is the true catastrophe. It is this loss that evokes the words "Nothing will remain, everything's finished."

Shahid's is not the only lost map. In "The Story," Michael Ondaatje invokes another.

> For his first forty days a child
> is given dreams of previous lives,
> journeys, winding paths,

a hundred small lessons
and then the past is erased.

Some are born screaming,
some full of introspective wandering
into the past — that bus ride in winter,
the sudden arrival within
a new city in the dark.
And those departures from family bonds
leaving what was lost and needed.
So the child's face is a lake
of fast moving clouds and emotions.

A last chance for the clear history of the self.
All our mothers and grandparents here,
our dismantled childhoods
in the buildings of the past.

Some great forty-day daydream
before we bury the maps.

The old maps are gone, and two of the finest poets of our time, Michael Ondaatje and Agha Shahid Ali, exiles from twinned Edens, have borne witness to their loss; gone are Michael's "forty-day daydream" and Shahid's "longings without limit." Writers who look back, in the wake of that loss, can only build shrines to that past. And yet the mystery of the sorrow entombed in their work is that their grief is not just for a time remembered: they grieve also for the loss of the map that made the future thinkable.

Is there then another map to replace those that have been buried in the rubble of our daydreams? Once, six years ago, I thought I had a glimpse of one: this is how it came about. I had spent a sleepless night at a guerrilla camp in the thickly forested mountains of the Burma-Thailand border. The Myanmar army was entrenched a few miles away, fighting a fierce engagement with Karenni insurgents. My hosts had handed me a makeshift pillow, of a book wrapped in a towel. The bundle came undone at some point during the night and I discovered, switching on

my flashlight, that the book was called *The Transformation of War*.
It was written by a military historian called Martin Van Creveld.
I began to read and was still reading hours later. The next day,
I wrote in my diary:

> I am appalled by Van Creveld's vision of the future, yet over here,
> it makes more sense than anything I have read about this kind of
> conflict. Van Creveld is arguing that modern weaponry has been
> rendered obsolete by its very effectiveness. The destructiveness of
> these weapons is such as to make conventional military-based
> conflict impossible: hence fighting will increasingly take the form
> of low-intensity conflict, based upon "close intermingling with
> the enemy." Civilians will be in the front lines of the conflict; they
> will be the focus of attack and conventional distinctions between
> army, state, and civil society will break down. Groups such as pri-
> vate mercenary bands commanded by warlords and even com-
> mercial organs will become the main combatants: "future war-
> making entities will probably resemble the Assassins, the group
> which, motivated by religion and allegedly supporting itself on
> drugs, terrorized the Middle East for . . . centuries.

Till then I had taken for granted a pattern of the world that
divided the globe between a large number of nation-states. Now
suddenly it was as though a bucket had been upended on the
map, making the colors run. The camp and the disputed territory
around it was no longer on no man's land; it was a reality in its
own right, one that extended in an unbroken swath through
northern Burma and northeast India to western China and Kashmir, Afghanistan, Central Asia, and the Caucasus. In this immense
stretch of territory, Van Creveld's vision was not just one of many
possible forks in the road: it was a turn already taken. Nor could
I any longer regard Myanmar and its brutally despotic regime as
an aberration, a holdover from a preempted past. I was forced to
ask myself whether that country might not hold some portents
for the future. Burma is a country to which terrorism and insurgency came exceptionally early: within a few months of independ-

ence, in 1948, the Rangoon government was besieged by sixteen re-
bellions. Accounts of life in Burma in the 1950s are replete with
tales of derailed trains, bombs in stations, sudden ambushes, and
the like. Within a few years civil society collapsed, and there followed an absolute militarization of political life. The results are
well known. That this could happen elsewhere did not seem im-
probable.

Not unaware of the world's discontents, I took Van Creveld's
vision seriously and tried to incorporate his warnings into my
everyday life. I made a point, for example, of not trying to shield
my children from news of violence and terror. Yet no matter how
carefully we prepare ourselves for the future, the reality is always
far in excess of our imaginings.

On the morning of September 11, I was sitting at my desk in my
house in Brooklyn when my wife called from her office in midtown Manhattan to tell me about the attacks on the World Trade
Center. My ten-year-old daughter, Lila, was at school a couple of
miles away, and my eight-year-old son was at home: this was to
have been his first day in a new school, and I was scheduled to take
him there later that morning. But instead we rushed out together
to fetch Lila home from her school in Brooklyn Heights.

Downtown Brooklyn was choked with people, and in the distance we saw a plume of dust rising into the clear blue sky, darken-
ing the horizon like a thundercloud. Everyone was heading away
from the river; only the two of us seemed to be walking toward
the darkness in the distance. I held my son's hand and walked as
fast as I could. On arriving in Brooklyn Heights, we found Lila in
the basement of her school. Her eyes were bright, and she was
eager to tell me what had happened. "Where were you?" she said.
"I saw it all. From the window of our history class we had a clear
view."

We stepped out and joined the great wave of dust-caked evacuees that was pouring over the Brooklyn Bridge. I held my children's hands and tried to think of words of reassurance, some-

thing that would reattach the moorings that had come undone
that morning and restore their sense of safety. But words are not to
be had for the asking, and I could think of none.

Since then I have come to recognize that there is very little I
can say to broaden my children's understanding of what they saw
that day. As a writer I have tried to live by the credo that nothing
human should be alien to me. Yet my imagination stops short as
I try to think of the human realities of what it must mean to plan a
collective suicide over a span of years or to stand in a check-in line
with people whose murder has already been decided on; of what it
takes to speak of love on a cell phone moments before one's death
or to reach for a stranger's hand as one leaps from the topmost
floor of a skyscraper. These are new dimensions of human experience, and I realize that they will become a part of the generational
gap that separates me from my children: their imagining of the
world will be different from mine, and that very difference will create a new reality. From my own childhood I remember a day when
I stared at a newspaper, mesmerized by a picture of a Buddhist
monk burning at a crossroads in Saigon. At that time, this too represented a new addition to the armory of human motivation: this
was the moment that inaugurated the era of political suicide in the
modern world. Since then such suicides have become so commonplace as often to go unreported. They have become a part of the
unseen foundations of our awareness, present but unnoticed, like
the earth beneath a basement.

The thickening crust of our awareness is both a sign and a reminder of our unwitting complicity in the evolution of violence: if
that which mesmerized us yesterday ceases to interest us today,
then it follows that the act which will next claim our attention will
be even more horrific, even more resistant to yesterday's imagination, than the last. The horror of these acts is thus exactly cali-
brated to the indifference upon which they are inflicted. Their purpose is not warlike, in the sense of achieving specific ends through
violence; their purpose is horror itself.

In one of its aspects terror represents an epistemic violence, a radical interruption in the procedures and protocols that give the world a semblance of comprehensibility. This is why it causes not just fear and anger but also long-lasting confusion and utterly disproportionate panic; it tears apart the stories through which individuals link their lives to a collective past and present. Everyday life would be impossible if we did not act upon certain assumptions about the future, near and distant — about the train we will catch tomorrow as well as the money we pay into our pensions. Not the least of the terror of a moment such as that of September 11 is that it reveals the future to be truly what it is: unknown, unpredictable, and utterly inscrutable. It is this epistemic upheaval that Michael Ondaatje and Agha Shahid Ali point to when they mourn the maps of our longings and our forty-day daydreams: the pure intuition of poetry had led them to an awareness of this loss long before the world awakened to the knowledge that "nothing will be the same again."

On October 11, a month after the attacks on the World Trade Center, *The New Yorker* organized an evening of readings to raise money for the victims. I was one of those invited to read, and I chose to read two of Shahid's poems. Several of the other readers chose texts that hearkened back to the wars of the twentieth century: Winston Churchill on World War I; Remarque on the trenches of the western front; Auden on the declaration of war in September 1939. When it was my turn to read, I was struck by the sharpness of the contrast between Shahid's voice and those of the poets of the last century; by the vividness of emotion; by the almost palpable terror that comes of having looked into the obscurity of a time that will not permit itself to be mapped with the measures of the past. It was as though news of times to come had been carried to the capital of the world by a messenger from a half-forgotten hinterland. Time had turned on itself: the backward had preceded the advanced; the periphery had visited the present before the center; the "half-made" world had become the diviner of the fully formed.

Yet the message itself was neither a presaging nor a prediction;

it lay merely in the acknowledgment of the loss of a map. But to be aware of the death of a teleology is not to know of what will take its place. The truth is that on the morning of September 11, I had nothing to say to my children that had not been said in Michael Ondaatje's poem "The Story":

> With all the swerves of history
> I cannot imagine your future . . .
>
> I no longer guess a future.
> And do not know how we end
> nor where.
>
> Though I know a story about maps, for you.

"THE GHAT OF THE ONLY WORLD"

Agha Shahid Ali in Brooklyn

2003

THE FIRST TIME that Agha Shahid Ali spoke to me about his approaching death was on April 25, 2001. The conversation began routinely. I had telephoned to remind him that we had been invited to a friend's house for lunch and that I was going to come by his apartment to pick him up. Although he had been under treatment for cancer for some fourteen months, Shahid was still on his feet and perfectly lucid, except for occasional lapses of memory. I heard him thumbing through his engagement book, and then suddenly he said, "Oh dear. I can't see a thing." There was a brief pause and then he added, "I hope this doesn't mean that I'm dying . . ."

Although Shahid and I had talked a great deal over the past many weeks, I had never before heard him touch on the subject of death. I did not know how to respond; his voice was completely at odds with the content of what he had just said, light to the point of jocularity. I mumbled something innocuous: "No, Shahid — of course not. You'll be fine." He cut me short. In a tone of voice that was at once quizzical and direct, he said, "When it happens, I hope you'll write something about me."

I was shocked into silence, and a long moment passed before I could bring myself to say the things that people say on such occasions. "Shahid, you'll be fine; you have to be strong . . ."

From the window of my study I could see a corner of the building in which he lived, some eight blocks away. It was just a few months since he moved there; he had been living a few miles away, in Manhattan, when he had had a sudden blackout, in February 2000. After tests revealed that he had a malignant brain tumor, he decided to move to Brooklyn, to be close to his youngest sister, Sameetah, who teaches at the Pratt Institute — a few blocks away from the street where I live.

Shahid ignored my reassurances. He began to laugh, and it was then that I realized he was dead serious. I understood that he was entrusting me with a quite specific charge: he wanted me to remember him not through the spoken recitatives of memory and friendship but through the written word. Shahid knew all too well that for those writers for whom things become real only in the process of writing, there is an in-built resistance to dealing with loss and bereavement. He knew that my instincts would have led me to search for reasons to avoid writing about his death: I would have told myself that I was not a poet, that our friendship was of recent date, that there were many others who knew him much better and would be writing from greater understanding and knowledge. All this Shahid had guessed, and he had decided to shut off those routes while there was still time.

"You must write about me."

Clear though it was that this imperative would have to be acknowledged, I could think of nothing to say. What are the words in which one promises a friend that one will write about him after his death? Finally I said, "Shahid, I will. I'll do the best I can."

By the end of the conversation I knew exactly what I had to do. I picked up my pen, noted the date, and wrote down everything I remembered of that conversation. This I continued to do for the next few months. It is this record that has made it possible for me to fulfill the pledge I made that day.

I knew Shahid's work long before I met him. His 1997 collection, *The Country Without a Post Office*, had made a powerful impression on me. His voice was like none I had ever heard before, at once lyrical and fiercely disciplined, engaged and yet deeply inward. Not for him the mock-casual almost-prose of so much contemporary poetry: his was a voice that was not ashamed to speak in a bardic register. I knew of no one else who would even conceive of publishing a line like "Mad heart, be brave."

In 1998, I quoted a line from *The Country Without a Post Office* in an article that touched briefly on Kashmir. At the time all I knew about Shahid was that he was from Srinagar and had studied in Delhi. I had been at Delhi University myself, but although our time there had briefly overlapped, we had never met. We had friends in common, however, and one of them put me in touch with Shahid. In 1998 and 1999 we had several conversations on the phone and even met a couple of times. But we were no more than acquaintances until he moved to Brooklyn the next year. Once we were in the same neighborhood, we began to meet for occasional meals and quickly discovered that we had a great deal in common. By this time, of course, Shahid's condition was already serious, yet his illness did not impede the progress of our friendship. We found that we had a huge roster of common friends, in India, America, and elsewhere; we discovered a shared love of rogan josh, Roshanara Begum, and Kishore Kumar, a mutual indifference to cricket, and an equal attachment to old Bombay films. Because of Shahid's condition, even the most trivial exchanges had a special charge and urgency: the inescapable poignance of talking about food and half-forgotten figures from the past with a man who knew himself to be dying was multiplied, in this instance, by the knowledge that this man was also a poet who had achieved greatness—perhaps the only such that I shall ever know as a friend.

One afternoon the writer Suketu Mehta, who also lives in Brooklyn, joined us for lunch. Together we hatched a plan for an *adda*—by definition, a gathering that has no agenda other than conviviality. Shahid was enthusiastic, and we began to meet regularly. From time to time other writers would join us. On one occasion a crew arrived with a television camera. Shahid was not in the least bit put out: "I'm *so* shameless; I just *love* the camera."

Shahid had a sorcerer's ability to transmute the mundane into the magical. Once I accompanied Iqbal, his brother, and Hena, his sister, on a trip to fetch him home from hospital. This was on May 21; by that time he had already been through several unsuccessful operations. Now he was back in hospital to undergo a surgical procedure that was intended to relieve the pressure on his brain. His head was shaved, and the shape of the tumor was visible upon his bare scalp, its edges outlined by metal sutures. When it was time to leave the ward, a blue-uniformed hospital escort arrived with a wheelchair. Shahid waved him away, declaring that he was strong enough to walk out of the hospital on his own. But he was groggier than he thought, and his knees buckled after no more than a few steps. Iqbal went running off to bring back the wheelchair while the rest of us stood in the corridor, holding him upright. At that moment, leaning against the cheerless hospital wall, a kind of rapture descended on Shahid. When the hospital orderly returned with the wheelchair, Shahid gave him a beaming smile and asked where he was from. Ecuador, the man said, and Shahid clapped his hands gleefully together. "Spanish!" he cried, at the top of his voice. "I always wanted to learn Spanish. Just to read Lorca."

At this the tired, slack-shouldered orderly came suddenly to life. "Lorca? Did you say Lorca?" He quoted a few lines, to Shahid's great delight. "Ah! 'La Cinque de la Tarde,'" Shahid cried, rolling the syllables gleefully around his tongue. "How I love those words. 'La Cinque de la Tarde'!" That was how we made our way through the hospital's crowded lobby: with Shahid and the orderly in the vanguard, one quoting snatches of Spanish poetry and the other breaking in from time to time with exultant cries of "La Cinque de la Tarde, La Cinque de la Tarde . . ."

Shahid's gregariousness had no limit: there was never an evening when there wasn't a party in his living room. "I love it that so many people are here," he told me once. "I love it that people come and there's always food. I love this spirit of festivity; it means that I don't have time to be depressed."

His apartment was a spacious and airy split-level on the seventh floor of a newly renovated building. There was a cavernous study on the top floor and a wide terrace that provided a magnificent view of the Manhattan skyline, across the East River. Shahid loved this view of the Brooklyn waterfront slipping like a ghat into the East River, under the glittering lights of Manhattan.

The journey from the foyer of Shahid's building to his door was a voyage between continents. On the way up, the rich fragrance of rogan josh and haak would invade the dour gray interior of the elevator; against the background of the songs and voices that were always echoing out of his apartment, even the ringing of the door-bell had an oddly musical sound. Suddenly Shahid would appear, flinging open the door, releasing a great cloud of heeng into the frosty New York air. "Oh, how *nice*," he would cry, clapping his hands, "how *nice* that you've come to see your little Mos-lem!" In-variably there'd be some half-dozen or more people gathered in-side — poets, students, writers, relatives — and in the kitchen some-one would always be cooking or making tea. Almost to the very end, even as his life was being consumed by his disease, he was the center of a perpetual carnival, an endless *mela* of talk, laughter, food, and of course poetry.

No matter how many people there were, Shahid was never so distracted as to lose track of the progress of the evening's meal. From time to time he would interrupt himself to shout directions to whoever was in the kitchen: "Yes, now, add the dahi now." Even when his eyesight was failing, he could tell from the smell alone exactly which stage the rogan josh had reached. And when things went exactly as they should, he would sniff the air and cry out loud, "Ah! Khana ka kya mehek hai!"

Shahid was legendary for his prowess in the kitchen, frequently spending days over the planning and preparation of a dinner party. It was through one such party, given while he was in Arizona, that he met James Merrill, the poet who was to radically alter the direc-tion of his poetry: it was after this encounter that he began to ex-periment with strict metrical patterns and verse forms such as the canzone and the sestina. No one had a greater influence on Shahid's poetry than James Merrill; indeed, in the poem in which he most explicitly prefigured his own death, "I Dream I Am at the Ghat of the Only World," he awarded the envoy to Merrill: "SHA-HID, HUSH. THIS IS ME, JAMES. THE LOVED ONE AL-WAYS LEAVES."

"How did you meet Merrill?" I asked Shahid once.

"I heard he was coming down for a reading and I told the people in charge that I wanted to meet him. They said, 'Then why don't you cook for him?' So I did." Merrill loved the food, and on learning that Shahid was moving to Hamilton College in upstate New York, he gave him his telephone number and asked him to call. On the occasion of Shahid's first reading at the Academy of American Poets, Merrill was present—a signal honor, considering that he was one of America's best-known poets. "Afterward," Shahid liked to recall, "everybody rushed up and said, 'Did you know that Jim Merrill was here?' My stock in New York went up a thousandfold that evening."

Shahid placed great store on authenticity and exactitude in cooking and would tolerate no deviation from traditional methods and recipes; for those who took shortcuts he had only pity. He had a special passion for the food of his region, one variant of it in particular: "Kashmiri food in the Pandit style." I asked him once why this was so important to him, and he explained that it was because of a recurrent dream in which all the Pandits had vanished from the valley of Kashmir and their food had become extinct. This was a nightmare that haunted him, and he returned to it again and again, in his conversation and his poetry.

> At a certain point I lost track of you.
> You needed me. You needed to perfect me:
> In your absence you polished me into the Enemy.
> Your history gets in the way of my memory.
> I am everything you lost. You can't forgive me.
> I am everything you lost. Your perfect Enemy.
> Your memory gets in the way of my memory . . .

There is nothing to forgive. You won't forgive me.
I hid my pain even from myself; I revealed my pain
        only to myself.
There is everything to forgive. You can't forgive me.
If only somehow you could have been mine,
what would not have been possible in the world?

Once, in conversation, he told me that he also loved Bengali food. I protested: "But Shahid, you've never even been to Calcutta."

"No," he said. "But we had friends who used to bring us that food. When you ate it, you could see that there were so many things that you didn't know about, everywhere in the country . . ."

This was at a time when his illness had forced him into spending long periods in bed. He was lying prone on his back, shielding his eyes with his fingers. Suddenly he broke off and reached for my hand. "I wish all this had not happened," he said. "This dividing of the country, the divisions between people — Hindu, Muslim, Muslim, Hindu — you can't imagine how much I hate it. It makes me sick. What I say is, why can't you be happy with the cuisines and the clothes and the music and all these wonderful things?" He paused and added softly, "At least here we have been able to make a space where we can all come together because of the good things."

Of the many "good things" in which he took pleasure, none was more dear to him than the music of Begum Akhtar. He had met the great ghazal singer when he was in his teens, through a friend, and she had become an abiding presence and influence in his life. In his apartment there were several shrinelike niches that were filled with pictures of the people he worshipped: Begum Akhtar was one of these, along with his father, his mother, and James Merrill. "I loved Begum Akhtar," he told me once. "In other circumstances you could have said that it was a sexual kind of love — but I don't know what it was. I loved to listen to her, I loved to be with her, I couldn't bear to be away from her. You can imagine what it was like. Here I was in my midteens — just sixteen — and I couldn't bear to be away from her."

His love of Begum Akhtar was such as to spill over into a powerful sense of identification. He told me once that the singer Sheila Dhar, who had known Begum Akhtar well, had told him that he even bore a resemblance to Begum Akhtar: "It's something about our teeth and mouth."

I said, "I don't see a resemblance between you and Begum Akhtar."

He directed a wounded glance at me. "Yes, there is," he said. "Sheila Dhar told me so."

"Well" — I quickly corrected myself — "she knew Begum Akhtar, so I think she knows more about it than I do."

He nodded. "Yes," he said. "It's something about the teeth. Her teeth were a little prominent [*dant agey they*] — so are mine."

It may well have been this relationship with Begum Akhtar that engendered his passion for the ghazal as a verse form. Yet, ardent advocate of the form though he was, he had little time for the gushing ardor of some of its contemporary American fans: "Imagine me at a writer's conference where a woman kept saying to me, 'Oh, I just love guh-zaals, I'm gonna write a lot of g'zaals,' and I said to her, in utter pain, 'OH, PLEASE DON'T!'" Always the disciplinarian in such matters, he believed that the ghazal would never flourish if its structure were not given due respect: "Some rules of the ghazal are clear and classically stringent. The opening couplet (called *matlā*) sets up a scheme (of rhyme called *qafia;* and refrain — called *radif*) by having it occur in both lines — the rhyme *immediately* preceding the refrain — and then this scheme occurs only in the second line of each succeeding couplet. That is, once a poet establishes the scheme — with total freedom, I might add — she or he becomes its slave. What results in the rest of the poem is the alluring tension of a slave trying to master the master." Over a period of several years he took it on himself to solicit ghazals from a number of poets writing in English. The resulting collection,

Ravishing Disunities: Real Ghazals in English, was published in 2000. In establishing a benchmark for the form it has already begun to exert a powerful influence: the formalization of the ghazal may well prove to be Shahid's most important scholarly contribution to the canon of English poetry. His own summation of the project was this: "If one writes in free verse — and one should — to subvert Western civilization, surely one should write in forms to save oneself from Western civilization?"

For Shahid, Begum Akhtar was the embodiment of one such form, not just in her music but in many other aspects of her being. An aspect of the ghazal that he greatly prized was the latitude it provided for wordplay, wit, and *nakhra* (posturing): Begum Akhtar was a consummate master of all of these. Shahid had a fund of stories about her sharpness in repartee. On one occasion he had accompanied her to the studios of All India Radio for a recording session. On the way in they met a famous singer, a man who was reputed to be having an affair with his *dhobin* (washerwoman). Begum Akhtar greeted the *ustad* with a deep salaam, as befitted by his standing in the world of music. But then, in passing, she tossed off the line "Arrey Khan-sahib, what a very clean kurta you're wearing today." Later, once out of the maestro's sight, they fell over laughing.

Shahid was himself no mean practitioner of repartee. On one famous occasion, at Barcelona airport, he was stopped by a security guard just as he was about to board a plane. The guard, a woman, asked, "What do you do?"

"I'm a poet," Shahid answered.

"What were you doing in Spain?"

"Writing poetry."

No matter what the question, Shahid worked poetry into his answer. Finally the exasperated woman asked, "Are you carrying anything that could be dangerous to the other passengers?" At this Shahid clapped a hand to his chest and cried, "Only my heart."

This was one of his great Wildean moments, and it was to occasion the poem "Barcelona Airport." He treasured these moments; "I long for people to give me an opportunity to answer questions," he told me once. On May 7 I had the good fortune to be with him when one such opportunity presented itself. Shahid was teaching at Manhattan's Baruch College in the spring semester of 2000, and this was to be his last class — indeed, the last he was ever to teach. The class was to be a short one, for he had an appointment at the hospital immediately afterward. I had heard a great deal about the brilliance of Shahid's teaching, but this was the first and only time that I was to see him perform in a classroom. It was evident from the moment we walked in that the students adored him: they had printed a magazine and dedicated the issue to him. Shahid, for his part, was not in the least subdued by the sadness of the occasion. From beginning to end, he was a sparkling diva, Akhtar incarnate, brimming with laughter and *nakhra*. When an Indian student walked in late, he greeted her with the cry, "Ah my little subcontinental has arrived." Clasping his hands, he feigned a swoon. "It stirs such a tide of patriotism in me to behold another South Asian!"

Toward the end of the class, a student asked a complicated question about the difference between plausibility and inevitability in a poem. Shahid's eyebrows arched higher and higher as he listened. At last, unable to contain himself, he broke in. "Oh, you're such a *naughty* boy," he cried, tapping the table with his fingertips. "You always turn *everything* into an abstraction."

But Begum Akhtar was not all wit and *nakhra*: indeed, the strongest bond between Shahid and her was, I suspect, the idea that sorrow has no finer mask than a studied lightness of manner. Shahid often told a story about Begum Akhtar's marriage. Although her family's origins were dubious, her fame as a beauty was such that she received a proposal from the scion of a prominent Muslim family of Lucknow. The proposal came with the condition that the talented young singer would give up singing: the man's family was deeply conservative and could not conceive of one of its members performing onstage. Begum Akhtar — or Akhtaribai Faizabadi, as she was then — accepted, but soon afterward her mother died. Heartbroken, Akhtaribai spent her days weeping on her grave. Her condition became such that a doctor had to be brought in to examine her. He said that if she were not allowed to sing, she would lose her mind. It was only then that her husband's family relented and allowed her to sing again.

Shahid was haunted by this image of Begum Akhtar, as a bereaved and inconsolable daughter, weeping on her mother's grave; it is in this grief-stricken aspect that she is evoked again and again in his poems. The poem that was his farewell to the world, "I Dream I Am at the Ghat of the Only World," opens with an evocation of Begum Akhtar:

> A night of ghazals comes to an end. The singer
> departs through her chosen mirror, her one diamond
> cut on her countless necks. I, as ever, linger

It was Shahid's mother who had introduced him to the music of Begum Akhtar: "With her I'd heard — on 78 rpm — *Peer Gynt* . . . / and Ghalib's grief in the voice of Begum Akhtar." In Shahid's later poems, Begum Akhtar was to become an image for the embodiment of his own sorrow after his mother's death. Shahid's mother, a woman of striking beauty, happened to have a close, indeed startling, resemblance to Begum Akhtar. Shahid's walls were hung with many pictures of both, and I would frequently mistake the one for the other. What then of Shahid's belief that he resembled Begum Akhtar? There is a mystery here that I am content to leave untouched.

Shahid was born in New Delhi in 1949. Later, in one of the temporal inversions that marked his poetry, he was to relive his conception in his poem "A Lost Memory of Delhi":

> I am not born
> it is 1948 and the bus turns
> onto a road without name

There on his bicycle
my father
He is younger than I

At Okhla where I get off
I pass my parents
strolling by the Jamuna River

Shahid's father's family was from Srinagar, in Kashmir. They were Shiites, who are a minority among the Muslims of Kashmir. Shahid liked to tell a story about the origins of his family. The line was founded, he used to say, by two brothers who came to Kashmir from Central Asia. The brothers had been trained as *hakims*, specializing in Yunani medicine, and they arrived in Kashmir with nothing but their knowledge of medical lore; they were so poor that they had to share a single cloak between them. But it so happened that the then maharajah of Kashmir was suffering from terrible stomach pains, "some kind of colic." Learning that all the kingdom's doctors had failed to cure the ailing ruler, the two brothers decided to try their hand. They gave the maharajah a concoction that went through the royal intestines like a plunger through a tube, bringing sudden and explosive relief. Delighted with his cure, the grateful potentate appointed the brothers his court physicians. Thus began the family's prosperity. "So you see," Shahid would comment, in bringing the story to its conclusion, "my family's fortunes were founded on a fart."

By Shahid's account, his great-grandfather was the first Kashmiri Muslim to matriculate. The story went that to sit for the examination, he had to travel all the way from Srinagar to Rawalpindi in a *tonga*. Later, he too became an official at the court of the maharajah of Kashmir. He had special charge of education, and took the initiative to educate his daughter. Shahid's grandmother was thus one of the first educated women in Kashmir. She passed the matriculation examination, took several other degrees, and in time became the inspector of women's schools. She could quote poetry in four languages: English, Urdu, Farsi, and Kash-

miri. Shahid's father, Agha Ashraf Ali, continued the family tradition of public service in education. He taught at Jamia Millia University, in New Delhi, and went on to become the principal of the
Teacher's College in Srinagar. In 1961 he enrolled at Ball State
Teacher's College, in Muncie, Indiana, to do a Ph.D. in comparative education. Shahid was twelve when the family moved to the
United States, and for the next three years he attended school in
Muncie. Later the family moved back to Srinagar, and that was
where Shahid completed his schooling. But it was because of his
early experience, I suspect, that he was able to take America so
completely in his stride when he arrived in Pennsylvania as a graduate student. The idea of a cultural divide or conflict had no purchase in his mind: America and India were the two poles of his life,
and he was at home in both in a way that was utterly easeful and
unproblematic.

Shahid took his undergraduate degree at the University of
Kashmir, in Srinagar. Although he excelled there, graduating with
the highest marks in his class, he did not recall the experience with
any fondness. "I learned nothing there," he told me once. "It was
just a question of *ratto-maro*ing [learning by heart]." In 1968 he
joined Hindu College in Delhi University to study for an M.A. in
English literature. Once again he performed with distinction, and
he went on to become a lecturer at the same college. It was in this
period that he published his first collection of poems, with P. Lal of
the Writer's Workshop in Calcutta.

Shahid's memories of Delhi University were deeply conflicted:
he became something of a campus celebrity but also endured re-
buffs and disappointments that may well have come his way only
because he was a Muslim and a Kashmiri. Although he developed
many close and lasting friendships, he also suffered many betrayals
and much unhappiness. In any event, he was, I think, deeply relieved when Penn State University, in College Park, Pennsylvania,
offered him a scholarship for a Ph.D.

His time at Penn State he remembered with unmitigated pleasure: "I grew as a reader, I grew as a poet, I grew as a lover." He fell

in with a vibrant group of graduate students, many of whom were Indian. This was, he often said, the happiest time of his life. Later Shahid moved to Arizona to take a degree in creative writing. This in turn was followed by a series of jobs in colleges and universities: Hamilton College, the University of Massachusetts at Amherst, and finally the University of Utah, in Salt Lake City, where he was appointed professor in 1999. He was on leave from Utah, doing a brief stint at New York University, when he had his first blackout, in February 2000.

After 1975, when he moved to Pennsylvania, Shahid lived mainly in America. His brother was already here, and they were later joined by their two sisters. But Shahid's parents continued to live in Srinagar, and it was his custom to spend the summer months with them there every year: "I always move in my heart between sad countries." Traveling between the United States and India, he was thus an intermittent but firsthand witness (*shahid*) to the mounting violence that seized the region from the late 1980s onward:

> It was '89, the stones were not far, signs of change
> everywhere (Kashmir would soon be in literal
> flames) . . .

The steady deterioration of the political situation in Kashmir — the violence and counterviolence — had a powerful effect on him. In time it became one of the central subjects of his work; indeed, it could be said that it was in writing of Kashmir that he created his finest work. The irony of this is that Shahid was not by inclination a political poet. I heard him say once, "If you are from a difficult place and that's all you have to write about, then you should stop writing. You have to respect your art, your form — that is just as important as what you write about." Another time I was present at Shahid's apartment when his longtime friend Patricia O'Neill showed him a couple of sonnets written by a Victorian poet. The poems were political, trenchant in their criticism of the British government for its failure to prevent the massacre of the Armeni-

ans in Turkey. Shahid glanced at them and tossed them off-hand-
edly aside: "These are terrible poems." Patricia asked why, and he
said, "Look, I already know where I stand on the massacre of the
Armenians. Of course I am against it. But this poem tells me nothing of the massacre; it makes nothing of it formally. I might as well
just read a news report."

Anguished as he was about Kashmir's destiny, Shahid resolutely
refused to embrace the role of victim that could so easily have
been his. Had he not done so, he could no doubt have easily become a fixture on talk shows, news programs, and op-ed pages.
But Shahid never had any doubt about his calling: he was a poet,
schooled in the fierce and unforgiving arts of language. Such as
they were, Shahid's political views were inherited largely from his
father, whose beliefs were akin to those of most secular, left-lean-
ing Muslim intellectuals of the Nehruvian era. Although respectful of religion, he was a firm believer in the separation of politics
and religious practice.

Once when Shahid was at dinner with my family, I asked him
bluntly, "What do you think is the solution for Kashmir?" His answer was, "I think ideally the best solution would be absolute autonomy within the Indian Union in the broadest sense." But this
led almost immediately to the enumeration of a long list of ca-
veats and reservations. Quite possibly, he said, such a solution was
no longer possible, given the actions of the Indian state in Kashmir; the extremist groups would never accept the "autonomy" solution in any case, and so many other complications had entered
the situation that it was almost impossible to think of a solution.

The truth is that Shahid's gaze was not political in the sense of
being framed in terms of policy and solutions. In the broadest
sense, his vision tended always toward the inclusive and ecumeni-
cal, an outlook that he credited to his upbringing. He spoke often
of a time in his childhood when he had been seized by the desire to
create a small Hindu temple in his room in Srinagar. He was initially hesitant to tell his parents, but when he did, they responded
with an enthusiasm equal to his own. His mother bought him *mur-*

tis (religious icons) and other accoutrements, and for a while he was assiduous in conducting *pujas* (Hindu ceremonies of worship) at this shrine. This was a favorite story. "Whenever people talk to me about Muslim fanaticism," he said to me once, "I tell them how my mother helped me make a temple in my room. 'What do you make of that?' I ask them." There is a touching evocation of this in his poem "Lenox Hill": "and I, one festival, crowned Krishna by you, Kashmir / listening to my flute."

I once remarked to Shahid that he was the closest that Kashmir had to a national poet. He shot back: "A national poet, maybe. But not a *nationalist* poet—please, not that." If anything, Kashmir's current plight represented for him the failure of the emancipatory promise of nationhood and the extinction of the pluralistic ideal that had been so dear to intellectuals of his father's generation. In the title poem of *The Country Without a Post Office,* a poet returns to Kashmir to find the keeper of a fallen minaret:

> "Nothing will remain, everything's finished,"
> I see his voice again: "This is a shrine
> of words. You'll find your letters to me. And mine
> to you. Come soon and tear open these vanished
> envelopes" . . .
>
> This is an archive. I've found the remains
> of his voice, that map of longings with no limit.

The pessimism engendered by the loss of these ideals—*that map of longings with no limit*—resulted in a vision in which, increasingly, Kashmir became a vortex of images circling around a single point of stillness: the idea of death. In this figuring of his homeland, he himself became one of the images that were spinning around the dark point of stillness—both Sháhid and Shahíd, witness and martyr—his destiny inextricably linked with Kashmir's, each prefigured by the other.

> I will die, in autumn, in Kashmir,
> and the shadowed routine of each vein

will almost be news, the blood censored,
for the *Saffron Sun* and the *Times of Rain*

Among my notes is a record of a telephone conversation on May 5. The day before he had gone to the hospital for an important test, a scan that was expected to reveal whether or not the course of chemotherapy that he was then undergoing had had the desired effect. All other alternative therapies and courses of treatment had been put off until this report.

The scan was scheduled for 2:30 in the afternoon. I called his number several times in the late afternoon and early evening — there was no response. I called again the next morning, and this time he answered. There were no preambles. He said, "Listen, Amitav, the news is not good at all. Basically, they are going to stop all my medicines now — the chemotherapy and so on. They give me a year or less. They'd suspected that I was not responding well because of the way I look. They will give me some radiation a little later. But they said there was not much hope."

Dazed, staring blankly at my desk, I said, "What will you do now, Shahid?"

"I would like to go back to Kashmir to die." His voice was quiet and untroubled. "Now I have to get my passport, settle my will, and all that. I don't want to leave a mess for my siblings. But after that I would like to go to Kashmir. It's still such a feudal system there, and there will be so much support — and my father is there too. Anyway, I don't want my siblings to have to make the journey afterward, like we had to with my mother."

Later, because of logistical and other reasons, he changed his mind about returning to Kashmir: he was content to be laid to rest in Northampton, in the vicinity of Amherst, a town sacred to the memory of his beloved Emily Dickinson. But I do not think it was an accident that his mind turned to Kashmir in speaking of death. Already, in his poetic imagery, death, Kashmir, and Sháhid/Shahíd had become so closely overlaid as to be inseparable, like old photographs that have melted together in the rain.

Yes, I remember it,
the day I'll die, I broadcast the crimson,

so long ago of that sky, its spread air,
its rushing dyes, and a piece of earth

bleeding, apart from the shore, as we went
on the day I'll die, post the guards, and he,

keeper of the world's last saffron, rowed me
on an island the size of a grave. On

two yards he rowed me into the sunset,
past all pain. On everyone's lips was news

of my death but only that beloved couplet,
broken, on his:

"If there is a paradise on earth,
It is this, it is this, it is this."

Shahid's mother, Sufia Nomani, was from Rudauli, in Uttar Pradesh. She was descended from a family that was well known for its Sufi heritage. Shahid believed that this connection influenced her life in many intangible ways; "She had the grandeur of a Sufi," he liked to say.

Although Shahid's parents lived in Srinagar, they usually spent the winter months in their flat in New Delhi. It was there that his mother had her first seizure, in December 1995. The attack was initially misdiagnosed, and it was not till the family brought her to New York's Lenox Hill Hospital, in January 1996, that it was confirmed that she had a malignant brain tumor. Her condition was so serious that she was operated on two days after her arrival. The operation did not have the desired effect and resulted instead in a partial paralysis. At the time Shahid and his younger brother Iqbal were both teaching at the University of Massachusetts in Amherst. His sister Hena was working on a Ph.D. at the same institution. The siblings decided to move their mother to Amherst, and it was there that she died, on April 24, 1997. In keeping with her wishes, the family took her body back to Kashmir for burial. This long and traumatic journey forms the subject of a cycle of poems, "From Amherst to Kashmir," that was later included in Shahid's 2001 collection, *Rooms Are Never Finished*.

During the last phase of his mother's illness and for several months afterward, Shahid was unable to write. The dry spell was broken in 1998, with "Lenox Hill," possibly his greatest poem. The poem was a canzone, a form of unusual rigor and difficulty (the poet Anthony Hecht once remarked that Shahid deserved to be in the *Guinness Book of Records* for having written three canzones — more than any other poet). In "Lenox Hill," the architectonics of the form create a soaring superstructure, an immense domed enclosure, like that of the great mosque of Isfahan or the mausoleum of Sayyida Zainab in Cairo: a space that seems all the more vast because of the austerity of its proportions. The rhymes and half-rhymes are the honeycombed arches that thrust the dome toward the heavens, and the meter is the mosaic that holds the whole in place. Within the immensity of this bounded space, every line throws open a window that beams a shaft of light across continents, from Amherst to Kashmir, from the hospital of Lenox Hill to the Pir Panjal Pass. Entombed at the center of this soaring edifice lies his mother:

> . . . Mother,
> they asked me, *So how's the writing?* I answered *My mother*
> *is my poem.* What did they expect? For no verse
> sufficed except the promise, fading, of Kashmir
> and the cries that reached you from the cliffs of Kashmir
>
> (across fifteen centuries) in the hospital. *Kashmir,*
> *she's dying!* How her breathing drowns out the universe
> as she sleeps in Amherst.

The poem is packed with the devices that he had perfected over a lifetime: rhetorical questions, imperative commands, lines broken or punctuated to create resonant and unresolvable ambiguities. It ends, characteristically, with a turn that is at once disingenuous and wrenchingly direct.

> For compared to my grief for you, what are those of Kashmir,
> and what (I close the ledger) are the griefs of the universe
> when I remember you — beyond all accounting — O my mother?

For Shahid, the passage of time produced no cushioning from the shock of the loss of his mother: he relived it over and over again until the end. Often he would interrupt himself in mid-conversation: "I can't believe she's gone; I still can't believe it." The week before his death, on waking one morning, he asked his family where his mother was and whether it was true that she was dead. On being told that she was, he wept as though he were living afresh through the event.

In the penultimate stanza of "Lenox Hill," in a breathtaking, heart-stopping inversion, Shahid figures himself as his mother's mother:

> "As you sit here by me, you're just like my mother,"
> she tells me. I imagine her: a bride in Kashmir,
> she's watching, at the Regal, her first film with Father.
> If only I could gather you in my arms, Mother,
> I'd save you — now my daughter — from God. The universe
> opens its ledger. I write: How helpless was God's mother!

I remember clearly the evening when Shahid read this poem in the living room of my house. I remember it because I could not keep myself from wondering whether it was possible that Shahid's identification with his mother was so powerful as to spill beyond the spirit and into the body. Brain cancer is not, so far as I know, a hereditary disease, yet his body had, as it were, elected to reproduce the conditions of his mother's death. But how could this be possible? Even the thought appears preposterous in the bleak light of the Aristotelian distinction between mind and body, and the notions of cause and effect that flow from it. Yet there are traditions in which poetry is a world of causality entire unto itself, where meta-phor extends beyond the mere linking of words, into the conjuga-tion of a distinctive reality. In Shahid's last months I thought often of the death of Babar, who was not just the first of the Mogul em-perors but also a poet and writer of extraordinary distinction.

Shahid thought of his work as being placed squarely within a modern Western tradition. Yet the mechanics of his imagination —dreams, visions, an overpowering sense of identity with those he loved—as well as his life, and perhaps even his death, were fash-ioned by a will that owed more perhaps to the Sufis and the Bhakti poets than to the modernists. In his determination to be not just a writer of poetry but an embodiment of his poetic vision, he was, I think, more the heir of Rumi and Kabir than Eliot and Merrill.

The last time I saw Shahid was on the twenty-seventh of Octo-ber, at his brother's house in Amherst. He was intermittently able to converse, and there were moments when we talked just as we had in the past. He was aware, as he had long been, of his ap-proaching end, and he had made his peace with it. I saw no trace of anguish or conflict: surrounded by the love of his family and friends, he was calm, contented, at peace. He had said to me once, "I love to think that I'll meet my mother in the afterlife, if there is an afterlife." I had the sense that as the end neared, this was his supreme consolation. He died peacefully, in his sleep, at 2 A.M. on December 8.

Now, in his absence, I am amazed that so brief a friendship has resulted in so vast a void. Often when I walk into my living room, I remember his presence there, particularly on the night when he read us his farewell to the world: "I Dream I Am at the Ghat of the Only World." I remember how he created a vision of an evening of ghazals, drawing to its end; of the bediamonded singer vanishing through a mirror; I remember him evoking the voices he loved— of Begum Akhtar, Eqbal Ahmed, and James Merrill—urging him on as he journeys toward his mother: *love doesn't help anyone finally survive.* Shahid knew exactly how it would end, and he was meticu-lous in saying his farewells, careful in crafting the envoy to the last verses of his own life.

COUNTDOWN

1998

ON MAY 11, the Indian government tested several nuclear devices at a site near the small medieval town of Pokhran, on the edge of the Thar Desert, in the western state of Rajasthan. I traveled to the area three months later. My visit coincided with the fifty-first anniversary of independence, the start of India's second half-century as a free nation. As I was heading toward Pokhran, the prime minister, Atal Bihari Vajpayee, was addressing the nation from the ramparts of Delhi's Red Fort — an Independence Day tradition. Driving through the desert, I listened to him on the car radio.

Vajpayee belongs to the Bharatiya Janata Party (the BJP, or the Indian People's Party), which is the largest single group in the coalition that now rules India. The BJP came to power in March, and the Pokhran tests followed two months later. The tests occasioned outpourings of joy among the BJP's members and sympathizers. They organized festivities and handed out sweetmeats on the streets to commemorate the achievement. There was talk of sending sand from the test site around the country so that the whole nation could partake of the glow from the blasts. Some of the BJP's leaders were said to be thinking of building a monument at Pokhran, a "shrine of strength" that could be visited by pilgrims. Nine days after the first tests, the prime minister flew to Pokhran himself. A celebration was organized near the crater left by the blasts. The prime minister was photographed standing on the crater's rim, looking reverentially into the pit.

But now, three months later, speaking at Red Fort, the prime minister's voice sounded oddly subdued. The euphoria had faded. On May 28, Pakistan had tested its own nuclear devices. This had had a sobering effect. In the following weeks, the rupee fell to a historic low, the stock market index fell, prices soared. The BJP's grasp on power was now none too secure.

I was traveling to Pokhran with two men whom I'd met that morning. They were landowning farmers who had relatives in the town. A friend had assigned them the task of showing me around. One man was in his sixties, with hennaed hair and a bushy mustache. The other was his son-in-law, a soft-spoken, burly man in his early forties. Their Hindi had the distinctive lilt of western Rajasthan.

It was searingly hot, and the desert wind chafed like sandpaper against our eyes. The road was a long, shimmering line. There were peafowl in the thorny trees, and the birds took wing as the car shot past, their great tails iridescent in the sunlight. Otherwise, there was nothing but scrub to interrupt the view of the horizon. In the dialect of the region, my guides told me, this area was known as "the flatland."

In Pokhran, my guides were welcomed by their acquaintances. A town official said he knew exactly the man I ought to meet. This man was sent for. His name was Manohar Joshi, and he was thirty-six, bespectacled, with a ready smile. He'd grown up in Pokhran, he told me. He was twelve in 1974, when a nuclear device was first tested in the district. The prime minister then was Indira Gandhi.

"In the years after 1974, there was a lot of illness," Joshi said. "We had never heard of cancer before. But after the test people began to get cancer. There were strange skin diseases. Sores. And people used to scratch themselves all the time. If these things had happened anywhere else in the country, in Bihar or Kashmir, people would rise up and stop it. But people here don't protest. They'll put up with anything."

Growing up in Pokhran, Joshi had developed a strong interest in nuclear matters. His family hadn't had the resources to send him to college. After high school, he'd started to work in a shop. But all the while he'd wanted to write. He'd begun to send opinion pieces to Hindi newspapers. One of them had taken him on as a stringer.

On the afternoon of May 11, he was preparing for his siesta when the ground began to shake, almost throwing him off his cot. He knew at once that this was no earthquake. It was a more powerful jolt than that of 1974. He recognized it for what it was and called his paper immediately. This, Joshi said proudly, made him the first journalist in the world to learn of the tests.

Joshi told me about a village called Khetolai. It was just six miles from the test site, the nearest human habitation. The effects of the 1974 tests had been felt more severely there, he said, than anywhere else in the district.

We drove off into the scrub, along a dirt road. The village was small, but there were no huts or shanties: the houses were sturdily built, of stone and mortar.

Khetolai was an unusual village, Joshi explained. Its inhabitants were reasonably prosperous — they made their living mainly from tending livestock — and almost everyone was literate, women as well as men. Many were Bishnois, members of a small religious sect whose founder had forbidden the felling of trees and the killing of animals. They thought of themselves as the world's first conservationists.

We stopped to look at a couple of buildings whose walls had been split by the tests, and we were immediately surrounded by eager schoolchildren. They led us into a house where three turbaned elders were sitting on *charpoys,* talking.

On May 11, at about noon, they told me, a squad of soldiers drove up and asked the villagers to move to open ground. People who owned refrigerators and television sets carried them out-of-doors and set them down in the sand. Then they sat under trees and waited. It was very hot. The temperature was over 120 degrees Fahrenheit.

Some three and a half hours later, there was a tremendous shaking in the ground and a booming noise. They saw a great cloud of dust and black-and-white smoke shooting skyward in the distance. Cracks opened up in the walls of the houses. Some had underground water tanks for livestock. The blasts split the tanks, emptying them of water.

Later, the villagers said, an official came around and offered them small sums of money as compensation. The underground tanks had been very expensive. The villagers refused to accept the money and demanded more.

Party activists appeared and erected a colorful marquee. There was talk that the BJP would hold celebrations in Khetolai. By this time the villagers were enraged, and the marquee was removed for fear that the media would hear of the villagers' complaints.

"After the test," a young man said, "the prime minister announced that he'd been to Pokhran and that there was no radioactivity. But how long was he here? Radioactivity doesn't work in minutes." Since 1974, he said, some twenty children had been born with deformed limbs. Cows had developed tumors in their udders. According to the young man, calves were born blind, or with their tongues and eyes attached to the wrong parts of their faces. No one had heard of such things before.

The young man held a clerical job for the government. He was articulate, and the elders handed him the burden of the conversation. In the past, he said, the villagers had cooperated with the government. They hadn't complained, and they'd been careful when talking to the press. "But now we are fed up. What benefits do we get from these tests? We don't even have a hospital."

Someone brought a tray of water glasses. The young man saw me hesitate and began to laugh. "Outsiders won't drink our water," he said. "Even the people who come to tell us that everything is safe won't touch our water."

My guides were subdued on the drive back. Even though they lived in the neighboring district, it had been years since they were last in Pokhran. What we'd seen had come as a complete surprise to them.

I spent the rest of the day in the town of Bikaner, about a hundred miles away. That evening I walked around its royal palace. It was vast, empty, and beautiful, like a melancholy fantasy. Its pink stone seemed to turn translucent in the light of the setting sun. The palace was of a stupefying lavishness. It was built around the turn of the century by Maharajah Sir Ganga Singh of Bikaner, a luminary who had cut a very splendid figure in the British Raj. He entertained viceroys and sent troops to Flanders. He was a signatory of the Treaty of Versailles. There were photographs in the corridors showing Maharajah Ganga Singh in the company of Churchill, Woodrow Wilson, and Lloyd George.

In New Delhi, many people had talked to me about how nuclear weapons would help India achieve "great power status." I'd been surprised by the depth of emotion that was invested in that curiously archaic phrase "great power." What exactly would it mean, I'd asked myself, if India achieved "great power status"? What were the images that were evoked by this tag?

Now, walking through this echoing old palace, looking at the pictures in the corridors, I realized that this was what the nuclearists wanted: treaties, photographs of themselves with the world's powerful, portraits on their walls. They had pinned on the bomb their hopes of bringing it all back.

The leading advocate of India's nuclear policies is K. Subrahmanyam, a large, forceful man who is the retired director of the Institute for Defence Studies and Analyses in New Delhi. Subrahmanyam advocates an aggressive nuclear program based on the premise that nuclear weapons are the currency of global power. "Nuclear weapons are not military weapons," he told me. "Their logic is that of international politics, and it is a logic of a global nuclear order." According to Subrahmanyam, international security has been progressively governed by a global nuclear order made up of the five nuclear-weapons powers—the United States, Russia, China, Britain, and France. "India," Subrahmanyam said, "wants to be a player and not an object of this global nuclear order."

I had expected to hear about regional threats and the Chinese missile program. But as Subrahmanyam sees it, India's nuclear policies are only tangentially related to the question of India's security. They are ultimately aimed at something much more abstract and very much more grand: global power. India could, if it plays its cards right, parlay its nuclear program into a seat on the United Nations Security Council and earn recognition as a "global player."

Subrahmanyam told me a story about a film. It was called *The Million Pound Note*, and it featured Gregory Peck. In the film, Peck's character uses an obviously valueless piece of paper printed to look like a million-pound note to con tradesmen into extending credit.

"A nuclear weapon acts like a million-pound note," Subrahmanyam said, his eyes gleaming. "It is of no apparent use. You can't use it to stop small wars. But it buys you credit, and that gives you the power to intimidate."

Subrahmanyam bristled when I suggested that there might be certain inherent dangers to the possession of nuclear weapons. Like most Indian hawks, he considers himself a reluctant nuclearist. He says he would prefer to see nuclear weapons done away with altogether. It is the nuclear superpowers' insistence on maintaining their arsenals that makes this impossible.

Issues of safety, he told me, were no more pressing in India than anywhere else. India and Pakistan had lived with each other's nuclear programs for many years. "It was the strategic logic of the West that was madness. Think of the United States building seventy thousand nuclear weapons at a cost of $5.8 trillion. Do you think these people are in a position to preach to us?"

Subrahmanyam, like many other supporters of the Indian nuclear program, sees little danger of the deployment of nuclear weapons. In New Delhi, it is widely believed that the very immensity of the destructive potential of nuclear weapons renders them useless as instruments of war, ensuring that their deployment can never be anything other than symbolic. That nuclear war is unthinkable has, paradoxically, given the weapons an aura of harmlessness.

I went to see an old acquaintance, Chandan Mitra, a historian with an Oxford doctorate. I had come across an editorial of his entitled "Explosion of Self-Esteem," published on May 12. At Delhi University, when I first knew Chandan, he was a Marxist. He is now an influential newspaper editor and is said to be a BJP sympathizer.

"The bomb is a currency of self-esteem," Chandan told me, with disarming bluntness. "Two hundred years of colonialism robbed us of our self-esteem. We do not have the national pride that the British have, or the French, the Germans, or the Americans. We have been told that we are not fit to rule ourselves — that was the justification of colonialism. Our achievements, our worth, our talent, have always been negated and denied. Mahatma Gandhi's endeavor all during the freedom movement was to rebuild our sense of self-esteem. Even if you don't have guns, he said, you still have moral force. Now, fifty years on, we know that moral force isn't enough to survive. It doesn't count for very much. When you look at India today and ask how best you can overcome those feelings of inferiority, the bomb seems to be as good an answer as any."

For Chandan, as for many other Indians, the bomb is more than a weapon. It has become a banner of political insurgency, a kind of millenarian movement for all the unfulfilled aspirations and dreams of the past fifty years.

The landscape of India teems with such insurgencies: the country is seized, in V. S. Naipaul's eloquent phrase, with "a million mutinies now." These insurrections are perhaps the most remarkable product of Indian democracy: this enabling of once marginal groups to fight for places at the table of power. The bomb cult represents the uprising of those who find themselves being pushed back from the table. It's the rebellion of the rebelled against, an insurgency of an elite. Its leaders see themselves as articulating the aspirations of an immeasurably vast constituency: more than 900 million people, or "one sixth of humanity," in the words of the Indian prime minister. The reality, however, is that the number is very much smaller than this and is dwindling every day. The almost mystical rapture that greeted the unveiling of the cult's fetish has long since dissipated.

While in New Delhi, I visited the Lok Sabha, the lower house of India's parliament, to watch a debate on foreign policy consequences of the nuclear tests. Most of the speakers were vociferously critical of the government for permitting the tests. Several of the speeches were ringing denunciations of the BJP's nuclear policies. Later I went to see one of the speakers, Ram Vilas Paswan. Paswan is a Dalit—a member of a caste group that was once treated as untouchable by high-caste Hindus. He holds the distinction of winning his parliamentary seat by record margins and is something of a cultural hero among many of the country's 230 million Dalits.

Paswan is a wiry man with a close-cropped beard and gold-rimmed eyeglasses. "These nuclear tests were not in the Indian national interest," he told me. "They were done in the interests of a party, to keep the present government from imploding. In the last elections in Pakistan, Nawaz Sharif campaigned on a platform of better relations with India. For this he was pilloried by his opponent, Benazir Bhutto, but he still won. The people of Pakistan want friendship with India. But how did our government respond? It burst a bomb in the face of a man who had reached out to us in friendship. And this in a country where ordinary citizens don't have food to eat. Where villages are being washed away by floods. Where two hundred million people don't have safe drinking water. Instead, we spend thirty-five thousand crores of rupees a year [about $8 billion] on armaments."

On August 6, Hiroshima Day, I was in Calcutta. More than 250,000 people marched in the streets to protest the nuclear tests of May 11. It was plain that the cult of the bomb had few adherents here, that the tests had divided the country more deeply than ever.

·   ·   ·

In New Delhi, I went to see George Fernandes, the defense minister of India.

I have known Fernandes, from a distance, for many years. He has a long history of involvement in human rights causes, and when I was a student at Delhi University, he was one of India's best-known antinuclear activists.

New Delhi is a sprawling city of some 10 million people, but its government offices and institutions are concentrated in a small area. The capital was designed by Sir Edwin Lutyens in the waning years of the British Raj. Two gargantuan buildings form the bureaucratic core of the city. They are known simply as North Block and South Block, and they face each other across a broad boulevard. The buildings are of red sandstone and are ornamented with many turrets and gateways of Anglo-Oriental design. From this fantastically grandiose complex the power of the Indian state radiates outward in diminishing circles of effectiveness.

I was taken to Fernandes's office, in South Block, by Jaya Jaitly, the general secretary of Fernandes's political party, the Samata (Equality) Party. The idea of my striding into the Defense Ministry was no more unlikely than the thought that these offices were presided over by George Fernandes, that perennially indignant activist.

At the age of sixteen, Fernandes, who had harbored ambitions of becoming a Catholic priest, joined a lay seminary. At nineteen he left, disillusioned (he remembers being appalled that the rectors ate better food and sat at higher tables than the seminarians), and went to Bombay, where he joined the socialist trade union movement. For years he had no permanent address and lived with members of his union on the outskirts of the city. Disowned by his father, he did not visit his home again until he was in his forties.

Fernandes still considers himself a socialist. In India's most recent elections, last February, the Samata Party won a mere 12 seats out of a total of 545. There was a time when the Congress — the party of Mahatma Gandhi — regularly commanded a decisive majority. But today no single party controls a sufficient number of seats to form a stable government. The country has gone to the polls twice in the past three years. Last February's elections gave the BJP, with 181 seats, a slight edge over the Congress. For the first time, the BJP was able to form a government, but only after fashioning a coalition with smaller parties. (The Samata Party entered on very advantageous terms, securing two positions in the cabinet, Fernandes's included.) The BJP's program is based on an assertive, militant Hinduism. In 1992 members of the BJP were instrumental in organizing the demolition of a sixteenth-century mosque that stood upon a site that they believed to be sacred to Hindus. In the aftermath, there were riots across the Indian subcontinent and thousands of people died.

We went up to Fernandes's office in the minister's elevator. A soldier in sparkling white puttees and a red turban pressed the buttons.

Fernandes is sixty-eight but could pass for a man in his midforties — lean, with a full head of curly graying hair. He always dresses in long, handwoven cotton kurtas and loose pajamas. He wears leather sandals — no socks or shoes — and washes his clothes by hand.

Two officers marched in, and Fernandes turned to talk to them. It was clear at a glance that despite Fernandes's sandals and rumpled clothes and the officers' heel-clicking starchiness, there was a genuine warmth between him and the soldiers. It occurred to me that Fernandes too wore a kind of uniform. It was a statement of simplicity.

The room was large but dank. Two pictures hung high on a wall. One was a portrait of Mahatma Gandhi; the other was a photograph of the ruins of a church in Hiroshima. It was probably here, at this desk, under these pictures, that Fernandes had deliberated on the tests of May 11.

I thought back to India's first atomic test. I was eighteen, in my second year at Delhi University. The voices of dissent were few; all the major political parties, right and left alike, came out in support. Fernandes was one of the very few political figures who openly criticized the test. For those such as myself, people who were opposed to nuclear armaments in an instinctive, perhaps unreflective way, Fernandes became a kind of beacon.

It was lunchtime, and Fernandes led the way to a spiral staircase. I spotted a small, simian figure observing us from a landing. I stopped, startled. It was a monkey, a common rhesus, with a muddy-brown mantle and a bright red rump. The animal stared at me calmly, unalarmed, and then went bounding off down a corridor.

"Did you see that monkey?" I said.

Fernandes laughed. "Yes. There's a whole troop living on this staircase."

"Sometimes," one of his aides whispered, "they attack the generals."

At lunch I said to Fernandes, "Are you comfortable with the recent nuclear tests? I ask you this because I have read your antinuclear writings and seen you at peace marches."

"I was opposed to the bomb from day one till the nineteenth of July, 1996," Fernandes said. On that day, the Lok Sabha was debating the Comprehensive Test Ban Treaty banning further tests. "In these discussions there was one point of unanimity: that we should not sign this treaty. I went through deep anguish—an atom bomb was morally unacceptable. But why should the five nations that have nuclear weapons tell us how to behave and what weapons we should have? I said we should keep all our options open—every option." The implication was that even then, he hadn't been able to endorse nuclear weapons.

After lunch, as he was rising to leave, Fernandes told me that he was scheduled to visit military installations in the embattled state of Kashmir. From there, he planned to fly farther north, to Ladakh and the Siachen Glacier, in the Karakoram Mountains. Across these snows, at altitudes of up to 22,000 feet, Indian and Pakistani troops have been exchanging fire regularly for fourteen years. The trip was to be a tour of inspection, but Fernandes would also address some political meetings. If I wanted to join him, he said, I should tell his office.

· · ·

On the morning of August 24, I boarded an Indian Air Force plane with Fernandes and his entourage. The plane was a twin-engine AN-32, an elderly and unabashedly functional craft of Soviet manufacture.

We stopped for lunch at a large military base in eastern Kashmir. I found myself sharing a table with several major generals and other senior officers. I was interested to learn these senior officers' views of the nuclear tests, but I soon discovered that their curiosity exceeded mine. Did I know who was behind the decision to proceed with the tests? they asked. Who had issued the orders? Who had known in advance?

I could no more enlighten them than they could me. Only in India, I thought, could a writer and a tableful of generals ask each other questions like these. It was confirmation, at any rate, that the armed forces' role in the tests had been limited.

The views of the military personnel were by no means uniform. Many believed that India needed a nuclear deterrent; some felt that the tests had resulted in security benefits for both India and Pakistan — that the two countries would now exercise greater caution in their frequent border confrontations.

But others expressed apprehensions. "An escalation of hostilities along the border can happen very easily," a major general said to me. "It takes just one officer in the field to start it off. There's no telling where it will stop."

None of the generals, I was relieved to note, appeared to believe that nuclear weapons were harmless icons of empowerment. In the light of my earlier conversations, there was something almost reassuring in this.

After lunch we went by helicopter to Surankote, an army base in the neck of territory that connects Kashmir to India. It was set in a valley, between steep, verdant hills. The sunlight glowed golden and mellow on the surrounding slopes. We were whisked off the landing pad and taken to the base. I found myself riding in a vehicle with a young major.

"What's it like here?" I said.

"Bad." He laughed. "Bordering on terrible." The Pakistani frontlines were just a few miles away, he explained. It took just a day to walk over the hills.

At the base there was a crowd of a few hundred people. Fernandes had mounted a podium with several other politicians and local dignitaries. Behind them were green hills capped by clouds.

The major pointed at the hills. "While we're standing here talking, there are half a dozen operations going on in those hills, right there."

He led me aside. "Let the politicians talk," he said. "I'll show you what's happening here if you want to know." We went into a tent and the major seated himself at a radio set. "This is where we listen to them," he said. He scanned the wavelengths, tuning in to several exchanges. "Listen," he said, turning up the volume. "They're speaking Punjabi, not Kashmiri. They're mercenaries who've signed up on two-year contracts. They're right there, in those hills."

The voices on the radio had a slow, dreamlike quality; they were speaking to each other unhurriedly, calling out cheerful greetings in slow-cadenced rural Punjabi.

As we were leaving the tent, the major darted suddenly into a group of journalists and took some rolls of film from a photographer. "I don't know what they've taken pictures of," he said. "I can't trust anyone here."

We walked back to listen to the speeches. "The politicians talk so well," the major said. "But what we have is a war. Does anyone know that? Does anyone care?"

The next day we flew to Leh, the principal town in the Himalayan region of Ladakh. Ladakh is only a few hundred miles from the valley of Kashmir, but near Leh, in the east, it is a world apart, a niche civilization—a far outpost of Buddhist culture which has flourished in a setting as extreme, in climate, altitude, and topography, as that of Tibet.

Leh is at 11,500 feet. On landing, we were handed pills to prevent altitude sickness and warned of short-term memory loss. In the afternoon, driving toward the Siachen Glacier, we went over the 18,300-foot Khardung Pass. A painted sign announced this to be the world's highest motorable road. Ahead lay the Karakoram Range. Among the peaks in this range is the 28,250-foot K2, Mt. Godwin-Austen, the second highest mountain in the world.

The landscape was one of lunar desolation, with electric-blue skies and a blinding sun. Great sheets of glaciated rock rose sheer out of narrow valleys: their colors were the unearthly pinks and mauves of planetary rings and stellar moons. The mountains had sharp, pyramidal points, their ridges honed to fine, knifelike edges. Below, along the valley floors, beside ribbonlike streams, were trees with silver bark. On occasional sandbanks, dwarfed by the vastness of the landscape, were tidy monasteries and villages.

The Siachen Glacier is known as the Third Pole. Outside of the polar wastelands, there is perhaps no terrain on earth that is less hospitable. There are no demarcated borders. Kashmir has what was once called the cease-fire line, which serves as a de facto border, but it stops short of this region, ending at a point on the map known as NJ 9842. The line was created in 1949, after the first war between India and Pakistan. At the time, neither India nor Pakistan conceived of needing to extend it into the high Karakorams, beyond NJ 9842. "No one had ever imagined," a Pakistani academic told me later, when I visited Lahore, "that human beings would ever wish to claim these frozen places."

But in the late 1970s several international mountaineering expeditions ventured into this region. They came through Pakistan and used Pakistani-controlled areas as their trailheads. This raised suspicions in India. It was discovered that maps were being published with lines drawn through the region, suggesting delineated borders where none existed. There was talk of "cartographic aggression."

It was these notional lines, on maps used by mountaineers, that transformed the Siachen Glacier into a battleground. It is generally agreed that the glacier, an immense mass of compacted snow and ice, seventy miles long and more than a mile deep, has no strategic, military, or economic value whatsoever.

In 1984 the Indian Army launched a large-scale airlifting operation and set up a number of military posts. Pakistan responded by putting up a parallel line of posts. There was no agreement on where the posts should be: shoving was the only way to decide. Since that time the Indian and Pakistani armies have regularly exchanged artillery fire at heights that range from 10,000 to 20,000 feet.

On the glacier we stopped to visit a dimly lighted hospital ward. There were a dozen men inside. None of them had been injured by "enemy action": their adversary was the terrain. They were plainsmen, mainly. In the normal course of things, snow would play no part in their lives. Most of the men were in their late thirties or early forties — family men. They stared at us mutely. One had tears in his eyes.

Every year a thousand soldiers are injured on the glacier — about the equivalent of an infantry battalion. "We allow at least ten extra men per battalion for wastage," an officer told me.

At some posts on the glacier, temperatures routinely dip to 40 degrees below zero. At these altitudes, wind velocities are very high. The soldiers spend much of their time crammed inside tents that are pitched on the surface of the glacier or on ledges of rock. Such heat as they have comes from small kerosene stoves, which produce a foul-smelling, grimy kind of soot. The soot works itself slowly into the soldiers' clothes, their hair, their eyes, their nostrils. When they return to base camp after a three-month tour of duty, they are enveloped in black grime.

The Siachen Glacier costs India, I was told, $2 million a day. The total cost of defending this mass of ice is beyond estimate, but it certainly exceeds several billion dollars.

In the evening I ate with a group of junior officers. I was interested to note that Indian soldiers always spoke of their Pakistani counterparts with detachment and respect. "Most of us here are from North India," a blunt-spoken major said to me. "We have more in common with the Pakistanis, if you don't mind my saying so, than we do with South Indians or Bengalis."

The next morning, in a Cheetah helicopter, I followed Fernandes through the gorges that lead up to the glacier. It was cloudy, and the brilliant colors of the rock faces had the blurred quality of a water-washed print. There was a majesty to the landscape that I had never seen before.

On our return, we drove to the snout of the glacier. A *bara khana* — a kind of feast — had been arranged under an open hangar, in Fernandes's honor. Fernandes left the officers' table and began to serve the other ranks, taking the dishes out of the hands of the kitchen staff. The men were visibly moved, and so was Fernandes. It was clear that in this job — arrived at fortuitously, late in his career — Fernandes had discovered some kind of vocation, a return, perhaps, to the austerity and brotherhood of his days as a seminarian or a trade unionist.

I was introduced to an officer who had just returned from three months on the glacier. He was proud of his men and all they had accomplished: they had dug caves in the ice for shelter, injuries had been kept to a minimum, no one had gone mad. He leaned closer. While on the glacier, he said, he'd thought of a plan for winning the war. He wanted to convey it to the defense minister. Could I help?

And the plan? I asked.

A thermonuclear explosion at the bottom of the glacier, a mile deep. The whole thing would melt, he explained, and the resulting flood would carry Pakistan away and put an end to the glacier as well. "We can work wonders."

He'd just come off the glacier, I reminded myself. This was just another kind of altitude sickness.

The next day, sitting in the air force plane, I talked to Fernandes about Pakistan. "Isn't it possible for both sides to disengage from the glacier?" I asked. "Can't some sort of solution be worked out?"

"Does anyone really want a solution?" he said quietly. "Things will just go on like this." In his voice there was a note of despair.

I came to be haunted by an image of two desperately poor protagonists balancing upon a barren mountaintop, each with a pickax stuck in the other's neck, each propping the other up, waiting to bleed to death.

In Leh, late one night in an empty dining room, Fernandes made the cryptic comment, "There are no Indians left."

"What do you mean?"

"There are no Indian parties today. There are only groups gathered around individuals."

He was referring to the powerful sectional and regional interests that have prevented any stable government from forming, precipitating the several elections in quick succession.

I asked him about his alliance with the BJP. "You were always a secular politician," I said. "How did you come to link yourself to a religious party?"

Fernandes spoke of an old political mentor who had urged him to maintain a dialogue with every segment of the political spectrum. He spoke of a bitter feud with a former protégé, Laloo Yadav, a powerful Bihar politician. Then, suddenly, he cut himself off. "Look," he said, "I'm rationalizing."

He had gone to the BJP as a last resort, he explained. He had tried to reach agreements with various secular left-wing parties. He tried many doors, he said, and "only when all other doors were closed" did he go to the BJP.

The causes of Fernandes's despondency were suddenly clear. He had spent a lifetime in politics, and the system had spun him around and around until what he did and what he believed no longer had the remotest connection. I knew that he still possessed a certain kind of idealism and personal integrity. But what had prevailed finally was vanity — the sheer vanity of power.

Fernandes is not alone. This sense of deadlock is an essential part of the background of the nuclear tests of May 11. To the leaders of the BJP, hanging on to power by the goodwill of a tenuous coalition, the tests must have appeared as one means of blasting a way out of a dead end. But if the BJP bears the principal responsibility for the tests, the blame is not its alone: it was Indira Gandhi and her Congress Party who set the precedent for using nuclear technology as political spectacle. Since then, many other Indian politicians have battled with the same temptation. Two other recent prime ministers, Narasimha Rao and I. K. Gujral, resisted, to their great credit, but they both came very close to succumbing. In the end, it is in the technology itself that the real danger lies. As long as a nuclear establishment exists, it will always tempt a politician desperate to keep a hold on power.

That night in Leh, I thought of something Fernandes had said to me earlier: "Someday we will sink, and this is not anything to do with China or with Pakistan. It is because this country is cursed to put up with a leadership that has chosen to sell it for their own personal aggrandizement." This seemed now like an unconscious self-indictment.

There are, in fact, many reasons to fear nuclear catastrophe in South Asia.

Both India and Pakistan have ballistic missiles. Their nuclear warheads will necessarily be produced in only a few facilities, because of limited resources. India's nuclear weapons, for instance, are thought to be produced at a single unit: the Bhabha Atomic Research Center, in Bombay. Both sides are therefore realistically able to destroy each other's production capacities with not much more than a single strike.

Several major cities in India and Pakistan are within a few hundred miles of each other, so once launched, a missile would take approximately five minutes to reach its target. Given the short flight time, military planners on both sides almost certainly have plans to retaliate immediately. In other words, if either nation believed itself to be under attack, it would have to respond instantly. In moments of crisis, the intelligence services of both India and Pakistan have historically had unreliable perceptions of threat. They have also been known to produce outright faulty intelligence.

The trouble will probably start in Kashmir. India and Pakistan have already fought two wars over the state. In recent months the conflict has spilled into other parts of India, with civilian populations coming under attack in the neighboring state of Himachal Pradesh, for example. The Indian government once mooted the idea of launching "hot pursuit" attacks across the border, against insurgents sheltering in Pakistani-held territory. In Pakistan, such assaults are likely to be perceived as an invasion. The risks of escalation are very real.

Zia Mian, a Pakistani-born nuclear expert at Princeton, said to me, "There are soldiers on both sides who have a hankering for a grand act of heroic erasure. A day might well come when these people would say, 'Let's get it over with forever, once and for all, no matter what the cost.'"

On a hot and humid August day, I drove around New Delhi with an old friend, Kanti Bajpai, trying to picture the damage the city would sustain during a nuclear explosion. Kanti has a doctorate in strategic studies from the University of Illinois, and he was among the many antinuclear activists who, on learning of the tests of May 11, immediately went to work. At the time, the BJP's cadres were organizing celebrations in the streets of several Indian cities. Opposition politicians looked on in stunned silence, struggling to gather their wits. It fell to citizens' associations to take on the task of articulating a critical response. Kanti came to national attention at this time.

Kanti believes that India, in pursuing a nuclear program, has gambled away its single greatest military advantage over Pakistan: the overwhelming superiority of its conventional forces. In legitimatizing Pakistan's nuclear program, India's military planners have in effect rendered their ground troops redundant. Kanti sees no threat from China. There is no history of persistent antagonism. No Chinese emperor ever invaded India; no Indian ever sought to conquer any part of China. In thousands of years of close coexistence, Chinese and Indian soldiers have fought only once, during the war of 1962.

Along with a number of other academics, Kanti has been trying to assess the consequences of a nuclear war in South Asia. A friend of his, M. V. Ramana, a research fellow at the Center for Energy and Environmental Studies at Princeton University, had recently computed the possible effects of a nuclear attack on Bombay. It was one of the first such studies to be done of a South Asian city. Ramana's findings caused some surprise: the casualty rates that he cited, for instance, were lower than expected — about 200,000. This was because in his calculations Ramana assumed that neither India nor Pakistan would use bombs much greater than what was dropped on Hiroshima — with a yield of about fifteen kilotons.

We set out on our journey through New Delhi armed with a copy of Ramana's seminal paper. Kanti wanted to apply the same calculations to New Delhi.

We drove up Rajpath, the grand thoroughfare that separates North Block from South Block. Ahead lay the domed residence of the president. This was once the palace of the imperial British viceroy; it is now known as Rashtrapati Bhavan. The palace looks down Rajpath toward a monument called India Gate. In the distance lie the ramparts of the Purana Qila, a sixteenth-century fort.

Ground zero, Kanti said, will probably lie somewhere near here: in all likelihood, between North and South Blocks.

On detonation, a nuclear weapon releases a burst of high-energy X-rays. These cause the temperature in the immediate vicinity to rise very suddenly to tens of millions of degrees. The rise in temperature causes a fireball to form, which shoots outward in every direction, cooling as it expands. By the time it reaches the facades of North Block and South Block, it will probably have cooled to about 300,000 degrees — enough to kill every living thing within several hundred feet of the point of explosion. Those caught on open ground will evaporate; those shielded by the buildings' thick walls will be incinerated.

South Block and North Block, like many of the ceremonial buildings in New Delhi, are made principally of pink Rajasthan sandstone. In Hiroshima and Nagasaki, granite surfaces and ceramic tiles up to several hundred feet from the explosion melted. Sandstone is considerably less dense than granite. The facades of the two blocks will probably melt like candle wax; so will the dome and walls of Rashtrapati Bhavan, and possibly even a portion of India Gate.

As the fireball expands, it generates a shock wave called the Mach front, which delivers a massive blow to everything in its path. This in turn is followed by an enormous increase in air pressure and very high wind velocities. The pressure of the air in the wake of the Mach front can reach several thousand pounds per square inch: it's like being inside a pressure cooker, but with pressure that is many thousands of times greater. The shock can generate winds that blow at speeds of more than 2000 miles per hour.

"Human beings will become projectiles," Kanti said. "If you're here and you're not incinerated immediately, you will become a human cannonball."

We drove toward the Jamuna River, passing the enormous circular building that houses India's parliament. Everyone here, Kanti said, will be either incinerated or killed by the radiation.

We proceeded to the National Archives and the vast bureaucratic warrens that house the government's principal administrative offices. These too will be destroyed. The recorded basis of government, Kanti said, will vanish. Land records, taxation documents — almost everything needed to reconstruct a settled society — will perish from the blast.

The changes in pressure caused by the explosion, Kanti explained, even a small one, will make your lungs burst. You won't necessarily die of burns or poisoning. "Your internal organs will rupture, even if you survive the initial blasts and flying objects."

Later I asked Gautam Bhatia, a New Delhi architect, about the effects of the blast on the city's buildings. Many of the landmark buildings of British-era New Delhi, he wrote to me, have very thick walls and are laterally buttressed with cross walls. These are capable of withstanding great pressure. But many of the city's contemporary public buildings, like some of its five-star hotels, have glass curtain walls. "Such structures have a poor rating for withstanding pressure, poor facilities for egress, and virtually no firefighting equipment."

New Delhi's newer residences will fare very badly. Most of the buildings are designed to withstand winds of about a hundred miles per hour: in the event of a nuclear explosion, they will face wind speeds of up to twenty times that. "The walls would be blown away instantly; if columns and slabs remain, the pressure will rip the building out of its foundations and overturn it."

In Indian cities, many households use canisters of liquid petroleum gas for everyday cooking. For about a mile around ground zero, Ramana estimates, these canisters will explode.

Kanti explained to me that the geographical spread of New Delhi is such that a single fifteen-kiloton nuclear explosion could not destroy the whole area. He estimated that the casualty figures for New Delhi would be much lower than those that Ramana had cited for Bombay: as low, potentially, as 60,000. Only the central parts of the city would be directly affected. "The city would continue to function in some way," Kanti said, "but its municipal, medical, and police services would be in total chaos. The infrastructure would disappear."

Fatalities, however, will account for only a small part of the human toll. Several hundreds of thousands of people will suffer burn injuries.

In New Delhi, I met with Dr. Usha Shrivastava, a member of a group called International Physicians for the Prevention of Nuclear War. She told me that over the past few decades, while New Delhi's population has more than doubled, the total number of hospital beds in the city has increased only slightly. She estimated that there are only 6000 to 7000 beds in the government-run hospitals that serve the majority of the city's population. These hospitals are already so crowded that in some wards two or three patients share a single bed. But the major hospitals—including the only one with a ward that specializes in burn injuries—are all within a few miles of the city's center, and they will not survive the blast anyway.

In the event of a nuclear explosion in New Delhi, Dr. Shrivas-tava said softly, "The ones who will be alive will be jealous of the dead ones."

When it's over, millions and millions of people will be with-out homes. They will begin to walk. The roads will soon be too clogged to accommodate cars or buses. Everyone will walk, rich and poor, young and old. Many will be nursing burn wounds and other severe injuries. They will be sick from radiation. There will be no food, no clean water, and no prospect of medical care. The water from the mountains will be contaminated. The rivers will be ruined. Epidemics will break out. Hundreds of thousands will die.

I had always imagined that a nuclear blast was a kind of apoca-lypse, beyond which no existence could be contemplated. Like many Indians, I associated the image of *pralay*—the mythological chaos of the end of the world—with a nuclear explosion. Listen-ing to Kanti that day as we drove around New Delhi, I realized that I, like most people, had been seduced into a species of nuclear ro-manticism, into thinking of nuclear weapons in symbolic and mythic ways. The explosion that Kanti was describing would not constitute an apocalyptic ending: it would be a beginning. What would follow would make the prospect of an end an object of uni-versal envy.

My journey would not be complete without a trip to Pakistan. It was to be my first visit, and the circumstances looked far from pro-pitious. The week before, the United States had fired Tomahawk missiles at terrorist camps in southern Afghanistan. Some had landed near the border of Pakistan. There were reports of Indian and American flags being burned in the streets.

At the airport in Lahore, I steeled myself for a long wait. My In-dian passport would lead, I was sure, to delays, questions, perhaps an interrogation. But nothing happened: I was waved through with a smile.

When Indians and Pakistanis visit each other's countries, there is often an alchemical reaction, a kind of magic. I had heard ac-counts of this from friends: they had spoken of the warmth, the hospitality, the intensity of emotion, the sense of stepping back into an interrupted memory, as though an earlier conversation were being resumed. Almost instantly these tales were confirmed — in taxi drivers' smiles, in the stories that people sought me out to tell, in the endless invitations to meals.

At mealtimes, though, there were arguments about how long it would be before Taliban-like groups made a bid for power. After dessert, the talk would turn to the buying of Kalashnikovs.

I went to see Qazi Hussain Ahmed, the leader of the Jamaat-e-Islami, the country's principal religious party. The Jamaat's headquarters are on the outskirts of Lahore, in a large and self-sufficient compound, surrounded by a high wall and manned by sentries.

Ahmed has a well-trimmed white beard, twinkling eyes, and a manner of great affability. "Other than the army," he said, "all the institutions in this country are more or less finished. These are all institutions of a Westernized elite, of people who are corrupt. We are now paying the price of their corruption. All the problems we have now — the economic crisis and so on — are the fruit of their corruption."

I was hearing a strange echo of voices from India.

"We are not for nuclear weapons," Ahmed told me. "We are ourselves in favor of disarmament. But we don't accept that five nations should have nuclear weapons and others shouldn't. We say, 'Let the five also disarm.'"

On one issue, however, his views were very different: the probability of a nuclear war. "When you have two nations," he said, "between whom there is so much ill will, so much enmity, and they both have nuclear weapons, then there is always the danger that these weapons will be used if war breaks out. Certainly. And in war people become mad. And when a nation fears that it is about to be defeated, it will do anything to spare itself the shame."

Almost without exception, the people I spoke to in Pakistan — hawks and doves alike — were of the opinion that the probability of nuclear war was high.

I spent my last afternoon in Lahore with Pakistan's leading human rights lawyer, Asma Jahangir. Asma is forty-eight, the daughter of an opposition politician who was one of the most vocal critics of the Pakistani Army's operations in what is now Bangladesh. She spent her teenage years briefing lawyers on behalf of her frequently imprisoned father. Today she cannot go outside without an armed bodyguard.

"Is nuclear war possible?" I asked.

"Anything is possible," she said, "because our policies are irrational. Our decision-making is ad hoc. We are surrounded by disinformation. We have a historical enmity and the emotionalism of jihad against each other. And we are fatalistic nations who believe that whatever happens — a famine, a drought, an accident — it is the will of God. Our decision-making is done by a few people on both sides. It's not the ordinary woman living in a village in Bihar whose voice is going to be heard, who's going to say, 'For God's sake, I don't want a nuclear bomb — I want my cow and I want milk for my children.'"

I often think back to the morning of May 12. I was in New York at the time. I remember my astonishment both at the news of the tests and also at the response to them: the tone of chastisement, the finger-wagging by countries that still possessed tens of thousands of nuclear warheads. Had they imagined that the technology to make a bomb had wound its way back into a genie's lamp because the cold war had ended? Did they think that it had escaped the world's attention that the five peacekeepers of the United Nations Security Council all had nuclear arms? If so, then perhaps India's nuclear tests served a worthwhile purpose by waking the world from this willed slumber.

So strong was my response to the West's hypocrisy that I discovered an unusual willingness in myself to put my own beliefs on nuclear matters aside. If there were good arguments to be made in defense of the Indian and Pakistani nuclear tests, then I wanted to know what they were: I wanted to hear them for myself.

I didn't hear them. What I heard instead was a strange mix of psychologizing, grandiose fantasy, and cynicism. The motivation behind India's nuclear program is summed up neatly in this formula: it is status-driven, not threat-driven. The intention is to push India into an imagined circle of twice-born nations — "the great powers." In Pakistan, the motivation is similar. Status here means parity with India. That the leaders of these two countries should be willing to risk economic breakdown, nuclear accidents, and nuclear war in order to indulge these confused ambitions is itself a sign that some essential element in the social compact has broken down; the desires of the rulers and the well-being of the ruled could not be further apart.

I think of something that George Fernandes said to me: "Our country has already fallen to the bottom. Very soon we will reach a point where there is no hope at all. I believe that we have reached that point now." I think also of the words of I. A. Rehman, of the Human Rights Commission of Pakistan: "This is the worst it's ever been. Everything is discredited. Everything is lost, broken into pieces."

I have never had so many utterly depressing conversations, so many talks that ended with the phrase "We have hit rock bottom." There was the college student who said, "Now even Bill Gates will take us seriously." There was the research scientist who believed that now his papers would get more international attention. And there were the diplomats looking forward to a seat on the Security Council. Has the gap between the realities of the subcontinent and the aspirations of its middle classes ever been wider? Talking to nuclear enthusiasts, I had the sense that what they were really saying was, "The country has tried everything else to get ahead. Nothing worked. This is our last card, and this is the time to play it." I am convinced that support for India's nuclear program is occasioned by a fear of the future. The bomb has become the weapon with which the rulers of the subcontinent wish to avert whatever is ahead.

THE MARCH OF THE NOVEL
THROUGH HISTORY

The Testimony of My Grandfather's Bookcase

1998

As a child I spent my holidays in my grandfather's house in Calcutta, and it was there that I began to read. My grandfather's house was a chaotic and noisy place, populated by a large number of uncles, aunts, cousins, and dependants, some of them bizarre, some merely eccentric, but almost all excitable in the extreme. Yet I learned much more about reading in this house than I ever did in school.

The walls of my grandfather's house were lined with rows of books, neatly stacked in glass-fronted bookcases. The bookcases were prominently displayed in a large hall that served, among innumerable other functions, as playground, sitting room, and hallway. The bookcases towered above us, looking down, eavesdropping on every conversation, keeping track of family gossip, glowering at quarreling children. Very rarely were the bookcases stirred out of their silent vigil. I was perhaps the only person in the house who raided them regularly, and I was in Calcutta for no more than a couple of months every year. When the bookcases were disturbed in my absence, it was usually not for their contents but because some special occasion required their cleaning. If the impending event happened to concern a weighty matter like a delicate marital negotiation, the bookcases got a very thorough scrubbing indeed. And well they deserved it, for at such times they were important props in the little plays that were enacted in their presence. They let the visitor know that this was a house in which books were valued; in other words, that we were cultivated people. This is always important in Calcutta, for Calcutta is an oddly bookish city.

Were we indeed cultivated people? I wonder. On the whole I don't think so. In my memory my grandfather's house is always full — of aunts, uncles, cousins. I am astonished sometimes when I think of how many people it housed, fed, entertained, educated. But my uncles were busy, practical, and, in general, successful professionals, with little time to spend on books.

Only one of my uncles was a real reader. He was a shy and rather retiring man, not the kind of person who takes it upon himself to educate his siblings or improve his relatives' taste. The books in the bookcases were almost all his. He was too quiet a man to carry much weight in family matters, and his views never counted for much when the elders sought each other's counsel. Yet despite the fullness of the house and the fierce competition for space, it was taken for granted that his bookcases would occupy the place of honor in the hall. Eventually tiring of his noisy relatives, my book-loving uncle decided to move to a house of his own in a distant and uncharacteristically quiet part of the city. But oddly enough the bookcases stayed; by this time the family was so attached to them that they were less dispensable than my uncle.

In the years that followed, the house passed into the hands of a branch of the family that was definitely very far from bookish. Yet their attachment to the bookcases seemed to increase inversely to their love of reading. I had been engaged in a secret pillaging of the bookcases for a very long time. Under the new regime my depredations came to a sudden halt; at the slightest squeak of a hinge, hordes of cousins would materialize suddenly around my ankles, snapping dire threats.

It served no purpose to tell them that the books were being consumed by maggots and mildew, that books rotted when they were not read. Arguments such as these interested them not at all: as far as they were concerned, the bookcases and their contents were a species of property and were subject to the usual laws.

This attitude made me impatient, even contemptuous at the time. Books were meant to be read, I thought, by people who valued and understood them. I felt not the slightest remorse for my long years of thievery. It seemed to me a terrible waste that nonreaders should succeed in appropriating my uncle's library. Today I am not so sure. Perhaps those cousins were teaching me a lesson that was important on its own terms: they were teaching me to value the printed word. Would anyone who had not learned this lesson well be foolhardy enough to imagine that a living could be made from words? I doubt it.

In another way they were also teaching me what a book is, a proper book, that is, not just printed paper gathered between covers. However much I may have chafed against the regime that stood between me and the bookcases, I have not forgotten those lessons. For me, to this day, a book, a proper book, is and always will be the kind of book that was on the bookshelves.

And what exactly was this kind of book?

Although so far as I know no one had ever articulated any guidelines about them, there were in fact some fairly strict rules about the books that were allowed onto those shelves. Textbooks and schoolbooks were never allowed; nor were books of a technical or professional nature — nothing to do with engineering, or medicine, or law, or indeed any of the callings that afforded my uncles their livings. In fact, the great majority of the books were of a single kind; they were novels. There were a few works of anthropology and psychology, books that had in some way filtered into the literary consciousness of the time: *The Golden Bough,* for example, as well as the *Collected Works of Sigmund Freud,* Marx and Engels's *Manifesto,* Havelock Ellis and Malinowski on sexual behavior, and so on.

But without a doubt it was the novel that weighed most heavily on the floors of my grandfather's house. To this day I am unable to place a textbook or a computer manual upon a bookshelf without a twinge of embarrassment.

This is how Nirad Chaudhuri, that erstwhile Calcuttan, accounts for the position that novels occupy in Bengali cultural life:

> It has to be pointed out that in the latter half of the nineteenth century Bengali life and Bengali literature had become very closely connected and literature was bringing into the life of educated Bengalis something which they could not get from any other source. Whether in the cities and towns or in the villages, where the Bengali gentry still had the permanent base of their life, it was the mainstay of their life of feeling, sentiment and passion ... Both emotional capacity and idealism were sustained by it ... When my sister was married in 1916, a college friend of mine presented her with fifteen of the latest novels by the foremost writers and my sister certainly did not prize them less than her far more costly clothes and jewellery. In fact, sales of fiction and poetry as wedding presents were a sure standby of their publishers.

About a quarter of the novels in my uncle's bookcases were in Bengali — a representative selection of the mainstream tradition of Bengali fiction in the twentieth century. Prominent among these were the works of Bankim Chandra, Sarat Chandra, Tagore, Bibhuti Bhushan, and so on. The rest were in English. But of these only a small proportion consisted of books that had been originally written in English. The others were translations from a number of other languages, most of them European: Russian had pride of place, followed by French, Italian, German, and Danish. The great masterpieces of the nineteenth century were dutifully represented: the novels of Dostoevsky, Tolstoy, and Turgenev, of Victor Hugo, Flaubert, Stendhal, Maupassant, and others. But these were the dustiest books of all, placed on shelves that were lofty but remote.

The books that were prominently displayed were an oddly disparate lot — or so they seem today. Some of those titles can still be seen on bookshelves everywhere: Joyce, Faulkner, and so on. But many others have long since been forgotten: Marie Corelli and Grazia Deledda, for instance, names that are so little known today, even in Italy, that they have become a kind of secret incantation for me, a password that allows entry into the brotherhood of remembered bookcases. Knut Hamsun too was once a part of this incantation, but unlike the others his reputation has since had an immense revival — and with good reason.

Other names from those shelves have become, in this age of resurgent capitalism, symbols of a certain kind of embarrassment or unease — the social realists, for example. But on my uncle's shelves they stood tall and proud, Russians and Americans alike: Maxim Gorky, Mikhail Sholokhov, John Steinbeck, Upton Sinclair. There were many others too whose places next to each other seem hard to account for at first glance: Sienkiewicz (of *Quo Vadis?*), Maurice Maeterlinck, Bergson. Recently, looking through the mildewed remnants of those shelves, I came upon what must have been the last addition to that collection. It was Ivo Andrić's *Bridge on the Drina,* published in the sixties.

For a long time I was at a loss to account for my uncle's odd assortment of books. I knew their eclecticism couldn't really be ascribed to personal idiosyncrasies of taste. My uncle was a keen reader, but he was not, I suspect, the kind of person who allows his own taste to steer him through libraries and bookshops. On the contrary, he was a reader of the kind whose taste is guided largely by prevalent opinion. This uncle, I might add, was a writer himself, in a modest way. He wrote plays in an epic vein with characters borrowed from the Sanskrit classics. He never left India and indeed rarely ventured out of his home state of West Bengal.

The principles that guided my uncle's taste would have been much clearer to me had I ever had an interest in trivia. To the quiz show adept, the link between Grazia Deledda, Gorky, Hamsun, Sholokhov, Sienkiewicz, and Andrić will be clear at once: it is the Nobel Prize for literature.

Writing about the Calcutta of the twenties and thirties, Nirad Chaudhuri says:

> To be up to date about literary fashions was a greater craze among us than to be up to date in clothes is with society women, and this desire became keener with the introduction of the Nobel Prize for literature. Not to be able to show at least one book of a Nobel Laureate was regarded almost as being illiterate.

But of course the Nobel Prize was itself both symptom and catalyst of a wider condition: the emergence of a notion of a universal "literature," a form of artistic expression that embodies differences in place and culture, emotion and aspiration, but in such a way as to render them communicable. This idea may well have had its birth in Europe, but I suspect it met with a much more enthusiastic reception outside. I spent a couple of years studying in England in the late seventies and early eighties. I don't remember ever having come across a bookshelf like my uncle's: one that had been largely formed by this vision of literature, by a deliberate search for books from a wide array of other countries.

I have, however, come across many such elsewhere, most memorably in Burma in the house of the late Mya Than Tint, one of the most important Burmese writers of the twentieth century.

Mya Than Tint was an amazing man. He spent more than a decade as a political prisoner. For part of that time he was incarcerated in the British-founded penal colony of Cocos Island, an infamous outcrop of rock where prisoners had to forage to survive. On his release he began to publish sketches and stories that won him a wide readership and great popular esteem in Burma. These wonderfully warm and vivid pieces have recently been translated and published under the title *Tales of Everyday People*.

I met Mya Than Tint in 1995, at his home in Rangoon. The first thing he said to me was, "I've seen your name somewhere." I was taken aback. Such is the ferocity of Burma's censorship regime that it seemed hardly possible that he could have come across my books or articles in Rangoon. "Wait a minute," Mya Than Tint said. He went to his study, fetched a tattered old copy of *Granta*, and pointed to my name on the contents page.

"Where did you get it?" I asked, open-mouthed. He explained, smiling, that he had kept his library going by befriending the rag pickers and paper traders who picked through the rubbish discarded by diplomats.

Looking through Mya Than Tint's bookshelves, I soon discovered that this determined refusal to be beaten into parochialism had its genesis in a bookcase that was startlingly similar to my uncle's. Knut Hamsun, Maxim Gorky, Sholokhov — all those once familiar names came echoing back to me from Calcutta as we sat talking in that bright, cool room in Rangoon.

I also once had occasion to meet the Indonesian novelist Pramoedya Ananta Toer, another writer of astonishing fortitude and courage. Of the same generation as Mya Than Tint, Pramoedya has lived through similar experiences of imprisonment and persecution. Unlike Mya Than Tint, he works in a language that has only recently become a vehicle of literary expression, Bahasa Indonesia. Pramoedya is thus widely thought of as the founding figure in a national literary tradition.

At some point I asked what his principal literary influences were. I do not know what I had expected to hear, but it was not the answer I got. I should not have been surprised, however; the names were familiar ones — Maxim Gorky and John Steinbeck.

Over the past few years, the world has caught up with Mya Than Tint and Pramoedya Ananta Toer. Today the habits of reading that they and others like them pioneered are mandatory among readers everywhere. Wherever I go today, the names that I see on serious bookshelves are always the same, no matter the script in which they are spelled: García Márquez, Vargas Llosa, Nadine Gordimer, Michael Ondaatje, Marguerite Yourcenar, Günter Grass, Salman Rushdie. That this is ever more true is self-evident: literary currents are now instantly transmitted around the world and instantly absorbed, like everything else. To mention this is to cite a jaded commonplace.

But the truth is that fiction has been thoroughly international for more than a century. In India, Burma, Egypt, Indonesia, and elsewhere this has long been obvious. Yet curiously, this truth has nowhere been more stoutly denied than in those places where the novel has its deepest roots; indeed, it could be said that this denial is the condition that made the novel possible.

The novel as a form was vigorously international from the start; we know that Spanish, English, French, and Russian novelists have read each other's work avidly since the eighteenth century. And yet the paradox of the novel as a form is that it is founded upon a myth of parochialism, in the exact sense of a parish — a place named and charted, a definite location. A novel, in other words, must always be set somewhere: it must have its setting, and within the evolution of the narrative this setting must, classically, play a part almost as important as those of the characters themselves. Location is thus intrinsic to a novel; we are at a loss to imagine its absence, no matter whether that place be Mrs. Gaskell's Cranford or Joyce's Dublin. A poem can create its setting and atmosphere out of verbal texture alone; not so a novel.

We carry these assumptions with us in much the same way that we assume the presence of actors and lights in a play. They are both so commonplace and so deeply rooted that they preempt us from reflecting on how very strange they actually are. Consider that the conceptions of location that made the novel possible came into being at exactly the time when the world was beginning to experience the greatest dislocation it has ever known. When we read *Middlemarch* or *Madame Bovary*, we have not the faintest inkling that the lives depicted in them are made possible by global empires (consider the contrast with that seminal work of Portuguese literature, Camões's *Lusiads*). Consider that when we read Hawthorne, we have to look very carefully between the lines to see that the New England ports he writes about are sustained by a far-flung network of trade. Consider that nowhere are the literary conventions of location more powerful than in the literature of the United States, itself the product of several epic dislocations.

How sharply this contrasts with traditions of fiction that predate the novel! It is true, for example, that the city of Baghdad provides a notional location for the *Thousand and One Nights.* But the Baghdad of Scheherazade is more a talisman, an incantation, than a setting. The stories could happen anywhere so long as our minds have room for an enchanted city.

Or think of that amazing collection of stories known as the *Panchatantra* or *Five Chapters.* These stories too have no settings to speak of, except the notion of a forest. Yet the *Panchatantra* is reckoned by some to be second only to the Bible in the extent of its global diffusion. Compiled in India early in the first millennium, the *Panchatantra* passed into Arabic through a sixth-century Persian translation, engendering some of the best-known of Middle Eastern fables, including parts of the *Thousand and One Nights.* The stories were handed on to the Slavic languages through Greek, then from Hebrew to Latin, a version in the latter appearing in 1270. Through Latin they passed into German and Italian. From the Italian version came the famous Elizabethan rendition of Sir Henry North, *The Morall Philosophy of Doni* (1570). These stories left their mark on collections as different as those of La Fontaine and the Grimm brothers, and today they are inseparably part of a global heritage.

Equally, the stories called the *Jafakas,* originally compiled in India, came to be diffused throughout southern and eastern Asia and even farther with the spread of Buddhism. The story, both in its epic form and in its shorter version, was vital in the creation of the remarkable cultural authority that India enjoyed in the Asia of the Middle Ages. Not until the advent of Hollywood was narrative again to play so important a part in the diffusion of a civilization.

Everywhere these stories went, they were freely and fluently adapted to local circumstances. Indeed, in a sense the whole point of the stories was their translatability—the dispensable and inessential nature of their locations. What held them together and gave them their appeal was not where they happened but how— the narrative, in other words. Or, to take another example, consider that European narrative tradition which was perhaps the immediate precursor of the novel: the story of Tristan and Isolde. By the late Middle Ages this Celtic narrative, which appears to have had its origins in Cornwall and Brittany, had been translated and adapted into several major European languages. Everywhere it went, the story of Tristan and Isolde was immediately adapted to new locations and new settings. The questions of its origins and its original locations are at best matters of pedantic interest.

In these ways of storytelling, it is the story that gives places their meaning. That is why Homer leaps at us from signs on the New York turnpike, from exits marked Ithaca and Troy; that is why the Ayodhya of the Ramayana lends its name equally to a street in Banaras and a town in Thailand.

This style of fictional narrative is not extinct — far from it. It lives very vividly in the spirit that animates popular cinema in India and many other places. In a Hindi film, as in a kung fu movie, the details that constitute the setting are profoundly unimportant, incidental almost. In Hindi films, the setting of a single song can take us through a number of changes of costume, each in a different location. These films, I need hardly point out, command huge audiences on several continents and may well be the most widely circulated cultural artifacts the world has ever known. When Indonesian streets and villages suddenly empty at four in the afternoon, it is not because of Maxim Gorky or John Steinbeck: it is because of the timing of a daily broadcast of a Hindi film.

Such is the continued vitality of this style of narrative that it eventually succeeded in weaning my uncle from his bookcases. Toward the end of his life, my book-loving uncle abandoned all of his old friends, Gorky and Sholokhov and Hamsun, and became a complete devotee of Bombay films. He would see dozens of Hindi films; sometimes we went together, on lazy afternoons. On the way home he would stop to buy fan magazines. Through much of his life he'd been a forbidding, distant man, an intellectual in the classic, Western sense; in his last years he was utterly transformed, warm, loving, thoughtful. His brothers and sisters scarcely recognized him.

Once, when we were watching a film together, he whispered in my ear that the star, then Bombay's reigning female deity, had recently contracted a severe infestation of lice.

"How do you know?" I asked.

"I read an interview with her hairdresser," he said. "In *Stardust*."

This was the man who'd handed me a copy of *And Quiet Flows the Don* when I was not quite twelve.

My uncle's journey is evidence that matters are not yet decided among different ways of telling stories: that if Literature, led by a flagship called the Novel, has declared victory, the other side, if there is one, has not necessarily conceded defeat. But what exactly is at stake here? What is being contested? Or, to narrow the question, what is the difference between the ways in which place and location are thought of by novelists and by storytellers of other kinds?

The contrast is best seen, I think, where it is most apparent: that is, in situations outside Europe and the Americas, where the novel is a relatively recent import. As an example, I would like to examine for a moment a novel from my own part of the world — Bengal. This novel is called *Rajmohun's Wife*, written in the early 1860s by the writer Bankim Chandra Chatterjee.

Bankim Chandra Chatterjee was a man of many parts. He was a civil servant, a scholar, a novelist, and a talented polemicist. He was also very widely read, in English as well as Bengali and Sanskrit. In a sense, his was the bookcase that was the ancestor of my uncle's.

Bankim played no small part in the extraordinary efflorescence of Bengali literature in the second half of the nineteenth century. He wrote several major novels in Bengali, all of which were quickly translated into other Indian languages. He was perhaps the first truly "Indian" writer of modern times, in the sense that his literary influence extended throughout the subcontinent. Nirad Chaudhuri describes him as "the creator of Bengali fiction and . . . the greatest novelist in the Bengali language." Bankim is also widely regarded as one of the intellectual progenitors of Indian nationalism.

Bankim Chandra was nothing if not a pioneer, and he self-consciously set himself the task of bringing the Bengali novel into being by attacking what he called "the Sanskrit school." It is hard today, looking back from a point of time when the novel sails as Literature's flagship, to imagine what it meant to champion such a form in nineteenth-century India. The traditions of fiction that Bankim was seeking to displace were powerful enough to awe its critics into silence. They still are; what modern writer, for example, could ever hope to achieve the success of the *Panchatantra*? It required true courage to seek to replace this style of narrative with a form so artificial and arbitrary as the novel; the endeavor must have seemed hopeless at the time. Nor did the so-called Sanskrit school lack for defendants. Bankim, and many others who took on the task of domesticating the novel, were immediately derided as monkeylike imitators of the West.

Bankim responded by calling for a full-scale insurrection. Imitation, he wrote, was the law of progress; no civilization was self-contained or self-generated, none could advance without borrowing. He wrote:

> Those who are familiar with the present writers in Bengali will readily admit that they all, good and bad alike, may be classed under two heads, the Sanskrit and the English schools. The former represents Sanskrit scholarship and the ancient literature of the country; the latter is the fruit of Western knowledge and ideas. By far the greater number of Bengali writers belong to the Sanskrit school; but by far the greater number of good writers belong to the other . . . It may be said that there is not at the present day anything like an indigenous school of writers, owing nothing either to Sanskrit writers or to those of Europe.

How poignantly ironic this passage seems a hundred years later, after generations of expatriate Indians, working mainly in England, have striven so hard to unlearn the lessons taught by Bankim and his successors in India. So successfully were novelistic conventions domesticated in the late nineteenth and early twentieth centuries that many Indian readers now think of them as somehow local, homegrown, comforting in their naturalistic simplicity, while the work of such writers as G. V. Desani, Zulfikar Ghose, Salman Rushdie, Adam Zameenzad, Shashi Tharoor, and others appears, by the same token, stylized and experimental.

Yet Bankim's opinions about the distinctiveness of Indian literature were much more extreme than those of his apocryphal Sanskrit school. In 1882 Bankim found himself embroiled in a very interesting controversy with a Protestant missionary, W. Hastie. The exchange began after Hastie had published a couple of letters in a Calcutta newspaper, *The Statesman*. I cannot resist quoting from one of these:

> Notwithstanding all that has been written about the myriotheistic idolatry of India, no pen has yet adequately depicted the hideousness and grossness of the monstrous system. It has been well described by one who knew it as "Satan's masterpiece . . . the most stupendous fortress and citadel of ancient error and idolatry now in the world . . ." With much that was noble and healthy in its early stages, the Sanskrit literature became infected by a moral leprosy which gradually spread like a corrupting disease through almost all its fibres and organs. The great Sanskrit scholars of Bengal know too well what I mean . . . Only to think that this has been the principal pabulum of the spiritual life of the Hindus for about a thousand years, and the loudly boasted lore of their semideified priests! Need we seek elsewhere for the foul disease that has been preying upon the vitals of the national life, and reducing the people to what they are? "Shew me your gods," cried an ancient Greek apologist, "and I will show you your men." The Hindu is just what his idol gods have made him. His own idolatry, and not foreign conquerors, has been the curse of his history. No people was ever degraded except by itself, and this is most literally so with the Hindus.

Bankim responded by advising Mr. Hastie to "obtain some knowledge of Sanskrit scriptures in the *original*

> . . . [for] no translation from the Sanskrit into a European language can truly or even approximately represent the original

. . . The English or the German language can possess no words or expressions to denote ideas or conceptions which have never entered into a Teutonic brain . . . A people so thoroughly unconnected with England or Germany as the old Sanskrit-speaking people of India, and developing a civilization and a literature peculiarly their own, had necessarily a vast store of ideas and conceptions utterly foreign to the Englishman or the German, just as the Englishman or the German boasts a still vaster number of ideas utterly foreign to the Hindu . . . [Mr. Hastie's position] is the logical outcome of that monstrous claim to omniscience, which certain Europeans . . . put forward for themselves . . . Yet nothing is a more common subject of merriment among the natives of India than the Europeans' ignorance of all that relates to India . . . A navvy who had strayed into the country . . . asked for some food from a native . . . The native gave him a cocoanut. The hungry sailor . . . bit the husk, chewed it . . . and flung the fruit at the head of the unhappy donor . . . The sailor carried away with him an opinion of Indian fruits parallel to that of Mr. Hastie and others, who merely bite at the husk of Sanskrit learning, but do not know their way to the kernel within.

He added: "I cheerfully admit the intellectual superiority of Europe. I deny, however . . . that intellectual superiority can enable the blind to see or the deaf to hear."

By the time he wrote the passages quoted above, Bankim was already an acclaimed novelist and a major figure in the Bengali literary world. But his experiments with the novel had begun some twenty years before, and his earliest efforts at novel writing were conducted in English. *Rajmohun's Wife* is the first known fictional work written by Bankim, and it was written in the early 1860s.

It will be evident from the above passages, abbreviated though they are, that Bankim wrote excellent English: his essays and letters are written in a style that is supple, light-handed, and effective. The style of *Rajmohun's Wife*, in contrast, is deliberate, uncertain, and often ponderous. What intrigues me most about this book, however, is the long passages of description that preface several of the chapters, bookending, as it were, some extremely melodramatic scenes.

Here are some examples:

The house of Mathur Ghose was a genuine specimen of mofussil magnificence united with a mofussil want of cleanliness.

From the far-off paddy fields you could descry through the intervening foliage, its high palisades and blackened walls. On a nearer view might be seen pieces of plaster of a venerable antiquity prepared to bid farewell to their old and weather-beaten tenement . . .

A mazy suite of dark and damp apartments led from a corner of this part of the building to the inner *mahal,* another quadrangle, on all four sides of which towered double-storeyed verandahs, as before . . . The walls of all the chambers above and below were well striped with numerous streaks of red, white, black, green, all colours of the rainbow, caused by the spittles of such as had found their mouths too much encumbered with paan, or by some improvident woman servant who had broken the *gola-handi* while it was full of its muddy contents . . . Numerous sketches in charcoal, which showed, we fear, nothing of the conception of (Michael) Angelo or the tinting of Guido (Reni), attested the art or idleness of the wicked boys and ingenious girls who had contrived to while away hungry hours by essays in the arts of designing and of defacing wall . . .

A thick and massive door led to the "godown" as the *mahal* was called by the males directly from outside . . .

A kitchen scene:

Madhav therefore immediately hurried into the inner apartments where he found it no very easy task to make himself heard in that busy hour of zenana life. There was a servant woman, black, rotund, and eloquent, demanding the transmission to her hand of sundry articles of domestic use, without however making it at all intelligible to whom her demands were addressed. There was another who boasted similar blessed corporal dimensions, but who thought it beneath her dignity to shelter them from view; and was busily employed broomstick in hand, in demolishing the little mountains of the skins and stems of sundry culinary vegetables which decorated the floors, and against which the half-naked dame never aimed a blow but coupled it with a curse on those whose duty it had been to prepare the said vegetables for dressing.

The questions that strike me when I read these lengthy and labored descriptions are, What are they for? For whom are they intended? Why did he bother to write them? Bankim must have known that this book was very unlikely to be read by anyone who did not know what the average Bengali landowner's house looked like — since by far the largest part of the literate population of Calcutta at that time consisted of landowners and their families. Similarly, anyone who had visited the Bengal of his time, for no matter how brief a period, would almost inevitably have been familiar with the other sights he describes: fishermen at work, cranes fishing, and so on.

Why then did Bankim go to the trouble of writing these passages? Did he think his book might be read by someone who was entirely unfamiliar with Bengal? The question is a natural and inevitable one, but I do not think it leads anywhere. For the fact of the matter is that I don't think Bankim was writing for anyone but himself. I suspect that he never really intended to publish *Rajmohun's Wife*; the novel has the most cursory of endings, as though he'd written it as an exercise and then thrown it aside once it had served its purpose. The book was not actually published until a decade or so after he'd stopped working on it. For Bankim, *Rajmohun's Wife* was clearly a rehearsal, a preparation for something else.

It is here, I think, that the answers lie. The passages of description in the book are not in fact intended to describe. Their only function is that they are there at all: they are Bankim's attempt to lay claim to the rhetoric of location, of place — to mount a springboard that would allow him to vault the gap between two entirely different conventions of narrative.

It is for a related reason, I think, that Bankim conducted his rehearsal in English rather than Bengali. To write about one's surroundings is anything but natural. Even to perceive one's immediate environment, one must somehow distance oneself from it; to describe it, one must assume a certain posture, a form of address. In other words, to locate oneself through prose, one must begin with an act of dislocation. It was this, perhaps, that English provided for Bankim: a kind of disconnected soapbox on which he could test a certain form of address before trying it out in Bengali.

This still leaves a question. Every form of address assumes a listener, a silent participant. Who was the listener in Bankim's mind when he was working on *Rajmohun's Wife*? The answer, I think, is the bookcase. It is the very vastness and cosmopolitanism of the fictional bookcase that requires novelists to locate themselves in relation to it, that demands of their work that it carry marks to establish their location.

This, then, is the peculiar paradox of the novel. Those of us who love novels often read them because of the eloquence with which they communicate a "sense of place." Yet the truth is that it is the very loss of a lived sense of place that makes their fictional representation possible.

THE FUNDAMENTALIST
CHALLENGE

1995

With the benefit of hindsight, I am ever more astonished by the degree to which, over the course of this century, religion has been reinvented as its own antithesis. At much the same time that one stream within modernism created a straw version of religion as a cloak of benighted ignorance that had to be destroyed with the weapons of literary, artistic, and scientific progressivism, another stream within this same movement created a no less fantastic version of religion as a bulwark against the dehumanization of contemporary life.

To a greater or lesser degree, most of us have felt the tug of both these currents. Indeed, it is hard to think of any contemporary, modern, or even not so modern thinker, writer, or artist who has not. Karl Marx, for instance, while writing his much-quoted sentence about religion being the opiate of the masses (itself not as dismissive as some of his followers have assumed), also wrote a less-known passage describing religion as the heart of a heartless world.

These are commonplaces, of course. We all know the stories of modernist figures who have swum from one of these currents into the other, a narrative best exemplified by the career of W. H. Auden. At the heart of these stories is a moment, often an extended moment, of conversion, and it is this moment that puzzles me now — with the benefit of hindsight, as I said. It puzzles me because it seems to me increasingly that the intellectual pedigrees of most versions of religious extremism around the world today can be traced to similar moments of conversion.

Let me cite a few examples. Swami Vivekananda, the late nineteenth-century thinker who is today claimed by Hindu extremists as a founding father, was famously a rationalist in the best positivist tradition, until he underwent a dramatic conversion. Or consider the Anagarika Dharmapala, who laid the foundations of Buddhist revivalism in Sri Lanka at the turn of the century. The Anagarika Dharmapala's early education was in Christian schools, and he is said to have learned the Bible by heart at an early age. He was reconverted to Buddhism by the American theosophist Henry Steel Olcott, who arrived in Sri Lanka in 1880. As with so many such figures, the first popular movement the Anagarika Dharmapala led was social rather than religious in nature — a temperance campaign.

In Iran, the figure who is thought to have played the most important part in the radicalization of Shiite youth in the recent past was neither a mullah nor an ayatollah but rather a Sorbonne-trained sociologist, Ali Shari'ati. In Shari'ati's writings, religion often assumes the aspect of a sociological instrument, a means to resist the versions of modernity he had witnessed in France.

Similarly the intellectual progenitors of religious extremism in Egypt, Hasan al-Banna and al-Sayyid Qutb, were not educated in traditional religious institutions. Both were graduates of the Dar al-Ulum, or House of Sciences, in Cairo, an institution that has been described as a "modernist teacher training institute." Al-Sayyid Qutb first made his name as a literary figure, a writer of fiction and critic who was actively involved in debates centered on questions of literary modernism in the Cairo of the 1930s and 1940s. Like the Anagarika Dharmapala in Sri Lanka before him, he began his career in the educational bureaucracy. His bosses in

Egypt's Ministry of Public Instruction sent him to America in 1948, apparently in the hope that he would be won over by American ways. His discovery of his religious mission is said to have occurred as he stood on the deck of the liner that was carrying him to New York. I have cited figures from Hinduism, Buddhism, and Islam; many similar figures could be cited from the Jewish and Christian traditions.

What do these moments of conversion signify? In trying to answer that question, we find ourselves reaching reflexively for the terms that float by on one or the other side of the modernist stream. On the one shore we find terms or phrases such as "atavism," "medievalism," "fear of uncertainty" coming all too readily to hand; on the other, our hands close upon "resistance," "alternative," "search for community," "thirst for meaning."

To a greater or lesser degree, moments of conversion such as those I have referred to are all of these things, but they are also something else: they mark a crossing from one current of modernism to another. It is too easy to forget that these reinvented forms of religion are not a repudiation of but a means of laying claim to the modern world. That is why the advance guards of these ideologies are never traditional religious specialists but rather young college graduates or engineering students — products, in other words, of secularly oriented, modernist institutions. It is for this reason that we find the same things valued on both shores but in diametrically opposed ways. Literature and art, for example, being regarded as the ultimate repository of value on one side, come to be excoriated on the other, in exact and equal measure, so that their destruction becomes a prime article of faith.

Where else are we to look for the sources of this antagonism except within the whirlpools that mark the meeting of these two currents? Certainly the conflict cannot be ascribed to religion in the broadest sense. For most of human history, religion and literature have been virtually inseparable, everywhere. I can think of nonreligious ideologies that have thought of literature as an enemy; I know of no religion that has historically held that position. That is why we must be rigorous and unrelenting in our rejection of the claims of those religious extremists who try to invoke historical and religious precedents for their attacks on writers. These claims are offered in bad faith. In fact, the roots of this hostility lie in the eminently modern pedigree of their own moments of conversion. The religions they invoke do not begin with a positive content of faith; they have their beginnings in acts of negation.

I have been using the phrase "religious extremism" with what may appear to be a reckless disregard for differences among the world's major religions. I do not do so unadvisedly. I do believe that the content of these ideologies is startlingly similar, across continents and cultures.

Consider, for example, that the rhetoric of religious extremism is everywhere centered on issues that would have been regarded as profane, or worldly, or largely secular, a few generations ago: issues of state power, control of the bureaucracy, school curricula, the army, the law courts, banks, and other such institutions. Consider also that religious extremists are everywhere hostile to mainstream traditions of dissent within whatever religion they claim to be speaking for. Muslim extremists in the Middle East are contemptuous of the traditional Sufi *tariqas* ("ways" of schools) that have so long been a mainstay within popular Islam; the political leadership of the Hindu extremist movement treats traditional mendicants and ascetics as a source of embarrassment. In both instances, this hostility has its roots in peculiarly bourgeois anxieties about respectability and rationality.

There is also much evidence to show that as the concerns of the major religions have grown more and more sociological, their doctrines and institutions have also increasingly converged. Yet while we speak of doctrine, we are still within a domain that is recognizably religious. But the truth is that in those areas of the world that are currently beset by religious turmoil, we very rarely hear anyone speak of doctrine or faith. In many of these areas, by a curious inversion, the language of religious hatred is not a religious language at all. The voices that spew hate invariably draw on more incendiary sources. One of these is the language of quantity, of number — statistics, in other words, that famous syntax of falsehood. Such and such a group is growing too fast, they declare, its birthrate is so and so; it will soon become a majority, overtake another group that has nowhere else to go; that group will then be swamped, washed into the sea by the rising tide of enemies within. Equally, these voices borrow the language of academic historiography. They produce archaeological data to prove that such and such a group has no right to be here, that they are invaders who arrived later than some other, more authentically located peoples, whose claim to the land is therefore greater.

One of the more curious elements of these bizarre but all too real discourses is what might be called the logic of competitive victimhood. Group X, incontestably a majority in its own area, will declare itself to be the real minority because it is outnumbered if the surrounding regions are taken into account. Its ideologues will cite this as the reason that, to preserve itself, it must drive members of Group Y off its territory: Group Y, which appears to be a minority, is actually a majority; the members of Group X are the real victims. And so on.

Most of these ideologies share similar discourses on women: what women should wear, how they should comport themselves, when and if they should reproduce. And all this, we are told, because scripture or custom has ordained it so. I remember very well an incident that dates back some fourteen years, to a time when I was living in a village in Egypt. One day a schoolboy of fifteen — one of the brightest and most likable in the village — said to me, "Do you know what I did today? I gave my mother and the womenfolk in the house a stern talking-to. I told them that they could not go to the burial ground anymore to pray at our family's tombs."

I was taken aback by this. So far as I knew, the custom of visiting tombs was a very old one, and it served the additional function of providing women with a place to meet their kinfolk and friends. "Why?" I asked the boy. "What made you do this?"

"Because it is against our religion, of course," he said. "Visiting a grave is nothing but irrational superstition."

It turned out, I later learned, that a schoolteacher with fundamentalist leanings had preached a fiery sermon in the mosque, urging the men of the village to put an end to this custom.

The image of that adolescent schoolboy lecturing his mother on what she could and could not do stayed with me for a long time. Where did he find that authority at the age of fifteen? Why did she allow him to speak to her like that? But wasn't he also right to do what he did? After all, is it not perhaps irrational to visit graves? But still, did she resent having to renounce her trips to the graveyard? I don't know. The outcome in any case was that she stayed at home. That is how religious extremism seems to work.

The issues around which these fundamentalist discourses are configured are not, of course, exclusively the concern of religious extremists. On the contrary, the concerns are precisely the same as those that animate certain kinds of conflict that have no religious referents at all: language conflicts, for example, or ethnic and tribal conflicts. In a sense, this is the most revealing aspect of these movements: that they all have recourse to the same language of difference—a language that is entirely profane, entirely devoid of faith or belief.

This was brought home to me very forcefully a couple of years ago when I was traveling in Cambodia. It so happened that the United Nations was then conducting a large-scale peacekeeping operation, and some 20,000 peacekeeping personnel from all over the globe had been deployed throughout the country. The principal obstacle to the peace was the Khmer Rouge, whose ideology had by that time been reduced to a nationalistic form of racism, directed at the Vietnamese and particularly the Vietnamese-speaking minority in Cambodia. A defector who had surrendered to UN officials a few months before the elections described his political training with the Khmer Rouge:

As far as the Vietnamese are concerned, whenever we meet them we must kill them, whether they are militaries or civilians, because they are not ordinary civilians but soldiers disguised as civilians. We must kill them, whether they are men, women, or children, there is no distinction, they are enemies. Children are not militaries, but if they are born or grow up in Cambodia, when they will be adult, they will consider Cambodian land as theirs. So we make no distinction. As to women, they give birth to Vietnamese children.

The Khmer Rouge carried out several massacres of civilians during the peacekeeping process, most of them directed against small Vietnamese fishing communities.

I arrived in Cambodia in January 1993, just six or seven weeks after my own country, India, had faced what was perhaps its most serious political crisis since it gained independence in 1947. The crisis was precipitated by the demolition of a mosque in the city of Ayodhya by Hindu extremists. The demolition of the mosque was followed by a wave of murderous attacks upon Muslim-minority communities in India. In a series of pogroms in various Indian cities, thousands of Muslims were systematically murdered, raped, and brutalized by Hindu extremists. In many respects, the language of the Hindu extremists, with the appropriate substitutions, was identical to that of the Khmer Rouge in Cambodia.

It was against the background of these tragic events that I found myself one day in Siem Reap, in northwestern Cambodia. In this town, famous for its proximity to the glorious temple complexes of Angkor Wat and Angkor Thorn, I came upon a group of Indian doctors who were running a small field hospital for the UN. By virtue of the camaraderie that links compatriots in a faraway place, I was invited to join them for a meal at their hospital. The doctors received me with the greatest cordiality in their prefabricated dining room. But no sooner had I sat down than they turned to me, smiling cordially across the rice and dal, and one of them said, "Mr. Ghosh, can you think of a good reason why we Hindus should not demolish every mosque in India? After all, we are the majority. Why should we allow minorities to dictate what is right for us?" I had not noticed until then that my hosts were all Hindus, from various parts of India.

Their line of reasoning was, of course, far from unfamiliar to me: it was the standard majoritarian argument trotted out by Hindu extremists in India. But here, in this context, with the gunshots of the Khmer Rouge occasionally audible in the distance, it provoked an extra dimension of outrage. In the first place, these doctors were not extremists, in any ordinary meaning of the term. On the contrary, they were the personification of middle-class normality. Second, they were probably not religious in any but the most private sense. For them, most likely, religion was no more than a mark of distinction, defining the borders of what they believed to be a majority. In the course of the furious argument that followed, I was amazed to discover — though perhaps I should not have been — that these doctors actually harbored a lurking admiration for the Khmer Rouge, an admiration that was in no way diminished by the fact that we were then under Khmer Rouge fire.

I was amazed because I could not immediately understand why extremist Hindu beliefs should translate so fluently into sympathy for a group that had no religious affiliations at all, a group whose ideological genealogy ought to have inspired revulsion in these middle-class professional men. It only became obvious to me later, reading reports from Bosnia, Croatia, Sudan, Algeria, Sri Lanka, and other strife-torn lands, that for this species of thinking, religion, race, ethnicity, and language have no real content at all. Their only significance lies in the lines of distinction they provide. The actual content of the ideology, whether it manifests itself in its religious avatar or its linguistic or ethnic one, is actually the same in every case, although articulated through different symbols. In several instances — Sri Lanka, for example — extremist movements have seamlessly shifted their focus from language to religion.

What, then, is this ideology that can travel so indifferently among such disparate political groups? I believe that it is an incarnation of a demon that has stalked liberal democracy everywhere throughout this century, an ideology that, for want of a better word, I shall call supremacism. It consists essentially in the belief that a group cannot ensure its continuity except by exerting absolute cultural and demographic control over a particular stretch of geography. The fascist antecedents of this ideology are clear and obvious. Some would go further and argue that nationalism of every kind must also be regarded as a variant of supremacism. This is often but not necessarily true. The nonsectarian, anti-imperialist nationalism of a Gandhi or a Saad Zaghloul was founded on a belief in the possibility of relative autonomy for heterogeneous populations and had nothing to do with asserting supremacy.

To return to where I began: it is my belief that extremist religious movements, whether in India or Israel or Egypt or the United States, are often supremacist movements, whatever their rhetoric. The movements that fit the pattern least perhaps are radical Muslim movements. Of all the world's religions, Islam remains today the least territorial, the least, as it were, nationalized. Yet it cannot be a coincidence that despite the critique of nationalism that is inherent in some branches of radical Islam, these movements have everywhere lapsed into patterns that are contained within the current framework of nation-states. Nor can it be a coincidence that in the Islamic world, as elsewhere, religious movements are at their most extreme in countries with large minority populations — Sudan and Egypt, for example. Indeed, such is the peculiar power of supremacist movements that they have actually conjured minorities into being where none actively existed before. Thus, in Algeria, Muslim extremists must now contend with an increasingly assertive minority Berber population.

In principle, it is not unreasonable that a population should have the right to live under religious law, with the proper democratic safeguards. But in practice, in contemporary societies, when such laws are instituted, they almost invariably become instruments of majoritarian domination. Consider, for example, the blasphemy laws enacted in Pakistan in the 1980s. A recently published Amnesty International report tells us that "at present several dozen people are charged with blasphemy, in Pakistan." The majority of these belong to the minority Ahmadiyya community. This sect, which considers itself Muslim, was declared heretical by the country's legislature, and its members were forbidden to profess, practice, or propagate their faith. According to Pakistani human rights activists, in a period of five years 108 Ahmadis were charged with blasphemy for practicing their faith. Over the past three years, according to the report, members of the Christian minority in Pakistan have also increasingly been charged with blasphemy. But here again, the meaning of blasphemy itself has changed. When a law such as this is available, it is unrealistic to expect that people will not use it in ways other than was intended. I quote from the report:

> In a number of cases, personal grudges against Christian neighbours seem to have led people to settle their disputes by bringing blasphemy charges. Anwar Masih, a Christian in Sammundri in Faisalabad district, had a quarrel with the local Muslim shopkeeper over a small debt and was subsequently charged with blasphemy . . . A 13-year-old Christian boy in Punjab was reported to have said that he had had a fight with the eight-year-old son of a Muslim neighbour. "It all started with some pigeons. The boys caught my pigeons and they didn't want to give them back to me . . . The little boy with whom I had a fight said he saw me write [blasphemous words] on the mosque . . ." [The boy], who has never learned to read or write, and two adult Christians were charged with blasphemy, in May 1993.

How far we are here from a reverence for the spirit of scripture!

I would like to turn now to a novel which, more than anything I have read recently, has forced me to confront the questions that contemporary religious extremism raises for writers. This is the Bengali novel *Lojja* (*Shame*), by the Bangladeshi writer Taslima Nasrin. I believe that this book, deeply flawed in many respects, is nonetheless a very important novel and a work of considerable insight. It is also a work that is literally much misunderstood, because at the moment it is available to most of the world in an English translation that can only be described as appalling. As a result the book has received many slighting and dismissive notices in America and Europe, probably because reviewers have assumed uncritically that the translation provides an accurate indication of the book's quality. It happens that although I write in English, my native language is Bengali, and having read the book in the original, I know this assumption to be untrue. It seems more and more unlikely now that the book will ever get a fair reading, partly because it has become a pawn within the religious conflicts of the Indian subcontinent, and partly because Taslima Nasrin is herself now a global "cause" for reasons that have little to do with her writing.

Lojja was apparently written at great speed, being completed in a couple of months. The book was later revised, but even in its revised version it remains a short novel—the new Bengali edition numbers 150 pages. The narrative is simple: through its protagonist, Suranjan Datta, it follows the fortunes of a Hindu family that finds itself engulfed in a wave of violence directed against the minority Hindu community in Bangladesh. The events it describes occur in the aftermath of the demolition of a mosque in Ayodhya on December 6, 1992. The narrative is punctuated throughout with paraphrased news reports, items from the files of human rights organizations, and other accounts detailing actual instances of violence. In particular it is a severe, because factual, indictment of certain groups of religious extremists in Bangladesh.

As is well known, the book caused an uproar when it was published in Bangladesh in 1993. It also became an instant bestseller on both sides of the border: that is, in Bangladesh as well as in the Bengali-speaking parts of India. A few months after its publication, the government of Bangladesh, in response to the demands of religious extremists, declared a ban on the book and had it removed from circulation. Shortly thereafter, an extremist Muslim leader declared Taslima Nasrin an apostate and issued a death warrant against her. The warrant carried a large bounty. A few months later, in response to certain remarks Taslima Nasrin was alleged to have made in a newspaper interview in Calcutta, the government of Bangladesh charged her officially with the crime of offending religious sentiments and began criminal proceedings. Taslima Nasrin then went into hiding for a period of two months. Thanks to the international outcry that followed, she was allowed to leave Bangladesh in August 1994. She is currently living in Sweden. In her short career in exile she has continued to rock governments. Last October the French foreign ministry refused her a visa, a gesture that created such an outburst of public indignation that the ministry was soon forced to reverse its decision. What I have sketched here is perhaps only the beginning of Taslima Nasrin's story. Even as I write, a government prosecutor in Bangladesh is appearing before a court to demand that she be sentenced in absentia for the crime of blasphemy.

However, religious extremists were not the only people in Bangladesh who objected to *Lojja* when it first appeared. Many nonsectarian, liberal voices were also fiercely critical of the book. Their objections were important ones and must be taken into account, because — and I cannot repeat this strongly enough — nonsectarian, broadly secularist voices do not by any means represent a weak or isolated strand of opinion in that country. Bangladeshi culture in particular, like Bengali culture in general, has a long and very powerful tradition of secularist thought; Taslima Nasrin is herself a product of this tradition. For all their visibility, the religious extremists represent a tiny minority of the population of Bangladesh. At present, for example, they control no more than 2 percent of the country's legislature.

Of the criticisms directed at *Lojja* by liberal, nonsectarian Bangladeshis and Indians, perhaps the most important is the charge that the novel, by limiting its focus to Bangladesh, profoundly distorts the context of the violence it depicts. Taken literally, this is, I think, true. By concentrating on the events in Dhaka, the book does indeed, by omission, distort the setting and causes of those events.

What, then, was this context? I shall try to sketch the chain of events as I see them, very briefly.

On December 6, 1992, several thousand Hindu supremacists tore down a four-hundred-year-old mosque in Ayodhya, claiming that the structure was built upon the birthplace of their mythical hero Sri Rama. The Indian government, despite ample warning, was culpably negligent in not taking action to prevent the demolition. Thus, through CNN, the whole world witnessed the destructive frenzy of a mob of Hindu fanatics attacking an archaeological site, in the service of an utter delusion. (After all, a legendary world-bestriding hero can only be diminished if his birthplace comes to be confined to a circumscribed geographical location.)

The destruction of the mosque was followed by tension and general unrest, in Pakistan and Bangladesh as well as India. In India this quickly escalated into violence directed against Muslims by well-organized mobs of Hindus. Riots broke out in several major cities, and within two days four hundred people had died. The overwhelming majority of the dead, as always in these situations in India, were Muslim. There is evidence that in many parts of the country the police cooperated with and even directed Hindu mobs. Within six days, according to the official reckoning, about twelve hundred people had died. Reports from all over the country attest to the unprecedented brutality, the unspeakable savagery, of the violence that was directed against innocent Muslims by Hindu supremacists. A month later, there was a second wave of anti-Muslim violence centered primarily in Bombay and Surat. The violence now assumed the aspect of systematic pogroms, with crowds hunting out Muslims from door to door in particular neighborhoods. I quote here a report from Surat, written by a Dutch observer:

> In a refugee camp which I visited a small boy, hardly six years of age, sits all alone in a corner staring in front of him. Before his

eyes he has seen first his father and mother murdered by the mob, then his grandfather and grandmother, and in the end three of his brothers. He is still alive but bodily not unscathed with 16 stitches in his head and burns on his back. The men who did it thought he was dead when they had finished with him . . . Page after page of my diary is filled with this sort of atrocity. Women between seven and 70 were up for grabs by male gangs roaming around the localities . . . People were also thrown into the flames and roasted alive. A high-ranking official told me how he had seen furniture coming down over the balcony from the opposite multistoreyed apartment building: mattresses, chairs, and then to his horror small children as well.

Such was the nature of the horror that visited India in the winter of 1992, in the name of religion.

In Bangladesh and Pakistan, the destruction of the Ayodhya mosque also led to violence. Temples were attacked and destroyed in both countries. In Bangladesh, which has a substantial Hindu population, a great many Hindu shrines were destroyed and desecrated; Hindu-owned businesses were attacked and looted; many Hindu families were driven from their homes. Yet it must also be noted that despite all that happened in Bangladesh, there was no actual loss of life, so far as I know. If accounts could be kept of such events, it would have to be said that the scale of violence in Bangladesh was small compared to what occurred in India.

But here we have to ask whether events such as these can be weighed at all on a scale of comparative horrors. For a minority family that is being harassed in Dhaka (or wherever), the horror of the situation is not mitigated by the knowledge that they are situated in the wings of the stage of violence, as it were, that far worse crimes are being visited upon minority groups in India. Equally, the terror of a middle-class Muslim family caught in a riot in Bombay is in no way lessened by the knowledge that there is greater violence still in Bosnia. To the Bosnian Serbs, in turn, the accounting of violence stretches back to the fourteenth century. To tinker with this calculus is really to enter into what I have called the logic of competitive victimhood: a discourse that ultimately serves only to fuel supremacism.

In inadvertently spotlighting events that were happening in the wings rather than at center stage, *Lojja* inevitably presents a partial view. As it happened, Hindu supremacists in India seized upon *Lojja* with undisguised glee. Pirated editions were quickly printed, and the book was even distributed free by Hindu activists in an attempt to whip up anti-Muslim feeling. This in turn led to accusations that Taslima Nasrin was a willing dupe of Hindu supremacists in India, that she was in the pay of a Calcutta publishing house, and so on.

In fact, *Lojja* is unequivocal in its condemnation of Hindu supremacists. It simply does not give them as much space as it does their Muslim counterparts in Bangladesh, which is unavoidable given the book's setting. Just as important, Taslima Nasrin can hardly be held responsible for the uses to which her book is put. In passing into the public domain, a book also passes beyond its author's control. I know of no way that an author can protect his or her text against abuse of this kind. The only option really is not to write about such matters at all.

We who write fiction, even when we deal with matters of public significance, have no choice, no matter how lush or extravagant our fictions, but to represent events as they are refracted through our characters. Our point of entry into even the largest of events is inevitably local, situated in and focused on details and particulars. To write of any event in this way is necessarily to neglect its political contexts. Consider by way of example a relatively simple kind of event: a mugging, let us say, in the streets of New York. If we write of the mugging of a white man by a black man, do we not in some way distort the context of the event if we do not accommodate the collective histories that form its background? Conversely, if, in defiance of stereotypes, we were to make our mugger a white female bank executive, would we not distort an equally important context? But where would our search for contexts end?

And would we not fatally disfigure the fictional texture of our work if we were to render all those broader contexts?

What, then, are the contexts that we, as writers of fiction, can properly supply? It seems to me that they must lie in the event itself, the scene, if you like: the aggressor's fear of his prey, the streetlamps above, the paper clip that drops from the victim's pocket as he reaches for his money. It must be in some part the reader's responsibility to situate the event within broader contexts, to populate the scene with the products of his or her experience and learning. A reader who reads the scene literally or mean-spiritedly must surely bear some part of the blame for that reading.

Read by an attentive reader, *Lojja* succeeds magnificently. Through a richness of detail it creates a circumstance that is its own context and in this sense is imaginatively available far beyond the boundaries of its location. I, for one, read *Lojja* not as a book about Hindus in Bangladesh but rather as a book about Muslims in India. It helped me feel on my own fingertips the texture of the fears that have prompted Muslim friends of mine to rent houses under false pretenses or buy train tickets under Hindu names. In short, it has helped me understand what it means to live under the threat of supremacist terror.

Lojja can be read in this way because it is founded on a very important insight, one that directly illustrates my main point. Almost despite herself, Taslima Nasrin recognizes that religious extremism today has very little to do with matters of doctrine and faith, that its real texts are borrowed from sociology, demography, political science, and so on. For a book that is said to be blasphemous, *Lojja* surprisingly contains no scriptural or religious references at all. Even words such as "Hindu" and "Muslim" figure in it but rarely. The words Taslima Nasrin uses are, rather, "minority" and "majority." There is nothing in *Lojja* that the most fastidiously devout reader could possibly object to from a theological point of view. That it succeeded nonetheless in enraging extremist religious opinion in Bangladesh, and bolstering opinion within the opposite religious camp in India, is a sign that it cut through to an altogether different kind of reality. Yet it is a fact that despite their outrage, the extremists could find no passage in it that could be indicted as blasphemous. That was why, perhaps, they later fell so gratefully on her throwaway remarks of doubtful provenance.

I would like to return now to some of the considerations with which I started. In particular I would like to go back to one of the images I offered at the beginning of this essay: that of W. H. Auden, breasting the modernist flow and crossing between currents. In offering this example I did not mean to suggest that Auden can in any way be associated with religious extremism as we know it today. To make such a suggestion would be plainly ludicrous. If there is an analogy here, it is a very limited one, and it consists only in this: that a conversion such as Auden's to Christianity was — among many other things — also an act of dissent, an opting out of what might be regarded as the mainstream of modernist consciousness.

It is finally undeniable, I think, that some kinds of contemporary religious extremism also represent a generalized, nebulous consciousness of dissent, an inarticulate, perhaps inexpressible critique of the political and moral economy of today's world. But the questions remain, even if this is true: why are these movements so easily pushed over the edge, why are they so violent, so destructive, and why is their thinking so filled with intolerance and hate?

Today, for the first time in history, a single ideal commands something close to absolute hegemony in the world: the notion that human existence must be permanently and irredeemably subordinated to the functioning of the impersonal mechanisms of a global marketplace. Realized in varying degrees in various parts of the world, this ideal enjoys the vigorous support of universities, banks, vast international corporations, and an increasingly interconnected global communications network. However, the market ideal as a cultural absolute, untempered by any other ethical, political, or spiritual ideals, is often so inhuman and predatory in its effects that it cannot but generate dissent. It is simply not conceivable that the majority of human beings will ever willingly give their assent to the idea that the search for profit should be the sole or central organizing principle of society.

By a curious paradox, the room for dissent has shrunk as the world has grown freer, and today, in this diminished space, every utterance begins to turn in on itself. This, I believe, is why we need to recreate, expand, and reimagine the space for articulate, humane, and creative dissent. In the absence of that space, the misdirected and ugly energies of religious extremism will only continue to flourish and grow.

What then, finally, of religion itself? Must we resign ourselves to the possibility that religious belief has everywhere been irreversibly cannibalized by this plethora of political, sociological, and in the end profane ideas? It is tempting to say no, that "real" Hindus, Buddhists, Christians, Jews, and Muslims continue to hold on to other values. Yet if it appears that the majority of the followers of a religion now profess ideas that are, as I have said, essentially political or sociological, then we must be prepared to accept that this is in fact what religion signifies in our time.

Still, I, for one, have swum too long in pre-postmodernist currents to accept that some part of the effort that human culture has so long invested in matters of the spirit will not, somehow, survive.

PETROFICTION

The Oil Encounter and the Novel

1992

IF THE SPICE TRADE has any twentieth-century equivalent, it can only be the oil industry. In its economic and strategic value as well as its ability to generate far-flung political, military, and cultural encounters, oil is clearly the only commodity that can serve as an analogy for pepper. In all matters technical, of course, the comparison is weighted grossly in favor of oil. But in at least one domain, it is the spice trade that can claim the clear advantage: in the quality of the literature that it nurtured.

Within a few decades of the discovery of the sea route to India, the Portuguese poet Luis de Camões had produced *The Lusiads,* the epic poem that chronicled Vasco da Gama's voyage and in effect conjured Portugal into literary nationhood. The Oil Encounter, in contrast, has produced scarcely a single work of note. In English, for example, it has generated little apart from some more or less second-rate travel literature and a vast amount of academic ephemera — nothing remotely of the quality or the intellectual distinction of the travelogues and narratives produced by such sixteenth-century Portuguese writers as Duarte Barbosa, Tomé Pires, and Caspar Correia. As for an epic poem, the very idea is ludicrous. To the principal protagonists in the Oil Encounter (which means, in effect, America and Americans on the one hand and the peoples of the Arabian Peninsula and the Persian Gulf on the other), the history of oil is a matter of embarrassment verging on the unspeakable, the pornographic. It is perhaps the one cultural issue on which the two sides are in complete agreement.

Still, if the Oil Encounter has proved barren, it is surely through no fault of its own. It would be hard to imagine a story that is equal in drama, or in historical resonance. Consider its Livingstonian beginnings: the Westerner with his caravan loads of machines and instruments, thrusting himself unannounced upon small, isolated communities deep within some of the most hostile environments on earth. And think of the postmodern present: city-states where virtually everyone is a "foreigner"; admixtures of peoples and cultures on a scale never before envisaged; vicious systems of helotry juxtaposed with unparalleled wealth; deserts transformed by technology, and military devastation on an apocalyptic scale.

It is a story that evokes horror, sympathy, guilt, rage, and a great deal else, depending on the listener's situation. The one thing that can be said of it with absolute certainty is that no one anywhere who has any thought for either his conscience or his self-preservation can afford to ignore it. So why, when there is so much to write about, has this encounter proved so imaginatively sterile?

On the American side, the answers are not far to seek. To a great many Americans, oil smells bad. It reeks of unavoidable overseas entanglements, a worrisome foreign dependency, economic uncertainty, risky and expensive military enterprises; of thousands of dead civilians and children and all the troublesome questions that lie buried in their graves. Bad enough at street level, the smell of oil gets a lot worse by the time it seeps into those rooms where serious fiction is written and read. It acquires more than just a whiff of that deep suspicion of the Arab and Muslim worlds that wafts through so much of American intellectual life. And to make things still worse, it begins to smell of pollution and environmental hazards. It reeks, it stinks, it becomes a Problem that can be written about only in the language of Solutions.

But there are other reasons why there isn't a Great American Oil Novel, and some of them lie hidden within the institutions that shape American writing today. It would be hard indeed to imagine the writing school that could teach its graduates to find their way through the uncharted firmaments of the Oil Encounter. In a way, the professionalization of fiction has had much the same effect in America as it had in Britain in another, imperial age: as though in precise counterpoint to the increasing geographical elasticity of the country's involvements, its fictional gaze has turned inward, becoming ever more introspective, ever more concentrated on its own self-definition. In other words, it has fastened upon a stock of themes and subjects, each of which is accompanied by a well-tested pedagogic technology. Try to imagine a major American writer taking on the Oil Encounter. The idea is literally inconceivable. It isn't fair, of course, to point the finger at American writers. There isn't very much they could write about: neither they nor anyone else really knows anything at all about the human experiences that surround the production of oil. A great deal has been invested in ensuring the muteness of the Oil Encounter: on the American (or Western) side, through regimes of strict corporate secrecy; on the Arab side, by the physical and demographic separation of oil installations and their workers from the indigenous population.

It is no accident, then, that the genre of "My Days in the Gulf" has yet to be invented. Most Western oilmen of this generation have no reason to be anything other than silent about their working lives. Their working experience of the Middle East is culturally a nullity, lived out largely within portable versions of Western suburbia.

In some ways the story is oddly similar on the Arab side, except that there it is a quirk of geography — of geology, to be exact — that is largely to blame for oil's literary barrenness. Perversely, oil chose to be discovered in precisely those parts of the Middle East that have been the most marginal in the development of modern Arab culture and literature — on the outermost peripheries of such literary centers as Cairo and Beirut.

Until quite recently, the littoral of the Gulf was considered an outlying region within the Arab world, a kind of frontier whose inhabitants' worth lay more in their virtuous simplicity than in their cultural aspirations. The slight curl of the lip that inevitably accompanies an attitude of that kind has become, if anything, a good deal more pronounced now that many Arab writers from Egypt and Lebanon—countries with faltering economies but rich literary traditions—are constrained to earn their livelihood in the Gulf. As a result, young Arab writers are no more likely to write about the Oil Encounter than their Western counterparts. No matter how long they have lived in the Gulf or in Libya, when it comes to the practice of fiction, they generally prefer to return to the familiar territories staked out by their literary forebears. There are, of course, some notable exceptions (such as the Palestinian writer Ghassan Kanafani's remarkable story "Men in the Sun"), but otherwise the Gulf serves all too often as a metaphor for corruption and decadence, a surrogate for the expression of the resentment that so many in the Arab world feel toward the regimes that rule the oil kingdoms.

In fact, very few people anywhere write about the Oil Encounter. The silence extends much further than the Arabic- or English-speaking worlds. Take Bengali, a language deeply addicted to the travelogue as a genre. Every year several dozen accounts of travel in America, Europe, China, and so on are published in Bengali, along with innumerable short stories and novels about expatriates in New Jersey, California, and various parts of Europe. Yet the hundreds of thousands of Bengali-speaking people who live and work in the oil kingdoms scarcely ever merit literary attention—or any kind of interest, for that matter.

As one of the few who have tried to write about the floating world of oil, I can bear witness to its slipperiness, to the ways in which it tends to trip fiction into incoherence. In the end, perhaps, it is the craft of writing itself—or rather writing as we know it today—that is responsible for the muteness of the Oil Encounter. The experiences that oil has generated run counter to many of the

historical imperatives that have shaped writing over the past couple of centuries and given it its distinctive forms. The territory of
oil is bafflingly multilingual, for example, while the novel, with
its conventions of naturalistic dialogue, is most at home within
monolingual speech communities (within nation-states, in other
words). Equally, the novel is never more comfortable than when it
is luxuriating in a "sense of place," reveling in its unique power to
evoke mood and atmosphere. But the experiences associated with
oil are lived out within a space that is no place at all, a world that
is intrinsically displaced, heterogeneous, and international. It is a
world that poses a radical challenge not merely to the practice of
writing as we know it but to much of modern culture: to such notions as the idea of distinguishable and distant civilizations, or recognizable and separate "societies." It is a world whose closest ana-
logues are medieval, not modern — which is probably why it has
proved so successful in eluding the gaze of contemporary global
culture. The truth is that we do not yet possess the form that can
give the Oil Encounter a literary expression.

For this reason alone, *Cities of Salt*, the Jordanian writer Abdelrahman Munif's monumental five-part cycle of novels dealing with
the history of oil, ought to be regarded as a work of immense significance. It so happens that the first novel in the cycle is also in
many ways a wonderful work of fiction, perhaps even in parts a
great one. Peter Theroux's excellent English translation of this
novel was published a few years ago under the eponymous title
Cities of Salt, and now its successor, *The Trench*, has appeared.
    Munif's prose is extremely difficult to translate, being rich in
ambiguities and unfamiliar dialectical usages, and so Theroux deserves to be commended for his translations — especially of the
first book, where he has done a wonderful job. He is scrupulously
faithful to both the letter and the spirit of the original, while sacrificing nothing in readability. Where Theroux has intervened, it is
in what would appear to be the relatively unimportant matters of
punctuation and typography. (He has numbered each chapter,

though the Arabic text does not really have chapters at all, but merely extended breaks between pages; and he has also eliminated Munif's favorite device of punctuation, a sentence or paragraph that ends with two period points rather than one, to indicate indeterminacy, inconclusivity, what you will . . .) These changes are slight enough, but they have the overall effect of producing a text that is much more "naturalistic" than the original. One day a professor of comparative literature somewhere will have fun using Theroux's translations to document the changes in protocol that texts undergo in being shaped to conform to different cultural expectations.

The Arabic title of Munif's first novel has the connotation of "the wilderness," or "the desert," and it begins with what is possibly the best and most detailed account of that mythical event, a First Encounter, in fiction — all the better for being, for once, glimpsed from the wrong end of the telescope. The novel opens, appropriately, on an oasis whose name identifies it as the source, or the beginning: Wadi al-Uyoun, an "outpouring of green in the harsh, obdurate desert." To the caravans that occasionally pass through it, as to its inhabitants, the wadi is an "earthly paradise," and to none more so than one Miteb al-Hathal ("the Troublemaker"), an elder of a tribe called al-Atoum:

> Left to himself to talk about Wadi al-Uyoun, Miteb al-Hathal would go on in a way no one could believe, for he could not confine himself to the good air and the sweetness of the water . . . or to the magnificent nights; he would tell stories which in some cases dated back to the days of Noah, or so said the old men.

But unsettling portents begin to intrude upon this earthly paradise. One evening at sunset, one of Miteb's sons returns from watering the family's livestock and tells his father of the arrival of "three foreigners with two marsh Arabs, and they speak Arabic" — "People say they came to look for water." But when Miteb goes to find out for himself, he sees them going to "places no one dreamed of going," collecting "unthinkable things," and writing "things no one understood," and he comes to the conclusion that "they certainly didn't come for water — they want something else. But what could they possibly want? What is there in this dry desert besides dust, sand and starvation?"

The people of the wadi hear the foreigners asking questions "about dialects, about tribes and their disputes, about religion and sects, about the rocks, the winds and the rainy season"; they listen to them quoting from the Koran and repeating the Muslim profession of faith; and they begin to "wonder among themselves if these were jinn, because people like these who knew all those things and spoke Arabic yet never prayed were not Muslims and could not be normal humans." Reading the portents, Miteb the Troublemaker senses that something terrible is about to befall the wadi and its people, but he knows neither what it is nor how to prevent it. Then suddenly, to everyone's relief, the foreigners leave, and the wadi settles back, just a trifle uneasily, to its old ways.

But soon enough the strangers come back. They are no longer unspecified "foreigners" but Americans, and they are everywhere, digging, collecting, and handing out "coins of English and Arab gold." Their liberality soon wins them friends in the wadi, but even the closest of their accomplices is utterly bewildered by their doings; "nothing was stranger than their morning prayers: they began by kicking their legs and raising their arms in the air, moving their bodies to the left and right, and then touching their toes until they were panting and drenched with sweat." Then a number of "yellow iron hulks" arrive, adding to the bewilderment of the wadi's inhabitants: "Could a man approach them without injury? What were they for and how did they behave — did they eat like animals or not?" Fearing the worst, the people of the wadi go to their emir to protest, only to be told that the Americans have "come from the ends of the earth to help us" — because "'there are oceans of blessings under this soil.'"

The protests are quickly suppressed, Miteb and other troublemakers are threatened with death, and before long the wadi's orchards and dwellings are demolished by the "yellow iron hulks."

After the flattening of his beloved wadi, Miteb mounts his white Omani she-camel and vanishes into the hills, becoming a prophetic spectral figure who emerges only occasionally from the desert to cry doom and to strike terror into those who collaborate with the oil men. As for Miteb's family and the rest of the wadi's inhabitants, they are quickly carried away by passing camel caravans. A number of them set out for a coastal settlement called Harran ("the Overheated"), where the new oil installations are to be built, a "cluster of low mud houses" — a place evidently very much as Doha and Kuwait were only a few decades ago.

The rest of Munif's narrative centers upon the early stages of Harran's transformation: the construction of the first roads, the gradual influx of people, the building of the oil installations, the port, and the emir's palace. Working in shifts, the newly arrived Arab workers and their American overseers slowly conjure two new townships into being, Arab Harran and American Harran. Every evening, after the day's work is done, the men drift home

> to the two sectorlike streams coursing down a slope, one broad and one small, the Americans to their camp and the Arabs to theirs, the Americans to their swimming pool, where their racket could be heard in the nearby barracks behind the barbed wire. When silence fell the workers guessed the Americans had gone into their air-conditioned rooms whose thick curtains shut everything out: sunlight, dust, flies, and Arabs.

Soon Harran no longer quite belongs to its people, and the single most important episode in the building of the new city has little to do with them. It is the story of an R-and-R ship that pays the city a brief visit for the benefit of the Americans living in the yet unfinished oil town:

> The astonished people of Harran approached [the ship] imperceptibly, step by step, like sleepwalkers. They could not believe their eyes and ears. Had there ever been anything like this ship, this huge

and magnificent? Where else in the world were there women like these, who resembled both milk and figs in their tanned whiteness? Was it possible that men could shamelessly walk around with women, with no fear of others? Were these their wives, or sweethearts, or something else?

For a whole day and night, the inhabitants of Harran watch the Americans of the oil town disporting themselves with the newly arrived women, and by the time the ship finally leaves "the men's balls are ready to burst." This event eventually comes to mark the beginning of the history of this city of salt:

> This day gave Harran a birth date, recording when and how it was built, for most people have no memory of Harran before that day. Even its own natives, who had lived there since the arrival of the first frightening group of Americans and watched with terror the realignment of the town's shoreline and hills — the Harranis, born and bred there, saddened by the destruction of their houses, recalling the old sorrows of lost travellers and the dead — remembered the day the ship came better than any other day, with fear, awe, and surprise. It was practically the only date they remembered.

The most sustained wrong note in *Cities of Salt* is reserved for its conclusion. The novel ends with a dramatic confrontation between the old Harran and the new: between a world where the emir sat in coffeehouses and gossiped with the Bedouins, where everybody had time for everyone else and no one was ever so ill that they needed remedies that were sold for money, and a universe in which Mr. Middleton of the oil company holds their livelihoods in his hands, where the newly arrived Lebanese doctor Subhi al-Mahmilji ("physician and surgeon, specialist in internal and venereal diseases, Universities of Berlin and Vienna") charges huge fees for the smallest service, where the emir spies on the townspeople with a telescope and needs a cadre of secret police to tell him what they are thinking. "Every day it's gotten worse," says one longtime resident of Harran, pointing toward the American enclave: "I told you, I told every one of you, the Americans are the disease, they're the root of the problem and what's happened now is nothing compared to what they have in store for us."

The matter comes to a head when a series of events — a killing by the secret police, sightings of the troublemaking Miteb, the laying off of twenty-three workers — prompts the workers of Harran to invent spontaneously the notion of the strike. They stop working and march through the town chanting:

> . . . The pipeline was built by beasts of prey,
> We will safeguard our rights,
> The Americans do not own it,
> This land is our land.

Then, led by two of Miteb the Troublemaker's sons, they storm the oil installation, sweeping aside the emir's secret police and the oil company's guards, and rescue some of their fellow workers who'd been trapped inside. And the book ends with an unequivocal triumph for the workers: the half-crazed emir flees the city after ordering the oil company to reinstate its sacked employees.

It is not hard to see why Munif would succumb to the temptation to end his book on an optimistic note. His is a devastatingly painful story, a slow, roundabout recounting of the almost accidental humiliation of one people by another. There is very little bitterness in Munif's telling of it. Its effectiveness lies rather in the gradual accumulation of detail. Munif's American oil men are neither rapacious nor heartless. On the contrary, they are eager, businesslike, and curious. When invited to an Arab wedding, they ask "about everything, about words, clothing and food, about the names of the bridegroom and his bride and whether they had known each other before, and if they had ever met . . . Every small thing excited the Americans' amazement." It is not through direct confrontation that the Harranis met their humiliation. Quite the opposite. Theirs is the indignity of not being taken seriously at all, of being regarded as an obstacle on the scale of a minor technical snag in the process of drilling for oil.

Better than any other, Munif's method shows us why so many people in the Middle East are moved to clutch at straws to regain some measure of self-respect for themselves — why so many Saudis, for example, felt the humiliation of Iraq's army almost as their own. But in fact the story is even grimmer than Munif's version of it, and the ending he chooses is founded in pure wish-fulfillment. It probably has more to do with its author's own history than with the story of oil in the Gulf.

Abdelrahman Munif was born in 1933, into a family of Saudi Arabian origin settled in Jordan. (He was later stripped of his Saudi citizenship for political reasons.) He studied in Baghdad and Cairo and went on to earn a Ph.D. in oil economics at the University of Belgrade — back in the days of Titoite socialism, when books written by progressive writers always ended in working-class victories. Since then Munif's working life has been spent mainly in the oil industry in the Middle East, albeit in a rather sequestered corner of it: he has occupied important positions in the Syrian Oil Company, and he has served as editor in chief of an Iraqi journal called *Oil and Development*.

No one, in other words, is in a better position than Munif to know that the final episode in his story is nothing more than an escapist fantasy. He must certainly be aware that the workforces of the international oil companies in the Arabian peninsula have never succeeded in becoming politically effective. When they showed signs of restiveness in the 1950s, they were ruthlessly and very effectively suppressed by their rulers, with the help of the oil companies. Over the past couple of decades, the powers that be in the oil sheikdoms (and who knows exactly who they are?) have followed a careful strategy for keeping their workers quiescent: they have held the Arab component of their workforces at a strictly regulated numerical level while importing large numbers of migrants from several of the poorer countries of Asia.

The policy has proved magically effective in the short run. It has created a class of workers who, being separated from the indigenous population (and from each other) by barriers of culture and language, are politically passive in a way that a predominantly Arab workforce could never be within the Arab-speaking world — a class that is all the more amenable to control for living perpetually under the threat of deportation. It is, in fact, a class of helots, with virtually no rights at all, and its members are often subjected to the most hideous kinds of physical abuse. Their experience makes a mockery of human rights rhetoric that accompanied the Gulf War; the fact that the war has effected no changes in the labor policies of the oil sheikdoms is proof in the eyes of millions of people in Asia and Africa that the "new world order" is designed to defend the rights of certain people at the expense of others.

Thus the story of the real consequences of the sort of political restiveness that Munif describes in *Cities of Salt* is not likely to warm the heart quite as cozily as the ending he gives his novel. But if Munif can be accused of naiveté on this score, he must still be given credit for seeing that the workplace, where democracy is said to begin, is the site where the foundations of contemporary authoritarianism in the oil sheikdoms were laid.

Today it is a commonplace in the Western media that aspirations toward democracy in the Arabian peninsula are a part of the fallout of changes ushered in by oil and the consequent breakdown of "traditional" society. In fact, in several instances exactly the opposite is true: oil and the developments it has brought in its wake have been directly responsible for the suppression of whatever democratic aspirations and tendencies there were within the region.

Certain parts of the Gulf, such as Bahrain, whose commercial importance far predates the discovery of oil, have long possessed sizable groups of businessmen, professionals, and skilled workers —a stratum not unlike a middle class. On the whole, that class shared the ideology of the nationalist movements of various nearby countries such as India, Egypt, and Iran. It was their liberal aspirations that became the victims of oil's most bizarre, most murderous creation: the petro-despot, dressed in a snowy *dishdasha* and armed with state-of-the-art weaponry — the creature whose gestation and birth Munif sets out to chronicle in the second volume of the *Cities of Salt* cycle, *The Trench*.

Unfortunately, *The Trench* comes as a great disappointment. The narrative now moves away from Harran to a city in the interior called Mooran ("the Changeable"), which serves as the seat of the country's ruling dynasty. With the move to the capital, the focus of the narrative now shifts to the country's rulers.

The story of *The Trench* is common enough in the oil sheikdoms of the Arabian peninsula; it begins with the accession to power of a sultan by the name of Khazael, and it ends with his deposition, when he is removed from the throne by rival factions within the royal family. Munif describes the transformations that occur during Sultan Khazael's reign by following the career of one of his chief advisers, a doctor called Subhi al-Mahmilji (who earlier played an important part in the creation of the new Harran). The story has great potential, but Munif's voice does not prove equal to the demands of the narrative. It loses the note of wonder, of detached and reverential curiosity, that lent such magic to parts of *Cities of Salt*, while gaining neither the volume nor the richness of coloring that its material demands.

Instead Munif shifts to satire, and the change proves disastrous. He makes a valiant attempt — not for nothing are his books banned in various countries on the Arabian peninsula — but satire has no hope of success when directed against figures like Sultan Khazael and his family. No one, certainly no mere writer of fiction, could hope to satirize the royal families of the Arabian peninsula with a greater breadth of imagination than they do themselves. As countless newspaper reports can prove, factual accounts of their doings are well able to beggar the fictional imagination. Indeed, in the eyes of the world at large, Arab and non-Arab, the oil sheik scarcely exists except as a caricature; he is the late twentieth century's most potent symbol of decadence, hypocrisy, and corruption. He preempts the very possibility of satire. Of course, it isn't always so. The compulsions and the absurdities of an earlier generation of oil sheiks had their roots in a genuinely tragic history of predicament. But those very real dilemmas are reduced to caricature in Munif's Sultan Khazael.

Even where it is successful, moreover, Munif's satire is founded ultimately upon a kind of nostalgia, a romantic hearkening back to a pristine, unspoiled past. It is not merely Americans from the oil companies who are the intruders here: every "foreigner" is to some degree an interloper in Harran and Mooran. As a result, Munif is led to ignore those very elements of the history of the oil kingdoms that ought to inspire his curiosity, the extraordinary admixtures of cultures, peoples, and languages that have resulted from the Oil Encounter.

Workers from other parts of Asia hardly figure at all in Munif's story. When they do, it is either as stereotypes (a Pakistani doctor in *Cities of Salt* bears the name Muhammad Jinnah) or as faceless crowds, a massed symbol of chaos: "Once Harran had been a city of fishermen and travelers coming home, but now it belonged to no one; its people were featureless, of all varieties and yet strangely unvaried. They were all of humanity and yet no one at all, an assemblage of languages, accents, colours and religions." The irony of *The Trench* is that in the end it leaves its writer a prisoner of his intended victim. Once Munif moves away from the earliest stages of the Oil Encounter, where each side's roles and attributes and identities are clearly assigned, to a more complicated reality — to the crowded, multilingual, culturally polyphonic present of the Arabian peninsula — he is unable to free himself from the prison house of xenophobia, bigotry, and racism that was created by precisely such figures as his Sultan Khazael. In its failure, *The Trench* provides still one more lesson in the difficulties that the experience of oil presents for the novelistic imagination.

AT LARGE IN BURMA

1996

What Went Wrong?

Like many Indians, I grew up on stories of other countries: places my parents and relatives had lived in or visited before the birth of the Republic of India, in 1947. To me, the most intriguing of these stories were those that my family carried out of Burma. I suspect that this was partly because Burma had become a kind of lost world in the early sixties, when I was old enough to listen to my relatives' stories. It was in 1962 that General Ne Win, the man who would be Burma's longtime dictator, seized power in a coup. Almost immediately he slammed the shutters and switched off the lights: Burma became the dark house of the neighborhood, huddled behind an impenetrable, overgrown fence. It was to remain shuttered for almost three decades.

In retrospect, I am astonished by the degree to which the Ne Win regime succeeded in cutting the country off, even from the attention of its immediate neighbors. Burma is one of the larger countries in Southeast Asia, with a land area considerably greater than that of Thailand and a population of an estimated 46 million. It hangs like a mango between India, China, and Thailand, with the province of Tenasserim trailing like a tendril down into the Andaman Sea. Its border with India is hundreds of miles long. Calcutta, where I was born, is closer to Burma's principal urban centers, Rangoon and Mandalay, than it is to New Delhi. Yet while other neighboring countries — Pakistan, Bangladesh, Sri Lanka — figured in our newspapers to the point of obsession, Burma was scarcely mentioned. In defiance of the laws of proximity, General Ne Win was able to render his country invisible to both its neighbors and the world at large.

In my family, memories of Burma were kept alive by an old connection, and last December, on traveling to Rangoon, I found a trace of that connection in a small, nondescript temple in the commercial center of the city. The temple stands on a broad, straight road that was once known as Spark Street; it is now called Bo Aung Kyaw Street. This part of Rangoon was planned and built by British engineers in the late nineteenth century, and Spark Street still has a dark, gas-lit Victorian feel to it.

The temple on Spark Street is merely a hall on the ground floor of an old apartment building. It was built in 1887 and has served ever since as a community center for Hindu immigrants from Bengal. I had heard about the temple as a child, from an aunt who had married into a wealthy Bengali family that had settled in Burma. My aunt's husband ran a prosperous timber business. He was nicknamed "the Prince" because of his extravagant tastes. My aunt and the Prince left Burma in 1942, in the last, panic-stricken weeks before the Japanese Army marched into Rangoon. They managed to bribe their way onto a ship that was sailing for Calcutta.

The couple settled in Calcutta, and the Prince went back into the timber business. He was a distinguished-looking man, aquiline and ruddy-cheeked, always dressed in a starched cotton kurta and dhoti. In my earliest memories, he is a figure of truly princely munificence, driving up in his chauffeured Studebaker to sweep his relatives off to the most expensive shops in the city. This was not the way people did things in Calcutta; it was the Burmese side of him, and in the semisocialist India of that time, it couldn't last. He began to slide down the economic scale, slowly at first and then with gathering speed. By the time I was old enough to talk to him, his cars were gone and he was living in a small fourth-floor flat in a part of Calcutta where almost everyone was a refugee from some-where or other; he just happened to be from farther away than most.

The flat was crammed with books, from Mickey Spillane to Knut Hamsun. The Prince read voraciously and eclectically, mainly in English, a language I never heard him speak. When I went to visit him, he would lay aside his books and talk of Burma.

"It was a golden land," he would say. "The richest country in Asia, except for Japan. There are no people on earth to compare with the Burmese — so generous, so hospitable, so kind to strang-ers. No one goes hungry in Burma — you just have to ask and someone will feed you."

In college I discovered that the picture was not quite so simple. Indians had settled in Burma in large numbers in the late nine-teenth century, after the British completed their conquest of the country. Indians had occupied a disproportionate number of gov-ernment posts, and Indian merchants and moneylenders had come to dominate crucial sectors of the country's economy. I argued with the Prince. "But Indians were bitterly resented in Burma, weren't they?" I'd say. "Burmese nationalism practically started with anti-Indian riots."

He acknowledged this with a nod and a shrug. "But that's just one part of the story," he'd say. "There was a lot of friendship too." Then his eyes would light up again. "Ah, but it was a golden land . . ." It is impossible, I suspect, to imagine oneself being resented by a place to which one has given such unreserved love.

Neither the Prince nor my aunt ever returned to Burma, but my father, who had visited them there, went back once. The year was 1945, and he was an officer serving in the Allied Fourteenth Army. As the Allied forces advanced on Rangoon from the north, my father found himself both amazed and appalled by the scale of the destruction around him. The British had adopted a scorched-earth policy when they withdrew from Burma in 1942, demolish-ing bridges, setting fire to oil fields, and blocking the Irrawaddy's navigation channels with scuttled ships. Three years later, the retreating Japanese had reciprocated, destroying all that was left of Burma's infrastructure. "When buffaloes fight," goes a Burmese proverb, "the grass gets trampled." By the end of the war, after two bitterly fought campaigns, Burma was a devastated country.

My father found Rangoon virtually unrecognizable, but on making his way to Spark Street he discovered that the temple had survived, and he was able to trace a few distant relatives who had remained in the neighborhood. They would have starved, they told him later, but for the army rations he steered their way.

On the evening of my visit, the temple was all but empty: a handful of elderly men were seated around a table in the neon-lit hall. I went up to them and earned a warm welcome by mentioning the Prince's family name. Soon, as I sat with them at the table, the conversation turned to prewar Burma, and I found myself listening to echoes of the Prince's voice, intoning the very same words: "A golden land, the richest country in Asia, the envy of its neighbors, the kindest, most hospitable people on earth — even now, when everything is so scarce . . ."

How did it all go wrong? I asked. Fifty years earlier, Burma had been the most developed country in the region, with an impressive agricultural surplus and a superabundance of natural resources — oil, timber, minerals. It had had an important petroleum industry, a highly educated population, almost universal adult literacy, a lively independent press, a rich literary culture, and a framework of democratic institutions. Now it was one of the most impoverished countries in the world's fastest-developing region, one of the United Nations' ten least developed nations on earth, and a byword for repression, xenophobia, and civil abuse. How could any country travel so far back so fast?

The man seated next to me tapped my arm. He was well over seventy, a thin, upright man with a thatch of white hair. I shall call him Mr. Bose. Mr. Bose led me to the temple's entrance and pointed across the street to the dark, unlit compound of the Secretariat Building, a sprawling complex of decaying red brick offices built by the British at the turn of the century. "Do you see that veranda there?" he said, pointing to one on a second-floor walkway. "That was where Burma's future ended. Do you see that door? It leads to the room where General Aung San was assassinated, on July 19, 1947. I was just down the corridor—I saw his body lying there."

I had often heard my father speak of General Aung San; he had met him once at an army barracks in Rangoon during the war. General Aung San had said very little—he was famously a man of few words—but he had made a powerful impression on everyone present. He was twenty-nine years old at the time, a strikingly good-looking young man, with high cheekbones, a receding hairline, and a good-humored twinkle in his eye.

Despite his youth, Aung San was the country's acknowledged leader, the hero of its independence movement. A few years before, as a young student-politician, he had fled from British-ruled Burma and received military training from the Japanese. He was instrumental in organizing a militia of Burmese nationals in Thailand. In 1942 he marched back across the border at the head of the Burma Independence Army, accompanying the invading Japanese forces. Later, increasingly distrustful of the Japanese, he and his soldiers switched loyalties and joined the Allies. At the end of the war, it was widely believed that General Aung San would assume Burma's leadership once the British granted the country its independence, in 1948.

Aung San was by birth a Burman and thus a member of the country's largest ethnic group. The Burmans are predominantly Buddhist and form two-thirds of the country's population. There are four sizable minorities—the Karen, the Rakhine, the Shan, and the Mon—and many smaller groups. Some are Buddhist and are linked with the people of neighboring Thailand. Others, such as the Kachin, the Karen, and the Karenni, include Christians, mainly from families that were converted by American Baptist missionaries in the nineteenth century. And in the west there is also a substantial Muslim population.

What these different minorities have had in common, historically, is a fear of being dominated by the Burmans. Aung San, uniquely, was able to transcend this historical mistrust of Burman politicians. It probably helped that he was married to a Christian, Daw Khin Kyi, although he himself was a Buddhist.

In April 1947, Burma's colonial administration held elections to choose the government that would assume power when the country became independent. Aung San led his party, the Anti-Fascist People's Freedom League, to a resounding electoral victory. He was thirty-two; he had been married nearly five years and had fathered three children. The youngest, Suu Kyi, was two years old.

The events of July 19, 1947, were fresh in Mr. Bose's memory, kept alive by years of telling and retelling. He was then working as a clerical superintendent in the colonial administration. His job required him to sit at a desk in a large hall, overseeing a team of clerks. General Aung San and his kitchen cabinet were meeting in a room down the corridor; Mr. Bose knew that room well, for he often delivered files there.

Mr. Bose was sitting at his desk at ten-fifteen on the morning of July 19 when he heard an earsplitting noise. He looked up to find himself staring at a roomful of startled clerks. Then he heard feet thudding along the corridor and down the stairs. It took a moment before he realized that the earsplitting noise had been gunfire. By the time Mr. Bose reached the door, a crowd had gathered there. The room was full of smoke. Standing on tiptoe, he counted nine bodies inside, some sprawled on the floor, some slumped over a table. Six members of the cabinet had died with General Aung San. They were among the country's most respected politicians and included some of its most important minority leaders. Mr. Bose looked down and saw a thin trickle of blood winding past his feet.

Mr. Bose learned that a group of men dressed in battle fatigues had driven into the Secretariat compound in two jeeps, through the entrance on Dalhousie Street. They had run directly to the cabinet room, carrying guns; they had known exactly where to go. The soldiers ran back the way they had come, jumped into their jeeps, and drove away through the same gate. That was the last that was ever heard of them, although several suspects were rounded up and a right-wing politician was later charged with the assassination and hanged.

This is the end, Mr. Bose thought as he stood in the corridor, looking into the bloody room. Nothing will ever be the same again.

"Can you imagine the consequences in India or China if this had happened to Nehru and his cabinet or to Mao and the politburo?" Mr. Bose said to me. "That's something you have to remember when you think of Burma."

The new Union of Burma attained its independence on schedule, in January 1948. U Nu, a trusted friend of Aung San's who had assumed the leadership of the party after the general's assassination, was sworn in as Burma's first prime minister.

Three months later civil war broke out, with a vast Communist uprising. Serious ethnic insurgencies started the following year, when a group of Karen soldiers seized an armory on the outskirts of Rangoon and dug themselves in against government troops. Two Karen regiments of the Burma Army then mutinied, and they were soon joined by a regiment of Kachins.

In colonial times, British recruiting policies had favored minority groups over the ethnic Burmans. The British Burma Army was formed largely of units such as the Karen Rifles and the Kachin Rifles. As a result, the civil war began with the insurgents outnumbering government troops, and they made short work of the government's inexperienced, understaffed official army. They captured Mandalay, Burma's second city, within six weeks and then advanced on Rangoon, the capital, which was already under siege, caught between Communist insurgents and Karen rebels. A year after independence, the authority of the Burmese government extended no farther than the city's outskirts. The administration came to be nicknamed the Rangoon Six-Mile Government. It survived largely because an arms shipment from India arrived just in time to supply the government's troops.

In the following decades, the people of Burma learned to live with quotidian violence on a scale unimaginable elsewhere until the global advent of terrorism. The notoriously phlegmatic writer Norman Lewis traveled through Burma in 1951 and found that guerrilla warfare had become so widespread as to be commonplace: bridges were demolished within hours of being rebuilt; railway tracks were repaired and blown up at clockwork intervals; trains and riverboats were fired upon with mechanical regularity. "In the situation of this unfortunate country," he wrote, "there is an element of grim Wellsian prediction come to fulfillment."

General Aung San may indeed have been the only Burmese leader who could have averted the civil war. A few months before his death, he had negotiated a landmark treaty with several minority groups, having been able to persuade them that their rights would be protected in a quasi-federal union. The treaty, known as the Panglong Agreement, laid the groundwork for what could well have been a viable federal union. With General Aung San's assassination, the agreement foundered.

In his death, General Aung San became Burma's most pervasive icon. It is easy to imagine that the people of Rangoon, beset on every side by civil strife, needed a symbol to remind them that Burma was more than a flag and a fantasy — that an eventual Union of Burma was indeed thinkable, even achievable. Aung San became the embodiment of that possibility. Despite the strains of the civil war, Burma clung fast to its parliamentary constitution: through the next decade, elections were held regularly, and the press flourished.

Then, in 1962, General Ne Win, the chief of the army, abruptly took control of the government and suspended the constitution. The new regime met with immediate civilian resistance. Students sealed off Rangoon University and declared it a "fortress of democracy." The police opened fire, killing an unknown number, blew up the student union building, and then closed the university. Many students went underground; many fled to insurgent-controlled areas on the border.

Soon after General Ne Win took power, it was announced that the ideology of the new regime was to be "the Burmese Way to Socialism." The general had a history of peculiar behavior and soon became famous for his tantrums and an obsession with the number nine. He was said by many to be mad and had undergone psychiatric treatment in Vienna. His professed ideology proved to be no ideology at all but a bizarre mix of xenophobia and astrology, with a smattering of Marxism. General Ne Win's one claim to legitimacy was a connection to Aung San, who had once been his comrade in exile, and the general made the most of the link. As the reality of Burma grew ever more distant from Aung San's vision, his image proliferated: on coins and banknotes, on street corners, in marketplaces.

It takes a military dictator to believe that symbols are inert and can be manipulated at will. Forty years after his assassination, Aung San had his revenge. In a strange, secular reincarnation, his daughter, Suu Kyi, came back to haunt those who had sought to make use of his death. In 1988, when Burma's decades of discontent culminated in an antimilitary uprising, Aung San Suu Kyi (pronounced *Awng Sahn Soo Chee*) emerged from obscurity as one of the country's most powerful voices, the personification of Burma's democratic resistance to military rule.

A Penguin on an Ice Floe

The first time I met Suu Kyi was in 1980, at Oxford, where I was then a graduate student. I had been given a package for her by a mutual friend in New Delhi; Suu Kyi went to high school and college in Delhi before going on to Oxford. She still has many friends in India. Her mother served as Burma's ambassador to India for several years.

In 1980, Suu Kyi was thirty-five and was leading a life of quiet, exiled domesticity on a leafy street in North Oxford, bringing up two sons, then aged seven and three, and writing occasional articles for scholarly journals.

I saw her next in a magazine photograph, eight years later: she was speaking into a microphone. It was August 26, 1988, and she was addressing a vast crowd in the shadow of the great golden spire of the Shwedagon Pagoda, in Rangoon. She was instantly recognizable and yet utterly transformed.

I learned later that her presence in Burma was largely fortuitous. In the course of a peripatetic life, spent in many countries abroad, Suu Kyi had returned regularly to visit her aging mother in Rangoon, and news that her mother had suffered a stroke was what took her back in 1988.

Mass protests against military rule had started a couple of weeks before Suu Kyi arrived in Rangoon. In March a brawl in a tea shop provoked a clash between university students and riot police, and forty-one students died of suffocation while being detained in a police van. The other students responded by taking to the streets in protest against the regime. The demonstrations continued over several weeks. Three months later, in June, student protests erupted again, eventually forcing the resignation of General Ne Win. The scale of the protests increased after the dictator's departure, culminating in a nationwide general strike on August 8. In commemoration of this day, many Burmese still refer to the democracy agitation as the Four Eights Movement, because of the date — 8/8/88. Thousands of people — not just students but teachers, monks, children, doctors, and workers of all kinds — joined the demonstrations. That day the army made its first determined attempt to crush the movement, and hundreds of unarmed demonstrators were shot dead. The killings went on for a week, but demonstrators continued to flood the streets.

Pictures of General Aung San were a prominent feature of the student-led demonstrations. He had himself begun his political career as a student leader, and the generation that formed the nucleus of the democracy movement was quick to lay claim to his legacy. Suu Kyi's family house, on University Avenue, became a center of political activity, and on August 26, in her speech at the Shwedagon Pagoda, she announced that she was joining the movement. "I could not, as my father's daughter, remain indifferent to all that was going on," she told the hundreds of thousands of people who had gathered to listen to her. "This national crisis could, in fact, be called the second struggle for national independence."

A bloody denouement was a few weeks away. On September 18, a group of senior military officers took over the government. The junta called itself the State Law and Order Restoration Council; it rules under that name to this day, although some of its senior members have changed. In Burma, the regime is universally referred to by the almost comically sinister acronym SLORC. The word is pronounced with an appropriately slurping, swallowing sound — "like Ian Fleming's SMERSH," as a diplomat once observed.

The junta's first move was to eliminate the democracy movement. Army units took control of the streets, machine-gunning any large gatherings, and arrested hundreds of activists. A mass exodus resulted: as many as six thousand students fled to insurgent-held areas on the border. Many joined the insurgents; some are still fighting.

Once SLORC had secured power, it announced that it would hold elections. In response, Suu Kyi and her associates formed a political party, the National League for Democracy. Over the next several months, Suu Kyi toured the country, campaigning. She drew vast crowds at every appearance, and her popularity became a matter of increasing concern for the new regime. On July 20, 1989, the day after the forty-second anniversary of her father's death, she was put under house arrest and barred from taking part in the elections. Her disenfranchisement did not have the effect the junta had hoped for. When elections were eventually held, the following year, her party won more than 80 percent of the seats. Faced with the prospect of being ousted from power, SLORC ignored the result. Suu Kyi was offered safe passage out of the country on the condition that she never return. She chose to remain in Rangoon under house arrest and became the living symbol of Burma's predicament. In 1991 she was awarded the Nobel Peace Prize, but she was unable to collect it: she was still under detention.

Suu Kyi's house arrest ended on July 11, 1995. Within hours of the announcement, a crowd gathered outside her house. She made a brief appearance, but the crowd wanted more. A larger crowd gathered the next day and a still larger one the day after that, waiting in silent vigil until she appeared at the gates. After making such impromptu appearances for several days, Suu Kyi decided that her daily addresses were taking too much of her time, so she resolved to hold regular meetings on weekend afternoons instead. Thus was invented a unique political institution: Suu Kyi's gateside meetings in Rangoon.

Before traveling to Burma, I had often wondered how SLORC had succeeded in keeping its hold on power for the past eight years, despite the overwhelming popular support for Suu Kyi and the National League for Democracy. The answers became evident once I was there. Military rulers in impoverished countries are frequently brutal, but they are rarely able to muster either the resources or the expertise required to operate complex systems of social control. Burma is an exception. Despite the country's meager resources, its successive military regimes have succeeded in creating systems of surveillance that are unsurpassed in the scope of their intrusiveness.

To take just one example: every household in Burma must register its members with the local authority; no one may spend the night at another household without obtaining permission from the local ward chairman. Members of ethnic minorities frequently have difficulty registering changes in their "guest lists." In Rangoon, I met a woman who, after three years of wedlock, still had to queue for weekly permission to stay at her husband's apartment.

References in the press to poverty are automatically censored, and so are references to corruption, bribery, and even disease. "The censors live in a world of illusion," a well-known writer told me. "On the one hand, they know everything; they have informers everywhere. They know how much people earn, how much they spend. But in an authoritarian culture people lead two-track lives."

At the end of our harrowing conversation, I asked, "What would you write about if there were no censorship?"

He threw up his hands in a gesture of helplessness. He had spent almost ten years in Burma's prisons, most of them in an island concentration camp, where he had had to forage for his food. "Since 1962, we have lived through the Dark Ages," he said. His voice shook as he tried to control his rage. "Torture, murder, poverty . . . I have never been able to write about any of these things."

The country's chief censoring body is the Press Scrutiny Board. Among the items that attracted its ire last year were two magazine covers: one featured a penguin on an ice floe, and the other pictured a young woman seated among fallen flowers; both were interpreted as oblique references to Suu Kyi.

A Secular Reincarnation

The first time I attended one of Suu Kyi's weekend meetings, early this year, I was taken aback by her public manner. I was startled by how much she laughed. At times she would break up in giggles, with a hand over her mouth; at other times she would laugh full-throatedly, throwing her head back. I had expected, I suppose, a certain solemnity of demeanor—if for no other reason than merely as an acknowledgment of the atmosphere of intimidation that surrounds those meetings. The people in the crowd didn't seem to care: they laughed with her, uproariously.

The meetings are held at four in the afternoon. Crowds start gathering at midday, and they vary in size from four thousand to ten thousand. Suu Kyi addresses them as she stands at her gate. People sit in orderly rows opposite her, hugging their *longyi*-shrouded knees, while venders hawk cheroots, betel, and skewers of blackened chicken. Vans, cars, and minibuses throng the avenue, squeezing slowly through the crowd. The passengers try to look nonchalant, but their composure dissolves once they spot Suu Kyi, and they smile and wave, craning their necks to get a full view. From time to time, intelligence men holding video cameras stand up and pan slowly over the crowd.

The form of the meetings is simple. Suu Kyi answers written

questions given to her by members of the crowd. The questions range from matters of food and health to politics and literature. On Sundays she is joined by at least one senior member of her party, a reminder that the National League for Democracy is a party and not an individual.

University Avenue is a curving, tree-shaded street that skirts the picturesque Inya Lake. Suu Kyi's house, screened by a mass of unkempt greenery, is not visible from the street. When I later walked through the house's blue gates to meet her, I was surprised by how modest and dilapidated the building was: a plain but solid two-story bungalow, with a portico and veranda overlooking a garden and the lake.

I was shown to a large room on the ground floor. A portrait of her father hung on a flaking, mildewed wall, slightly askew. Close by was an orange banner bearing the symbol of the National League for Democracy, a fighting peacock. Through a barred window I caught a glimpse of the lake, its sunbathed surface speckled with lotus pads.

When Suu Kyi entered the room, dressed, as usual, in a Burmese sarong, I knew why she had made such an impression on me when I first met her. It is not her beauty, although her beauty is considerable. It is that she emanates an almost mystical quality of solitude — not solemnity, for she is always animated, either laughing or driving a point home with an upraised finger, but a sovereign, inviolate aloneness.

I had prepared a long list of questions, but now, in her presence, I didn't know where to begin. The unexpectedly complicated business of entering her house had unsettled me: the taxi driver who dropped me at a distance and sped away; the camera-wielding intelligence agents who loitered by her gate; the smiling policeman who inquired politely after the name of my hotel. After these sinister preliminaries, the normalcy of her house and the calm authority of her presence came almost as a jolt.

I glanced at my notes. Most of my questions were about her party's policies, SLORC's machinations, and so on. I knew now what her answers would be. She meets with foreign reporters almost daily, and her answers are unvarying; they could hardly be otherwise, considering how often the questions are repeated.

She never leaves any doubt about her opposition to foreign investment in Burma under the current regime, although at the time we spoke she stopped short of calling for economic sanctions. Also by implication she is critical of attempts to lure tourists to Burma. She is unequivocal in her criticism of a so-called constitutional convention that was called by SLORC three years ago; the constitution that was proposed, she points out, would effectively institutionalize military rule, since it reserves a large proportion of seats for military appointees. At the same time, she is generally nonconfrontational in her references to the current regime; she rarely even uses the term "SLORC," preferring to use the phrase "the authorities."

As I listened to these answers, I knew what I really wanted to ask: I wanted to know what it was like to be under house arrest for six years; what it meant to be separated from one's spouse and one's children, to be offered the option of leaving and turning it down. I thought of my own family, thousands of miles away, and the pain of even a brief separation; of the times I'd found myself looking at my watch and wondering whether my children were asleep or at play.

Her gateside meetings, I'd noticed, were attended by dozens of foreigners. Only a few were reporters and journalists; most were tourists and travelers. They were people like me, members of the world's vast, newspaper-reading middle class, people who took it for granted that there are no heroes among us. But Suu Kyi had proved us wrong. She lived the same kind of life, attended the same classes, read the same books and magazines, got into the same arguments. And she had shown us that the apparently soft and yielding world of books and words could sometimes forge a very fine kind of steel.

I too had come on a pilgrimage of sorts. What I really wanted to know was, "Where did you find the courage to do what you have done? What gave you the strength?" And what could one possibly learn of this in an hour — or two hours, or even a hundred? It would take a poet or a novelist years of labor to find a way of understanding what she had done.

The futility of my prepared questions made them inevitable. "So many people around the world marvel at how you survived those years of house arrest," I said. "In a way, house arrest must be worse than prison — "

She interrupted me with a laugh. "Sometimes I thought it would be better in prison," she said, "because I wouldn't have to cope with keeping the house clean."

Every time it rained, she said, the roof sprang new leaks, and she had to run up and down the stairs positioning buckets. "It was a great nuisance. Sometimes I thought, I wonder if it leaks at Insein jail? Whether the prisoners have to run around with buckets to catch the leaks?"

"Did Buddhism help?" I asked.

"Yes," she said. "Buddhist meditation helped because it created a sense of awareness and a sense of calm."

"What was it like," I asked, "the first time you saw your children after those years of house arrest?"

She paused to reflect. "I didn't see them together," she said. "My elder son came first, you see. He was fifteen when I last saw him, and he had already taken on his adolescent shape. But my younger son was eleven, and he was still a little boy. When I saw him again, he had changed completely. He had changed physically. If I had seen him out on the street, I would not have known he was my son. I was very happy that nothing had happened — that nothing had really affected the closeness between us."

She stopped. She evidently found it difficult, possibly distasteful, to talk about her family to a stranger. I felt that I had trespassed, in a small way. Like Suu Kyi, I was brought up to believe in the appropriateness of a strict separation between the public and the private, the political and the domestic. In this view, it is wrong as well as unseemly to reduce a vast political movement to the career of a single leader — to identify the aspirations of millions of people with the life of an individual.

The irony is that nothing better illustrates the passing of these values than Suu Kyi's predicament. In the postmodern world, politics is everywhere a matter of symbols, and the truth is that Suu Kyi is her own greatest political asset. It is only because Burma's 1988 democracy movement had a symbol, personified in Suu Kyi, that the world remembers it and continues to exert pressure on the current regime. Otherwise, the world would almost certainly have forgotten Burma's slain and dispersed democrats just as quickly as it has forgotten many others like them in the past.

The golf-playing generals who run Burma are, of course, well aware of this situation. If it were not for Suu Kyi and the increasingly vocal support for her abroad, SLORC's leaders would have scarcely a worry as they tee off on the links. Under house arrest, Suu Kyi was a living reproach to the regime and a bar to many foreign investors. By releasing her, the junta achieved a minor propaganda coup.

SLORC is headed by four of the Burmese Army's senior generals. The man who is widely believed to be the brains behind the regime's adroit maneuverings over the past several years is Lieutenant General Khin Nyunt, the longtime chief of Burma's intelligence apparatus and a political operator of formidable skill. After the events of 1988, SLORC moved quickly to "liberalize" the economy and invite foreign investment. No one knows exactly how much money the regime has attracted (the government claims to have got $3 billion), but the single largest investment is a billion-dollar gas pipeline financed by the French company Total and the American energy conglomerate Unocal.

SLORC takes particular pride in what it has done to end the forty-eight-year-old civil war with the country's ethnic insurgents. Again through shrewd political maneuvering, SLORC has forced many of the country's insurgents to negotiate. Fifteen groups have concluded ceasefire agreements with Rangoon, and the official press frequently claims that these agreements show that the insurgents have entered "the legal fold."

When I mentioned the ceasefires, Suu Kyi said, "There were reports in the Thai papers a couple of weeks ago that there is a constant flow of arms across the border, which indicates that the insurgents are continuing to accumulate arms. That does not sound very much as though they were preparing for permanent peace." I had already decided that I wanted to investigate the government's claims for myself.

In SLORC's official usage, Burma is now Myanmar, Rangoon is now Yangon, Karenni is now Kayah, and so on. But most of the people I spoke to used the old forms. As I was rising to leave, I asked Suu Kyi to resolve the dilemma; since she is effectively the country's elected leader, she had as good a right as anyone to decide what it should be called.

"I think it's very foolish," she said. "The excuse [that the authorities] gave was that Burma was a colonial name and referred only to the Burmese people, and Myanmar included all the other ethnic groups. This is just not true. Myanmar is a literary form of *Bama*, which means Burmese. So what it is all about I do not know. Some people say it is *yedea* — a propitiatory rite, something to prevent bad fortune. The authorities believe a lot in astrology."

"Would you rather I used the old names?" I asked.

She laughed. "Yes, please use the old forms," she said. "As support for a sensible way of looking at things. I do not like narrowmindedness. Even if these names were given by the British colonialists, so what? After all, India is called India and not Bharat, and China is China. I think if you have enough confidence in yourself, you should not worry about what you are called."

Among the Insurgents

Two days after my meeting with Aung San Suu Kyi, I heard that fighting had broken out between the Burmese Army and a contingent of Karenni insurgents. The Karenni were supported by a regiment of dissident Burmese students, and the fighting was concentrated in a remote and mountainous border region adjoining northwestern Thailand. The official Burmese media had listed the

Karenni among the groups that had been brought back into the legal fold through SLORC's ceasefire policy. There was no mention of any fighting.

I found myself wondering, What is Burma (or Myanmar, for that matter)? Who are the Karenni insurgents? What has driven them to fight for so long, with such tenacity? Are the two aspects of Burma — the areas under the control of Rangoon and those claimed by the insurgents — really so distant from each other? I recalled an anecdote told to me by a senior diplomat in Bangkok, about Thailand's immensely revered monarch, King Bhumibol, who had personally overseen his country's passage to democracy. The king had remarked that an overhasty transition to democracy in Burma might produce a situation similar to the one in Bosnia, only worse. If this was so, what were the prospects of democracy in any multiethnic society?

When the Burmese offensive was in its second week, I flew to the border town of Mae Hong Son, in northwestern Thailand. It was a clear day, and I watched in awe as the red riverine plains of the south changed into jagged, densely forested mountains, a pristine landscape of misted valleys and towering ridges. I could see no sign of any habitation until Mae Hong Son itself appeared suddenly in my window, a string of teakwood buildings nestled in a deep valley.

At first glance, Mae Hong Son seemed to be a quiet and prosperous frontier town. It was hard to imagine that a war was being fought in the surrounding mountains. I was surprised by the number of hotels on offer. I picked a Holiday Inn. From my room I glimpsed a turquoise swimming pool ringed by European tourists sipping vividly colored drinks in umbrellaed glasses. Within half an hour, my contacts in Mae Hong Son, members of a Burmese student group, sent a guide to take me back across the Burma border into a Karenni-held area that was currently under attack.

We rented a motor scooter and went rattling off down a dirt track that ended at a village near the foot of the mountains. We waded across a stream and started climbing. It was about five in the afternoon, and the sun had already dipped behind a ridge. Following a steeply ascending trail, we stepped from twilight into the darkness of a densely canopied forest. Neither my guide nor I had thought to bring a flashlight; he was wearing rubber sandals and I a pair of thin-soled leather shoes.

I began to regret my precipitate departure from the Holiday Inn. Clawing at the undergrowth to keep from falling, I feared I would end up with a snake in my fist. By the time we stumbled into the students' base camp, hours later, exhaustion had erased every thought from my mind. It was all I could do to stay on my feet.

Half a dozen young guerrillas dressed in camouflage fatigues were squatting around a campfire by a bamboo hut, playing guitars. A heavyset, thickly bearded man detached himself from the group and stepped over to meet me. He introduced himself as the commander of the regiment. He looked me over as I sat panting on a rock. After a moment's hesitation, he asked, a little shyly, "Are you Indian?" I then noticed that his spoken English sounded oddly like my own. I nodded and, through a veil of exhaustion, took another look at him. Suddenly I sat up. "And you?" I asked.

"My parents were Indian," he said with a smile. "But I'm Burmese."

After my ordeal in the jungle, I was not quite prepared for such an eminently postmodern encounter. My astonishment must have been evident in my face, for the commander began to laugh.

He was called Ko Sonny, but his given name, I learned, was Mahinder Singh. He was in his early thirties and had been "in the jungle" almost eight years. His family had been settled in Burma for three generations. His parents were born there; his father was Sikh and his mother Hindu, both from families of well-to-do Indian businessmen.

I was disconcerted listening to Sonny in the flickering firelight. I was sure that our relatives had known one another once in Burma; his had chosen to stay and mine hadn't. Except for a few years and a couple of turns of fate, each of us could have been in the other's place.

I spent the night on a bamboo pallet in Sonny's hut. The next day I was jolted awake before dawn by the sound of a Burmese Army artillery barrage. After groping for a match, I stepped outside to find Sonny talking into a walkie-talkie. The Burmese Army had launched an assault on a Karenni position in an adjoining valley.

The fighting was a good distance away, but the sound of gunfire came rolling up the misted mountainside with uncanny clarity, the rattle of small-arms fire clearly audible in the lulls between exploding artillery shells. The noise sent flocks of parakeets shooting out of the mountainside's tangled canopy.

With daybreak I had my first look at the camp — a string of thatched bamboo huts arranged along a mountain stream. A great deal of thought had gone into the camp's planning. The plumbing was far from rudimentary: water was piped directly into bathrooms and showers from the stream. There was a dammed pond teeming with fish and, nearby, a pen full of pigs.

Next to each hut was a vegetable patch. Once Sonny had ascertained that the fighting was not headed our way, he picked up a watering can and waded into a patch of bok choy. Following his lead, the others put aside their battle gear and disappeared into their pumpkin trellises and mustard beds like a troop of Sunday gardeners.

"Growing food is as important to our survival as fighting," Ko Sonny explained apologetically. "We do this before we go on patrol."

We set out an hour or so later, a detachment of half a dozen student fighters, with Sonny in the lead. Once we had crossed the border, an unmarked forest trail, Sonny and his men reclaimed a cache of aging M-16s and slung them over their shoulders.

We climbed onto a ridge, where I found myself gazing at a majestic spectacle of forested gorges, mountain peaks, and a sky of crisp, pellucid blue. The shelling was sporadic now: occasionally the forest canopy would silently sprout a mushroom cloud of smoke, the accompanying blast climbing leisurely up the slope moments later.

Mae Hong Son was clearly visible, a smudge in the floor of a

tip-tilted valley. While Sonny counted off the caliber of the exploding shells — 120mm, 81mm — I turned his binoculars on the town
and spotted my hotel.

Sonny pointed to the Karenni post we were to visit. It was
called Naung Lon and was built around a peak that reared high
above the surrounding spurs and ridges. We entered through a
gate hidden in a wall of bamboo stakes. After crossing a moat and
a barbed-wire barrier, we made our way cautiously past a ring of
heavily sandbagged gun emplacements and were met by a Karenni
officer, a tall, stooped man with melancholy eyes and an air of re-
gretful doggedness. The officer and his men, like most Karenni
insurgents, were devout Christians. The officer himself happened
to be a Baptist. His eyes flickered constantly as we spoke. His
arm describing a semicircle, he pointed to the Burmese Army positions on the mountaintops around us. The Burmese Army had
concentrated ten thousand men in the area, he explained. The
Karenni army had a force of about six hundred. He knew that he
was defending a hopeless position and had already made plans to
evacuate.

Later, on the way back to the student camp, I remarked to
Sonny that I didn't see how the Karenni army could possibly escape defeat.

Sonny laughed. The Karenni, he pointed out, had been fighting
against dire odds for fifty years. Many regarded the war against
SLORC as a direct continuation of the war against the Japanese.
Some Karenni families had been at war for three generations, and
many of their fighters had spent their entire lives in refugee camps.

What does it take, I found myself wondering, to sustain an insurgency for fifty years, to go on fighting a war that the rest of the
world has almost forgotten? What did freedom mean to the Karenni — democracy or simply the right to set up an ethnic enclave
of their own?

The next day I returned to Mae Hong Son and went to see Mr.
Abel Tweed, the foreign minister of the Karenni National Progressive Party, in his small back-alley office. A voluble square-jawed

man, Mr. Tweed delved into a makeshift archive housed in a cupboard. "We have always been independent," he announced, "and we have the documents to prove it."

Leafing through the papers he handed me, I saw that he was right: the British had clearly recognized Karenni autonomy in the late nineteenth century and had rejected the option of annexing the Karenni territories to Burma proper. Their reasons were not altruistic. "It is evident that the country is perfectly worthless in itself," one British administrator wrote of the Karenni area. "It is almost impracticable, for even an elephant."

It was the Second World War that thrust the Karenni's "impracticable" country center stage. Looking for Asian partners in the struggle against the Japanese, the Allied powers encouraged several ethnic groups along the borders of Burma to rise against the occupying army. The Karenni, the Karen, and the Kachin eagerly embraced the Allies. A number of British and American military personnel took up residence in their villages, and some of them virtually assumed the role of tribal elders.

The Karenni, along with the Karen and the Kachin, were spectacularly effective guerrillas, and their loyalty proved to be important to the Allies. The payment that these groups expected was independence. To this day they nurture a bitter historical grievance that the debt was never paid.

Abel Tweed was born long after the war, but his voice shook as he talked of the British departure from Burma. "The British knew that the Karenni were not a part of Burma," he said. "But the Karenni are a small people; they forgot us."

There are six thousand or so displaced Karenni refugees, and they are divided among five camps. Until fairly recently, these camps were in Burma, on a narrow tract of land controlled by the insurgents, but the steady advance of Burmese troops has gradually pushed the camps back over the border into Thailand. The camps are now clustered around Mae Hong Son, a tourist town that promotes an activity known as "hill-tribe trekking." The camps have come to be linked to this tourist entertainment through an odd symbiosis. The women of one Karenni subgroup have traditionally worn heavy brass rings to elongate their necks, and these women are now ticketed tourist attractions, billed as "giraffe women"; their refugee camps are a feature of the hill-tribe trekking routes. In effect, tourism has transformed these camps, with their tragic histories of oppression, displacement, and misery, into counterfeits of timeless rural simplicity — waxwork versions of the very past that their inhabitants have irretrievably lost. Karenni fighters returning from their battles on the front lines become, as it were, mirrors in which their visitors can discover an imagined Asian innocence.

I had come to the border hoping to find that democracy would provide a solution to Burma's unresolved civil war. By the time I left, I was no longer sure what the solution could be.

"The majority of Burmans think that democracy is the only problem," a member of the powerful Kachin minority reminded me. "But ethnic groups took up arms when Rangoon had a democratic government. A change to democracy won't help. The outside world expects too much from Suu Kyi. From our point of view, we don't care who governs — the weaker, the better."

There are thousands of putative nationalities in the world today; at least sixteen of them are situated on Burma's borders. It is hard to imagine that the inhabitants of these areas would be well served by becoming separate states. A hypothetical Karenni state, for example, would be landlocked, with the population of a medium-sized town: it would not be less dependent on its larger neighbors simply because it had a flag and a seat at the UN.

Burma's borders are undeniably arbitrary, the product of a capricious colonial history. But colonial officials cannot reasonably be blamed for the arbitrariness of the lines they drew. All boundaries are artificial: there is no such thing as a "natural" nation, which has journeyed through history with its boundaries and ethnic composition intact. In a region as heterogeneous as Southeast Asia, any boundary is sure to be arbitrary. On balance, Burma's best hopes for peace lie in maintaining intact the larger and more inclusive entity that history, albeit absent-mindedly, bequeathed to its population almost half a century ago.

Aung San Suu Kyi is the one figure in Burma who has popular support, both among ethnic Burmans and among many minorities, to start a process of national reconciliation. But even Suu Kyi would find it difficult to alter the historical borders. In the event of a total military withdrawal, it is possible that some insurgent groups would attempt to reclaim the territories they once controlled. A rekindling of the insurgencies would almost certainly lead to a rapid erosion of Suu Kyi's popular support. Suu Kyi is aware that she cannot govern effectively without the support of the army, and she has been at pains to build bridges with middle-ranking officers as well as with the rank and file, repeatedly stressing her heritage as the daughter of the army's founder.

Somewhere in the unruffled reaches of her serenity, Suu Kyi has probably prepared herself for the ordeal that lies ahead: the possibility that she, an apostle of nonviolence, may yet find herself constrained to wage war.

I spent a lot of time with Sonny. He was very good company: always witty, ready to laugh, enormously intelligent, and so devoid of macho posturing that it was easy to forget he was a hardened combatant. When we were in the mountains, he would go striding along at the head of a column, looking every inch the guerrilla, with his dangling cheroot and his cradled M-16. When he came down to visit Mae Hong Son, he would exchange his fatigues for jeans and a T-shirt, and it was hard to tell him apart from a holiday-ing business executive.

I asked him once, "As someone of Indian descent, do you ever feel out of place as the commander of a regiment of Burmese students?"

"You don't understand," he said. "I don't think of myself as Indian. I hated being Indian. As a child, everywhere I went people would point to me and say *kala* [foreigner], although I had never left Burma in my whole life. I hated that word. I wanted to show them: that is not what I am; I am not a *kala*. This is why I am here now."

Sonny had grown up in a tiny provincial town, Loikaw, the capital of Burma's erstwhile Karenni province. While he was attending the university in Rangoon (he studied physics there for four years), he championed the cause of Karenni and other minority students. With the start of the democracy movement, in 1988, he returned home and helped to organize peaceful demonstrations in Loikaw. He was arrested on September 18 and released ten days later. Fearing rearrest, he immediately planned his escape to the border.

On the night of October 6, Sonny left Loikaw with a group of activists. They made their way to a rebel base, where Karenni insurgents gave them a warm welcome and provided them with land and supplies so that they could set up bases of their own. Sonny and his fellow activists had never held a gun.

After eight years of fighting, Sonny has no illusions about the "armed struggle." "We're fighting because there is no other way to get SLORC to talk," he told me. "For us, armed struggle is just a strategy. We are not militants here — we can see how bad war is."

I asked, "Have you ever thought of trying other political strategies?"

"Of course," he said. "Do you think I like to get up in the morning and think of killing? Killing someone from my own country, who is forced to fight by dictators? I would like to try other things — politics, lobbying. But the students chose me to command this regiment. I can't just leave them."

Sonny has paid a price for his decision to leave Loikaw. His girlfriend, a Burmese in Rangoon, gave up waiting for him and married someone else. In 1994 his mother died of a heart attack; Sonny found out months afterward from a passing trader. She was, he said, the person he was closest to.

The student dissidents are now in their late twenties or early thirties. They had once aspired to become technicians and engineers, doctors and pharmacists. Those hopes are gone. They have no income to speak of, and their contacts with Thai society are few.

The truth is that they now have very limited options. Legally, they are not allowed either to work or to study in Thailand; to seek asylum abroad as refugees, they would have to enter a holding camp in southern Thailand while their papers were processed. Those whose applications were rejected would risk being deported to Burma, and once there they would almost certainly be imprisoned, or worse. The alternative is to join the underworld of illegal foreign workers in Thailand, vanishing into a nightmarish half-life of crime, drugs, and prostitution. They have been pushed into a situation where the jungle is the sanest choice available.

For the insurgents, Aung San Suu Kyi offers the only remaining hope of returning to their country with dignity and reclaiming their lives. When Sonny heard that I had met Aung San Suu Kyi in Rangoon, he wanted to know exactly what she had said. I played him some of my tape, including a segment in which she answered a question about her commitment to nonviolence.

"I do not think violence will really get us what we want," she said. "Some of the younger people disagree. In 1988, a lot of them went across the border because they said the only way you can topple this government is by force of arms. And not just the younger people. Even very mature, seasoned people have said to me, 'You can't do it without arms. This government is the type that understands only violence.' But my argument is: All right, supposing that all those who wanted democracy decided that the only way was through force of arms and we all took up arms. Would we not be setting a precedent for more violence in the future? Would we not be endorsing the view that those who have the superior might of arms are those who will rule the country? That is something that I cannot support. But we have always said that we will never, never disown those who have decided to take up arms, because we understand how they feel. I tried to dissuade some of the young people who fled across the border, but who am I to force them to stay? If I could guarantee their liberty and their safety, if I could say to them, 'You will not be arrested, you will not be tortured,' I would. But since I could not, I did not even think I had the moral right to stop them leaving."

When the tape was finished, I asked Sonny what he would do if he was pushed out of Thailand as well. "What if the Thais decide to cut off your supplies or starve you out of Thailand?"

"It wouldn't be easy to starve us out," Sonny said. "We've been here a long time. We now have many connections with the people of this region; some Burmese students have married Thai villagers. We can survive in the jungle—we are used to it now. That is why our camps are self-sufficient. We could disappear into the jungle for a long time. We are not unprepared."

If it came to the worst, Sonny was saying, he and his men would disappear into the jungle to carry on their war from behind the lines. And it made sense: the poppy fields of the Golden Triangle, with their warring drug lords, were just a short walk away. Someone as resourceful as Sonny could disappear there indefinitely if he was pushed; the jungle was all too ready to claim him.

It was cold in the camp that night, with a bitter wind blowing through the slatted bamboo walls. I spent much of the night awake, trying to think of what it meant to live in a circumstance in which the jungle seemed to be the best of all available options.

I awoke next morning to find a pile of books by my head. Sonny had wrapped a few books in a towel as a makeshift pillow, and the bundle had come undone at night. The books were language primers, workbooks, and the like, except for one: a hardbound 1991 edition entitled *The Transformation of War*. The author, Martin van Creveld, I discovered later, is something of an oracle among doomsday theorists.

I flipped the book open, and I became riveted. I began to make notes in my diary. "Van Creveld is arguing that the state's historic monopoly of violence ended with the 'Thirty Years War of

1914–45'; that nuclear weapons have rendered war, as waged by states, nearly obsolete, because inconceivable; that the world will now be dominated by low-intensity conflict; that states in the conventional sense will give way to bands of warlords; that the distinction between government, army, and the people will begin to fall apart as never before, especially in the Third World; that groups such as private mercenary bands, commanded by warlords and even commercial agencies (like the old East India Company), will once again take over the function of war-making; that 'existing distinctions between war and crime will break down.'"

Outside the hut, Sonny and his men were busy in the crisp sunlight, tending their patches of cauliflower and mustard. Until then I had looked upon Sonny as an anachronistic remnant of a dwindling series of "dirty little Asian wars." I now saw that I was very likely wrong: what Sonny represented was not the past but a possible future.

Suddenly the question of Aung San Suu Kyi and Burma's future assumed an urgent, global dimension. Legitimate, consensual government is the one bulwark between us and the prospect of encroaching warlordism and ever-increasing conflict; in embodying that possibility, Aung San Suu Kyi represents much more than the aspirations of Burma's people.

Daughter of Destiny?

I returned to Burma during the last week of July. In the past couple of months there had been a number of disquieting developments. I wanted to see for myself what the consequences were, for both Aung San Suu Kyi and the country.

Last May a conference called by Suu Kyi to mark the anniversary of her party's victory in the 1990 election was disrupted when the government arrested more than 230 party delegates who planned to attend; many were arrested at their homes or on their way to Rangoon.

Suu Kyi, unable to convene all the delegates, held the conference anyway, as scheduled, between May 26 and May 28. Thousands gathered outside her gates, one of the largest crowds since her house arrest ended last year. On the last day she announced that her party would draft a new constitution—a democratic alternative to the one that was being slowly deliberated by the government. Like the party conference itself, the call for a new constitution was a provocative gesture, and for Aung San Suu Kyi an unusually confrontational one. For the first time since her release, Suu Kyi had wrested the initiative away from the government, pushing it onto the defensive. Her party was reinvigorated.

Two weeks later the government responded. It issued a decree that effectively banned Suu Kyi's gateside meetings: all speeches and any statements that were seen to undermine "the stability of the state" were prohibited. In case there was any doubt about its objective, the law also prohibited the drafting of a new constitution without the authorization of the state. The decree was issued on June 7, but it was not immediately put into effect. The government appears to have been unprepared for the vehemence of the international criticism that its actions provoked.

The criticism had been mounting since April, when, as part of an effort to harass and intimidate Suu Kyi's supporters, the authorities had arrested one of her close family friends, Leo Nichols, for operating an unauthorized fax machine. Nichols, an Anglo-Burmese businessman who had served as honorary consul for the Scandinavian countries, was sentenced to three years in prison on May 17. Five weeks later, he died while in police custody, and the government's account of his death was unsatisfactory. Protests widened. Denmark called for economic sanctions and asked the European Union to impose them; in the United States, a similar motion was debated in Congress.

The government's reaction was seen at the time to be oddly contradictory. There was even the suggestion that it might be ready to compromise. The likelihood is that the generals were largely indifferent to the international outcry; their concern was that the outcry might influence the leaders attending the July meeting of the Association of Southeast Asian Nations (ASEAN) in Jakarta. Burma was still not a member of the association — a legacy of its years of isolation — and membership was essential to establishing the country as a full trading partner in the region. Burma was seeking observer status, the first step in gaining membership. The talk among the Asian nations was now of "constructive engagement" — the soft diplomacy that only successful trade makes possible. On July 20, Burma got the recognition it sought. The regime, it seems, was set on buying its own legitimacy.

I arrived in Rangoon on Sunday, July 28, just in time to make it to the gateside meeting on University Avenue. The week before, the American secretary of state, Warren Christopher, had been in Jakarta and had censured the government of Burma, but his censure was largely rhetorical and ineffective. He stopped short of sanctions, and I wondered what Suu Kyi's response would be. In the past she had characteristically hesitated to call for any kind of economic boycott; she had now changed her position. The new wave of foreign investment, she had concluded, merely "put more money in the pockets of the privileged elite. Sanctions," she said, "would not hurt the ordinary people of Burma."

The meeting was a large one — about six thousand people. Looking around, I spotted the familiar faces of several people, some of them occupying the same spots as before, like restaurant regulars. Suu Kyi was, as before at the Sunday meetings, flanked by two senior colleagues from the National League for Democracy.

On my previous visit I had been astonished by her performance. She was full of merriment, giggling and flirtatious. Several months later she was still animated, but the lightheartedness was no longer there.

She had changed. So too had the city. The next day I went downtown, into the main business district, and found that an entire block had been transformed. The graceful but shabby old colonial arcades — untouched, like so much of Rangoon, for decades — had been torn down, and in a matter of months had been replaced with a maze of office buildings, hotels, and shops. In a nearby marketplace I discovered that the value of the currency had dropped by a third and that the price of foodstuffs had risen dramatically.

I was taken to one of Rangoon's new coffee bars by Ma Thanegi, a friend from my last visit. Ma Thanegi is an artist. She joined the democracy movement in 1988 and became an extremely active member; she even worked as an assistant to Aung San Suu Kyi and was a close friend. But then she was arrested and imprisoned for three years. By the time of her release, she had had enough of politics — she wanted to look after her own interests — and she opened an art gallery with an American expatriate.

Ma Thanegi was concerned about recent developments, especially Western trade sanctions. Her view was that a trade boycott would work only if it was a total boycott, involving all countries. And was that realistic? If only Western companies pulled out, there would be many Asian ones prepared to take their place. These new companies, Ma Thanegi said, would have less regard for Burmese workers and the local environment than those they had replaced.

Ma Thanegi had lived her whole life in Rangoon. She came of age during General Ne Win's Burmese Way to Socialism. "We lived under self-imposed isolation for decades," she said. "There was absolutely nothing, no opportunities at all, but we struggled on. Ma Ma," as she refers to Suu Kyi, "says we have to tighten our belts and think about politics. But there are no more notches to tighten on our belts."

Ma Thanegi wasn't a member of an especially privileged elite — she was middle-class. She wasn't a selfish international trader, eager to devour Burma's natural resources. She wasn't looking for a quick and easy return. Ma Thanegi was tired of coping with scarcity.

I saw Aung San Suu Kyi the next day. As I walked through the familiar blue gates, I noticed a striking new addition: a large bamboo-and-thatch pavilion. It had been built to house the delegates of the party conference; most of those who had originally been invited did not get to see it.

When Aung San Suu Kyi appeared, I congratulated her on the success of the conference. With a self-deprecating smile, she described it as "routine party work." The achievement, she said, was in SLORC's reaction: it showed "how nervous SLORC was of the democracy movement."

Suu Kyi's face seemed strained and tired. It was now more than a year since she'd been freed from house arrest, and I found myself wondering whether her freedom was not in its way as much a burden as a release. It seemed as though the impossibly difficult task of conducting a political life under the conditions imposed on her by SLORC had proved just as hard as the enforced solitude of the preceding years. Those conditions seemed to be making her into a different kind of political figure.

She was quick to confirm the change. After she was released, she said, she made a point of being conciliatory, "but SLORC did not respond. And we have to carry on with our work. We are not going to sit and wait for SLORC to decide what we want to do . . . That's not the way politics works."

Suu Kyi had not, as far I knew, responded publicly to the recent ASEAN meeting, in which Burma was granted its new observer status, and I was eager to know what her thoughts might be. I asked her if she was surprised by the warmth of Burma's welcome.

She dismissed my question. It was only normal that the association should welcome a new member.

Her reply surprised me.

No, she said, really. There was nothing unusual about it.

I persisted. At a time when many nations were talking about taking actions against Burma, the Southeast Asian leaders spoke about a policy of constructive engagement, which seemed like an endorsement of the regime.

Again I was dismissed. Picking her words carefully, Suu Kyi said, "I don't quite understand why one talks about constructive engagement as being such a problem. Each government has its own policy, and we accept that this is the policy of the ASEAN nations. I sometimes think that this problem is made out to be much bigger than it really is . . . Just because [these governments] have decided on a policy of constructive engagement, there is no need for us to think of them as our enemies. I do not think it's a case of us and them."

I was witnessing, I realized, Suu Kyi the tactician. She was choosing her words with such care because she wanted to ensure that she did not alienate the leaders of nations who might otherwise think of her as a threat.

I was struck by the differences in Suu Kyi's manner. That other time I had had several glimpses of her earlier selves — the writer and researcher, the scholar trying to reach for the right words to articulate subtle gradations of truth. She now seemed much more the politician, opaque and often abrupt in her answers. The change was inevitable, perhaps, and possibly necessary, but I still found myself mourning it.

Suu Kyi now had a party line. "We think," she said, "that sanctions are the right thing. Further investment in Burma is not helping the people." It is, she said, serving only a privileged elite. "It is increasingly obvious that investments made now in Burma only help to make SLORC richer and richer. And that is an obstacle to democratization."

I mentioned some of the arguments I had heard — that sanctions will lead only to the Western companies being replaced by their Asian counterparts — and this remark too was peremptorily dismissed. Without Western investment, she said, "I think you will find that confidence in the Burmese economy will diminish. It is not going to encourage the Asians to come rushing in. On the contrary."

At my previous meeting with Suu Kyi, I'd asked her whether she was contemplating a call for mass civil disobedience. She had remarked that she couldn't tell me even if she had been, but she'd gone on to add, on a note of barely disguised frustration, that if the people wanted democracy, then they were going to have to do something to get it. When I asked her about civil disobedience this time, my question was curtly dismissed. "We never discuss our plans in advance," she said. "You know that."

Even so, I was left wondering. That morning I had talked to a diplomat who was certain that if Suu Kyi called for civil disobedience, the country would follow. It would grind to a complete standstill, he said. I asked myself if that might be the future.

I left Rangoon the next day, feeling discouraged. The business-class section of the plane was full to capacity, its seats occupied by trim men in suits. They all looked as if they had flown in from the great boom centers of Asia. They were in town to do a deal. I looked down on the receding city, and I thought of a comment that Suu Kyi had made at the end of our meeting. "I've always told you," she said, "that we will win . . . that we will establish a democracy in Burma, and I stand by that. But as to when, I cannot predict. I've always said that to you."

Once the plane had sliced through the dark blanket of Rangoon's monsoon sky, the cabin filled with the whine of laptops logging on — that familiar buzzing sound, not unlike that of mosquitoes feasting in midflight.

THE GHOSTS OF MRS. GANDHI

1995

NOWHERE ELSE IN THE WORLD did the year 1984 fulfill its apocalyptic portents as it did in India. Separatist violence in the Punjab; the military attack on the great Sikh temple of Amritsar; the assassination of the prime minister, Mrs. Indira Gandhi; riots in several cities; the gas disaster in Bhopal — the events followed relentlessly on each other. There were days in 1984 when it took courage to open the New Delhi papers in the morning.

Of the year's many catastrophes, the sectarian violence following Gandhi's death had the greatest effect on my life. Looking back, I see that the experiences of that period were profoundly important to my development as a writer, so much so that I have never attempted to write about them until now.

At the time I was living in a part of New Delhi called Defence Colony — a neighborhood of large, labyrinthine houses, with little self-contained warrens of servants' rooms tucked away on rooftops and above garages. When I lived there, these rooms had come to house a floating population of the young and straitened — journalists, copywriters, minor executives, and university people like myself. We battened upon this wealthy enclave like mites in a honeycomb, spreading from rooftop to rooftop, our ramshackle lives curtained from our landlords by chiffon-draped washing lines and thickets of TV aerials.

I was twenty-eight. The city I considered home was Calcutta, but New Delhi was where I had spent all my adult life, except for a few years away in England and Egypt. I had returned to India two years before, upon completing a doctorate at Oxford, and recently found a teaching job at Delhi University. But it was in the privacy of my baking rooftop hutch that my real life was lived. I was writing my first novel, in the classic fashion, perched in a garret.

On the morning of October 31, the day of Mrs. Gandhi's death, I caught a bus to Delhi University as usual, at about half past nine. From where I lived it took an hour and a half: a long commute, but not an exceptional one for New Delhi. The assassination had occurred shortly before, just a few miles away, but I had no knowledge of this when I boarded the bus. Nor did I notice anything untoward at any point during the ninety-minute journey. But the news, traveling by word of mouth, raced my bus to the university.

When I walked into the grounds, I saw not the usual boisterous, Frisbee-throwing crowd of students but small groups of people standing intently around transistor radios. A young man detached himself from one of the huddles and approached me, his mouth twisted into the tight-lipped, knowing smile that seems always to accompany the gambit "Have you heard . . . ?"

The campus was humming, he said. No one knew for sure, but it was being said that Mrs. Gandhi had been shot. The word was that she had been assassinated by two Sikh bodyguards, in revenge for her having sent troops to raid the Sikhs' Golden Temple of Amritsar earlier that year.

Just before stepping into the lecture room, I heard a report on All India Radio, the national network: Mrs. Gandhi had been rushed to hospital after an attempted assassination.

Nothing stopped; the momentum of the daily routine carried things forward. I went into a classroom and began my lecture, but not many students had shown up, and those who had were distracted and distant; there was a lot of fidgeting.

Halfway through the class, I looked out through the room's single, slitlike window. The sunlight lay bright on the lawn below and on the trees beyond. It was the time of year when Delhi was at its best, crisp and cool, its abundant greenery freshly watered by the recently retreated monsoons, its skies washed sparking clean. By the time I turned back, I had forgotten what I was saying and had to reach for my notes.

My unsteadiness surprised me. I was not an uncritical admirer of Mrs. Gandhi. Her brief period of semi-dictatorial rule in the mid-seventies was still alive in my memory. But the ghastliness of her murder was a sudden reminder of the very real qualities that had been taken for granted: her fortitude, her dignity, her physical courage, her endurance.

Yet it was not just grief I felt at that moment. Rather, it was a sense of something coming loose, of a mooring untied some-where within.

The first reliable report of Mrs. Gandhi's death was broadcast from Karachi, by Pakistan's official radio network, at around 1:30 P.M. On All India Radio, regular broadcasts had been replaced by music.

I left the university in the late afternoon with a friend, Hari Sen, who lived at the other end of the city. I needed to make a long-distance phone call, and he had offered to let me use his family's telephone.

To get to Hari's house, we had to change buses at Connaught Palace, the elegant circular arcade that lies at the geographical heart of Delhi, linking the old city with the new. As the bus swung around the periphery of the arcade, I noticed that the shops, stalls, and eateries were beginning to shut down, even though it was still afternoon.

Our next bus was not quite full, which was unusual. Just as it was pulling out, a man ran out of an office and jumped on. He was middle-aged and dressed in shirt and trousers, evidently an em-ployee of one of the nearby government buildings. He was a Sikh, but I barely noticed this at the time.

He probably jumped on without giving the matter any thought, this being his regular, daily bus. But as it happened, on this day no choice could have been more unfortunate, for the route of the bus went past the hospital where Indira Gandhi's body then lay. Certain loyalists in her party had begun inciting the crowd gathered there to seek revenge. The motorcade of Giani Zail Singh, the president of the republic, a Sikh, had already been attacked by a mob.

None of this was known to us then, and we would never have suspected it; violence had never been directed at the Sikhs in Delhi.

As the bus made its way down New Delhi's broad, tree-lined avenues, official-looking cars with outriders and escorts overtook us, speeding toward the hospital. As we drew nearer, it became evident that a large number of people had gathered there. But this was no ordinary crowd: it seemed to consist mostly of red-eyed young men in half-unbuttoned shirts. It was now that I noticed that my Sikh fellow passenger was showing signs of increasing anxiety, sometimes standing up to look out, sometimes glancing at the door. It was too late to get off the bus; thugs were everywhere. The bands of young men grew more and more menacing as we approached the hospital. There was a watchfulness about them. Some were armed with steel rods and bicycle chains; others had fanned out across the busy road and were stopping cars and buses.

A stout woman in a sari sitting across the aisle from me was the first to understand what was going on. Rising to her feet, she gestured urgently at the Sikh, who was sitting hunched in his seat. She hissed at him in Hindi, telling him to get down and keep out of sight.

The man started in surprise and squeezed himself into the narrow footspace between the seats. Minutes later our bus was intercepted by a group of young men dressed in bright, sharp synthetics. Several had bicycle chains draped around their wrists. They ran along beside the bus as it slowed to a halt. We heard them call out to the driver through the open door, asking if there were any Sikhs on the bus.

The driver shook his head. No, he said there were no Sikhs on the bus.

A few rows ahead of me, the crouching, turbaned figure had gone completely still. Outside, some of the young men were jumping up to look through the windows, asking if there were any Sikhs on the bus. There was no anger in their voices; that was the most chilling thing of all.

No, someone said, and immediately other voices picked up the refrain. Soon all the passengers were shaking their heads and saying, No, no, let us go now, we have to get home.

Eventually the thugs stepped back and waved us through. Nobody said a word as we sped away down Ring Road.

Hari Sen lived in one of New Delhi's recently developed residential colonies. It was called Safdarjang Enclave, and it was neatly and solidly middle-class, a neighborhood of aspirations rather than opulence. Like most such New Delhi suburbs, the area has a mixed population; Sikhs were well represented.

A long street ran from end to end of the neighborhood, like the spine of a comb, with parallel side streets running off it. Hari lived at the end of one of those streets, in a fairly typical big one-story bungalow. The house next door, however, was much grander and uncharacteristically daring in design. An angular structure, it was perched rakishly on stilts. Mr. Bawa, the owner, was an elderly Sikh who had spent a long time abroad, working with various international organizations. For several years he had resided in Southeast Asia; thus the stilts.

Hari lived with his family in a household so large and eccentric that it had come to be known among his friends as Macondo, after Gabriel García Márquez's magical village. On this occasion, however, only his mother and teenage sister were at home. I decided to stay over.

The next morning was very bright. When I stepped out into the sunshine, I came upon a sight that I could never have imagined. In every direction columns of smoke rose slowly into a limpid sky. Sikh houses and businesses were burning. The fires were so carefully targeted that they created an impression quite differ-

ent from that of a general conflagration: it was like looking upward into the vault of some vast pillared hall.

The columns of smoke increased in number even as I stood
outside watching. Some were burning a short distance away. I
spoke to a passerby and learned that several nearby Sikh houses
had been looted and set on fire that morning. The mob had started
at the far end of the colony and was working its way in our direction. Hindus or Muslims who had sheltered or defended Sikhs
were also being attacked; their houses were being looted and
burned.

It was still and quiet, eerily so. The usual sounds of rush-hour
traffic were absent. But every so often we heard a speeding car or
motorcycle on the main street. Later we discovered that these
mysterious speeding vehicles were instrumental in directing the
carnage that was taking place. Protected by certain politicians, "organizers" were zooming around the city, assembling "mobs" and
transporting them to Sikh-owned houses and shops.

Apparently the transportation was provided free. A civil rights
report published shortly afterward stated that this phase of the
violence "began with the arrival of groups of armed young people in tempo vans, motorcycles, scooters or trucks," and went on to
say, "With cans of petrol they went around the localities and systematically set fire to Sikh houses, shops and gurdwaras . . . The
targets were primarily young Sikhs. They were dragged out, beaten
up and then burnt alive . . . In all the affected spots, a calculated
attempt to terrorize the people was evident in the common tendency among the assailants to burn alive the Sikhs on public roads."

Fire was everywhere; it was the day's motif. Throughout the
city, Sikh houses were being looted and set on fire, often with their
occupants still inside.

A survivor — a woman who lost her husband and three sons —
offered the following account to Veena Das, a Delhi sociologist:
"Some people, the neighbors, one of my relatives, said it would be
better if we hid in an abandoned house nearby. So my husband
took our three sons and hid there. We locked the house from out-

side, but there was treachery in people's hearts. Someone must have told the crowd. They baited him to come out. Then they poured kerosene on that house. They burnt them alive. When I went there that night, the bodies of my sons were on the loft — huddled together."

Over the next few days, some twenty-five hundred people died in Delhi alone. Thousands more died in other cities. The total death toll will never be known. The dead were overwhelmingly Sikh men. Entire neighborhoods were gutted; tens of thousands of people were left homeless.

Like many other members of my generation, I grew up believing that mass slaughter of the type that followed the partition of India and Pakistan, in 1947, could never happen again. But that morning, in the city of Delhi, the violence had reached the same level of intensity.

As Hari and I stood staring into the smoke-streaked sky, Mrs. Sen, Hari's mother, was thinking of matters closer at hand. She was about fifty, a tall, graceful woman with a gentle, soft-spoken manner. In an understated way, she was also deeply religious, a devout Hindu. When she heard what was happening, she picked up the phone and called Mr. and Mrs. Bawa, the elderly Sikh couple next door, to let them know that they were welcome to come over. She met with an unexpected response: an awkward silence. Mrs. Bawa thought she was joking, and wasn't sure whether to be amused or not.

Toward midday Mrs. Sen received a phone call: the mob was now in the immediate neighborhood, advancing systematically from street to street. Hari decided that it was time to go over and have a talk with the Bawas. I went along.

Mr. Bawa proved to be a small, slight man. Although he was casually dressed, his turban was neatly tied and his beard was carefully combed and bound. He was puzzled by our visit. After a polite greeting, he asked what he could do for us. It fell to Hari to explain.

Mr. Bawa had heard about Indira Gandhi's assassination, of course, and he knew that there had been some trouble. But he could not understand why these "disturbances" should impinge on him or his wife. He had no more sympathy for the Sikh terrorists than we did; his revulsion at the assassination was, if anything, even greater than ours. Not only was his commitment to India and the Indian state absolute, but it was evident from his bearing that he belonged to the country's ruling elite.

How do you explain to someone who has spent a lifetime cocooned in privilege that a potentially terminal rent has appeared in the wrappings? We found ourselves faltering. Mr. Bawa could not bring himself to believe that a mob might attack him.

By the time we left, it was Mr. Bawa who was mouthing reassurances. He sent us off with jovial pats on our backs. He did not actually say "Buck up," but his manner said it for him.

We were confident that the government would soon act to stop the violence. In India there is a drill associated with civil disturbances; a curfew is declared; paramilitary units are deployed; in extreme cases the army marches to the stricken areas. No city in India is better equipped to perform this drill than New Delhi, with its huge security apparatus. We later learned that in some cities — Calcutta, for example — the state authorities did act promptly to prevent violence. But in New Delhi and in much of northern India, hour followed hour without a response. Every few minutes we tuned to the radio, hoping to hear that the army had been ordered out. All we heard was mournful music and descriptions of Mrs. Gandhi's lying in state, of the comings and goings of dignitaries, foreign and national. The bulletins could have been messages from another planet.

As the afternoon progressed, we continued to hear reports of the mob's steady advance. Before long it had reached the next alley; we could hear the voices; the smoke was everywhere. There was still no sign of the army or the police.

Hari again called Mr. Bawa, and now, with the flames visible from his windows, he was more receptive. He agreed to come over with his wife, just for a short while. But there was a problem: how?

The two properties were separated by a shoulder-high wall, so it was impossible to walk from one house to the other except along the street.

I spotted a few of the thugs already at the end of the street. We could hear the occasional motorcycle cruising slowly up and down. The Bawas could not risk stepping out into the street. They would be seen; the sun had dipped low in the sky, but it was still light. Mr. Bawa balked at the thought of climbing over the wall; it seemed an insuperable obstacle at his age. But eventually Hari persuaded him to try.

We went to wait for them at the back of the Sens' house, in a spot that was well sheltered from the street. The mob seemed terrifyingly close, the Bawas reckless in their tardiness. A long time passed before the elderly couple finally appeared, hurrying toward us.

Mr. Bawa had changed before leaving the house: he was neatly dressed, dapper, even, in blazer and cravat. Mrs. Bawa, a small, matronly woman, was dressed in a salwar and kameez. Their cook was with them, and it was with his assistance that they had made it over the wall. The cook, who was Hindu, then returned to the house to stand guard.

Hari lead the Bawas into the drawing room, where Mrs. Sen was waiting, dressed in a chiffon sari. The room was large and well appointed, its walls hung with a rare and beautiful set of miniatures. With the curtains now drawn and the lamps lit, it was warm and welcoming. But all that lay between us and the mob in the street was a row of curtained French windows and a garden wall.

Mrs. Sen greeted the elderly couple with folded hands as they came in. The three seated themselves in an intimate circle, and soon a silver tea tray appeared. Instantly all constraint evaporated, and to the tinkling of porcelain, the conversation turned to the staples of New Delhi drawing-room chatter.

I could not bring myself to sit down. I stood in the corridor, distracted, looking out through the front entrance.

A couple of scouts on motorcycles had drawn up next door.

They had dismounted and were inspecting the house, walking in among the concrete stilts, looking up into the house. Somehow they got wind of the cook's presence and called him out.

The cook was very frightened. He was surrounded by thugs thrusting knives in his face and shouting questions. It was dark, and some were carrying kerosene torches. Wasn't it true, they shouted, that his employers were Sikhs? Where were they? Were they hiding inside? Who owned the house — Hindus or Sikhs?

Hari and I hid behind the wall between the two houses and listened to the interrogation. Our fates depended on this lone, frightened man. We had no idea what he would do — of how secure the Bawas were of his loyalties, or whether he might seek revenge for some past slight by revealing their whereabouts. If he did, both houses would burn.

Although stuttering in terror, the cook held his own. Yes, he said, yes, his employers were Sikhs, but they'd left town; there was no one in the house. No, the house didn't belong to them; they were renting from a Hindu.

He succeeded in persuading most of the thugs, but a few eyed the surrounding houses suspiciously. Some appeared at the steel gates in front of us, rattling the bars.

We went up and positioned ourselves at the gates. I remember a strange sense of disconnection as I walked down the driveway, as though I were watching myself from somewhere very distant.

We took hold of the gates and shouted back: Get away! You have no business here! There's no one inside! The house is empty.

To our surprise they began to drift away, one by one.

Just before this, I had stepped into the house to see how Mrs. Sen and the Bawas were faring. The thugs were clearly audible in the lamplit drawing room; only a thin curtain shielded the interior from their view.

My memory of what I saw in the drawing room is uncannily vivid. Mrs. Sen had a smile on her face as she poured a cup of tea for Mr. Bawa. Beside her, Mrs. Bawa in a firm, unwavering voice was comparing the domestic situations in New Delhi and Manila.

·   ·   ·

The next morning I heard about a protest that was being organized at the large compound of a relief agency. When I arrived, a meeting was already under way, a gathering of seventy or eighty people.

The mood was somber. Some of the people spoke about neighborhoods that had been taken over by vengeful mobs. They described countless murders — many by setting the victims alight — as well as terrible destruction: the burning of Sikh temples, the looting of Sikh schools, the razing of Sikh homes and shops. The violence was worse than I had imagined. It was declared at the meeting that an effective initial tactic would be to march into one of the badly affected neighborhoods and confront the rioters directly.

The group had grown to about a hundred and fifty men and women, among them Swami Agnivesh, a Hindu ascetic; Ravi Chopra, a scientist and environmentalist; and a handful of opposition politicians, including Chandra Shekhar, who became prime minister for a brief period several years later.

The group was pitifully small by the standards of a city where crowds of several hundred thousand were routinely mustered for political rallies. Nevertheless, the members rose to their feet and began to march.

Years before, I had read a passage by V. S. Naipaul that has stayed with me ever since. I have never been able to find it again, so this account is from memory. In his incomparable prose, Naipaul describes a demonstration. He is in a hotel room somewhere in Africa or South America; he looks down and sees people marching past. To his surprise, the sight fills him with an obscure longing, a kind of melancholy; he is aware of a wish to go out, to join, to merge his concerns with theirs. Yet he knows he never will; it is simply not in his nature to join crowds.

For many years I read everything of Naipaul's I could lay my hands on; I couldn't have enough of him. I read him with the intimate, appalled attention that one reserves for one's most skillful interlocutors. It was he who first made it possible for me to think of myself as a writer, working in English.

I remembered that passage because I believed that I too was not a joiner, and in Naipaul's pitiless mirror I thought I saw an aspect of myself rendered visible. Yet as this forlorn little group marched out of the shelter of the compound, I did not hesitate for a moment: without a second thought, I joined.

The march headed first for Lajpat Nagar, a busy commercial area a mile or so away. I knew the area. Though it was in New Delhi, its streets resembled the older parts of the city, where small, cramped shops tended to spill out onto the footpaths.

We were shouting slogans as we marched, hoary Gandhian staples of peace and brotherhood from half a century before. Then, suddenly, we were confronted with a starkly familiar spectacle, an image of twentieth-century urban horror: burned-out cars, their ransacked interiors visible through smashed windows; debris and rubble everywhere. Blackened pots had been strewn along the street. A cinema had been gutted, and the charred faces of film stars stared out at us from half-burned posters.

As I think back to that march, my memory breaks down, details dissolve. I recently telephoned some friends who had been there. Their memories are similar to mine in only one respect: they too clung to one scene while successfully ridding their minds of the rest.

The scene my memory preserved is of a moment when it seemed inevitable that we would be attacked.

Rounding a corner, we found ourselves facing a crowd that was larger and more determined-looking than any other crowds we had encountered. On each previous occasion we had prevailed by marching at the thugs and engaging them directly, in dialogues that turned quickly into extended shouting matches. In every instance we had succeeded in facing them down. But this particular mob was intent on confrontation. As its members advanced on us, brandishing knives and steel rods, we stopped. Our voices grew louder as they came toward us; a kind of rapture descended on us, exhilaration in anticipation of a climax. We braced for the attack, leaning forward as if into a wind.

And then something happened that I have never completely understood. Nothing was said; there was no signal, nor was there any break in the rhythm of our chanting. But suddenly all the women in our group — and the women made up more than half the group's numbers — stepped out and surrounded the men; their saris and kameezes became a thin, fluttering barrier, a wall around us. They turned to face the approaching men, challenging them, daring them to attack.

The thugs took a few more steps toward us and then faltered, confused. A moment later they were gone.

The march ended at the walled compound where it had started. In the next couple of hours an organization was created, the Nagarik Ekta Manch, or Citizen's Unity Front, and its work — to bring relief to the injured and the bereft, to shelter the homeless — began the next morning. Food and clothing were needed, and camps had to be established to accommodate the thousands of people with nowhere to sleep. And by the next day we were overwhelmed — literally. The large compound was crowded with vanloads of blankets, secondhand clothing, shoes, and sacks of flour, sugar, and tea. Previously hardnosed, unsentimental businessmen sent cars and trucks. There was barely room to move.

My own role was slight. For a few weeks I worked with a team from Delhi University, distributing supplies in the slums and working-class neighborhoods that had been worst hit by the rioting. Then I returned to my desk.

In time, inevitably, most of the front's volunteers returned to their everyday lives. But some members — most notably the women involved in the running of refugee camps — continued to work for years afterward with Sikh women and children who had been rendered homeless. Lalita Ramdas, Veena Das, Mita Bose, Radha Kumar: these women, each one an accomplished professional, gave up years of their time to repair the enormous damage that had been done in a matter of two or three days.

The front also formed a team to investigate the riots. I briefly considered joining but then decided that an investigation would be a waste of time, because the politicians capable of inciting violence were unlikely to heed a tiny group of concerned citizens.

I was wrong. A document eventually produced by this team — a slim pamphlet entitled "Who Are the Guilty?" — has become a classic, a searing indictment of the politicians who incited the riots and the police who allowed the rioters to have their way.

Over the years the Indian government has compensated some of the survivors of the 1984 violence and resettled some of the survivors. One gap remains: to this day, not one instigator of the riots has been charged. But the pressure on the government has never gone away, and it continues to grow; every year the nails hammered in by that slim document dig just a little deeper.

The pamphlets and others that followed are testaments to the only humane possibility available to people who live in multiethnic, multireligious societies like those of the Indian subcontinent. Human rights documents such as "Who Are the Guilty?" are essential to the process of broadening civil institutions: they are the weapons with which society asserts itself against a state that runs criminally amok, as this one did in Delhi in November of 1984.

It is heartening that sanity prevails today in the Punjab. But not elsewhere. In Bombay, local government officials want to stop people from painting buildings green — a color associated with the Muslim religion. And hundreds of Muslims have been deported from the city's slums — in at least one case for committing an offense no greater than reading a Bengali newspaper. It is imperative that governments ensure that those who instigate mass violence do not go unpunished.

The Bosnian writer Dzevad Karahasan, in a remarkable essay called "Literature and War" (published last year in his collection *Sarajevo, Exodus of a City*), makes a startling connection between modern literary aestheticism and the contemporary world's indifference to violence: "The decision to perceive literally everything as an aesthetic phenomenon—completely sidestepping questions about goodness and truth—is an artistic decision. That decision started in the realm of art, and went on to become characteristic of the contemporary world."

When I went back to my desk in November of 1984, I found myself confronting decisions about writing that I had never faced before. How was I to write about what I had seen without reducing it to mere spectacle? My next novel was bound to be influenced by my experiences, but I could see no way of writing directly about those events without creating them as a panorama of violence—"an aesthetic phenomenon," as Karahasan was to call it. At the time, the idea seemed obscene and futile; of much greater importance were factual reports of the testimony of the victims. But these were already being done by people who were, I knew, more competent than I could be.

Within a few months I started my novel, which I eventually called *The Shadow Lines*—a book that led me backward in time to earlier memories of riots, ones witnessed in childhood. It became a book not about any one event but about the meaning of such events and their effects on the individuals who live through them.

And until now I have never really written about what I saw in November of 1984. I am not alone; several others who took part in that march went on to publish books, yet nobody, so far as I know, has ever written about it except in passing.

There are good reasons for this, not least the politics of the situation, which leave so little room for the writer. The riots were generated by a cycle of violence, involving the terrorists in the Punjab, on the one hand, and the Indian government, on the other. To write carelessly, in such a way as to appear to endorse terrorism or repression, can add easily to the problem, and in such incendiary circumstances, words cost lives, and it is only appropriate that those who deal in words should pay scrupulous attention to what they say. It is only appropriate that they should find themselves inhibited.

But there is also a simpler explanation. Before I could set down a word, I had to resolve a dilemma, between being a writer and being a citizen. As a writer, I had only one obvious subject: the violence. From the news report, or the latest film or novel, we have come to expect the bloody detail or the elegantly staged conflagration that closes a chapter or effects a climax. But it is worth asking if the very obviousness of this subject arises out of our modern conventions of representation; within the dominant aesthetic of our time — the aesthetic of what Karahasan calls "indifference" — it is all too easy to present violence as an apocalyptic spectacle, while the resistance to it can easily figure as mere sentimentality or, worse, as pathetic and absurd.

Writers don't join crowds — Naipaul and so many others teach us that. But what do you do when the constitutional authority fails to act? You join and in joining bear all the responsibilities and obligations and guilt that joining represents. My experience of the violence was overwhelmingly and memorably of the resistance to it. When I think of the women staring down the mob, I am not filled with a writerly wonder. I am reminded of my gratitude for being saved from injury. What I saw at first hand — and not merely on that march but on the bus, in Hari's house, in the huge compound that filled with essential goods — was not the horror of violence but the affirmation of humanity: in each case, I witnessed the risks that perfectly ordinary people are willing to take for one another.

When I now read descriptions of troubled parts of the world, in which violence appears primordial and inevitable, a fate to which masses of people are largely resigned, I find myself asking, Is that all there was to it? Or is it possible that the authors of these descriptions failed to find a form — or a style or a voice or a plot — that could accommodate both violence *and* the civilized willed response to it?

The truth is that the commonest response to violence is one of repugnance and that a significant number of people try to oppose it in whatever ways they can. That these efforts rarely appear in accounts of violence is not surprising: they are too undramatic. For those who participate in them, they are often hard to write about for the same reasons that so long delayed my own account of 1984.

"Let us not fool ourselves," Karahasan writes. "The world is written first—the holy books say that it was created in words—and all that happens in it, happens in language first."

It is when we think of the world the aesthetic of indifference might bring into being that we recognize the urgency of remembering the stories we have not written.

AN EGYPTIAN IN BAGHDAD

1990

The last time I spoke to Nabeel was over a year ago. He was in Baghdad. I was in New York. It wasn't easy getting through. The directory listed a code for Baghdad, but after days of trying, all I'd got was a recorded message telling me that the number I'd dialed didn't exist.

In the end I had to book a call with the operator. She took a while, but eventually there was a voice at the other end, speaking in the blunt, rounded Arabic of Iraq: "Yes? Who is it?"

Nabeel's family had told me that he was working as an assistant in a photographer's shop. The owner was an Iraqi, and Nabeel had been working for him since 1986, when he left his village in Egypt and went to Iraq. There was a telephone in the shop and the owner was relatively kind, a relatively kind Iraqi, and he allowed Nabeel to receive calls.

I imagined him as a big, paunchy man, Nabeel's boss, sitting at the end of a counter, behind a cash box, with the telephone beside him and a Kodacolor poster of a snow-clad mountain on the wall above. He was wearing a blue jallabeyya and a white lace cap; he had a carefully trimmed mustache and a pair of sunglasses in his breast pocket. The telephone beside him was of the old-fashioned kind, black and heavy, and it had a brass lock fastened in its dial. The boss kept the key, and Nabeel and the other assistants had to ask for it when they wanted to make a call. It was late at night in New York, so it had to be morning in Baghdad. The shop must just have opened. They had probably had no customers yet.

"Is Nabeel there?" I asked.

"Who?" said the voice.

"Nabeel Idris Badawy," I said. "The Egyptian."

He grunted. *"Wa min inta?"* he said. "And who're you?"

"I'm a friend of his," I said. "Tell him it's his friend from India. He'll know."

"What's that?" he said. "From where?"

"From India, *ya raiyis,*" I said. "Could you tell him? And quickly if you please, for I'm calling from America."

"From America?" he shouted down the line. "But you said you're Indian?"

"Yes, I am—I'm just in America on a visit. Nabeel quickly, if you please, *ya raiyis . . .*"

I heard him shout across the room: *"Ya* Nabeel, somebody wants to talk to you, some Indian or something . . ."

I could tell from Nabeel's first words of greeting that my call had taken him completely by surprise. It was only natural. Eight years had passed since I'd left his village. He and his family had befriended me when I was living there in 1980 and 1981, doing research. I was then in my mid-twenties; Nabeel was a few years younger. We had become close friends, and for the first few years after I'd left, we had written letters back and forth between India and Egypt. But then he had gone to do his national service in the army, and he'd stopped writing. In time I had stopped writing too. He had no way of knowing that I would be in the United States on a visit that year. Until a few weeks ago I hadn't known that he was in Baghdad. I knew now because I had just been to Egypt and had visited his village and his family.

"Nabeel's not here, *ya* Amitab," his sister-in-law, Fawzia, had said to me, once she recovered from the shock of seeing me at the door. "He's not in the village—he's gone to Iraq."

Ushering me in, she fussed about distractedly, pumping her

kerosene stove, fetching tea and sugar. She was a pretty, good-humored woman who had always made me welcome in their house. I had been in the village when she was married to Nabeel's older brother Aly.

"Nabeel left about two years ago," she said. "He went with his cousin Ismail, do you remember him?"

I did. He was Nabeel's best friend as well as his cousin, although they could not have been more different. Ismail was lively, energetic, always ready with a joke or a pun; Nabeel, on the other hand, was thoughtful and serious, with a marked disinclination for vigorous activity of any kind. When he made his way down the lanes of the village, it was in a stately, considered kind of way, in marked contrast to the caperings of his cousin.

"They left for Iraq soon after they finished their national service," said Fawzia. "They went to make money."

They had rented a room in Baghdad with some other young men from the village, she said, and they all lived and cooked and ate together. She had taught Nabeel and Ismail to cook a few things before they left, so they managed all right. Ismail was a construction laborer. There was good money to be had in construction; Nabeel earned less as a photographer's assistant, but he liked his job. Ismail had been trying to get him to go into construction, but Nabeel wasn't interested.

"You know him," she said, laughing. "He always wanted a job where he wouldn't have to get his clothes dirty."

Later, when her husband, Aly, had come home from the fields and we had all had dinner, she gave me the number of the shop in Baghdad. Once every couple of months or so she and Nabeel's brothers would make a trip to a post office in a nearby town and telephone him in Baghdad.

"It costs a lot," she said, "but you can hear him like he was in the next house."

Nabeel couldn't telephone them, of course, but now and again he would speak into a cassette recorder and send them a tape. He and his brothers had all been through high school; Nabeel himself even had a college degree. But they still found the spoken word more reassuring than the written.

"You must hear his voice on the machine," said Aly, producing a tape. He placed it carefully inside a huge cassette recorder cum radio and we gathered around to listen. Nabeel's voice was very solemn, and he was speaking like a Cairene, almost as though he'd forgotten the village dialect.

"Does he always talk like that now?" I asked Fawzia.

"Oh no." She laughed. "He's talking like that because it's a cassette. On the telephone he sounds just like he used to."

Nabeel said almost nothing about himself and his life in Iraq, just that he was well and that his salary had gone up. He listed in detail the names of all the people he wanted them to convey his greetings to—members of his lineage, people in the village, his school friends. Then he told them about everyone from the village who was in Iraq—that so-and-so was well, that someone had moved to another city, and that someone else was about to go home. For the rest he gave his family precise instructions about what they were to do with the money he was sending them—about the additions they were to make to the house, exactly how the rooms should look, how much they should spend on the floors, the windows, the roof. His brothers listened, rapt, though they must have heard the tape through several times already.

Later Aly wrote down Nabeel's address for me. It consisted of a number on a numbered street in "New Baghdad." I pictured to myself an urban development project of the kind that flourishes in the arid hinterlands of Cairo and New Delhi—straight, treeless streets and blocks of yellow buildings divided into "Pockets," "Phases," and "Zones."

"You must telephone him," one of Nabeel's younger brothers said. "He'll be so pleased. Do you know, he's kept all your letters, wrapped in a plastic bag? He still talks of you, a lot. Tell me, didn't you once say to him . . ."

And then he recounted, almost word for word, a conversation I had once had with Nabeel. It was about something trivial, about my college in Delhi, but for some reason I had written it down in my diary that very day, while it was still fresh in memory. I had read through my diaries of that time again recently. That was why I knew that Nabeel's brother had repeated that conversation, or at least a part of it, almost verbatim, in near exact detail. I was amazed. It seemed to me an impossible, deeply moving defiance of time and the laws of hearsay and memory.

"You can be sure that I will telephone him," I said to Nabeel's brother. "I'll telephone him soon, from America."

"You must tell him that we are well and that he should send another cassette."

"Won't he be surprised," said Fawzia, "when he hears Amitab's voice on the phone? He'll think someone's playing a joke on him."

"We'll write and tell him," said Aly. "We'll write tomorrow so he won't be surprised. We'll tell him that you're going to phone him from America."

But they hadn't written: the surprise in Nabeel's voice as he greeted me over the phone was proof of that. And I, for my part, even though I had the advantage, was almost as amazed as Nabeel, though for a different reason. When I was living in their village, in 1980 and '81, Nabeel and Ismail had had very definite plans for their immediate future: they wanted salaried jobs in the Agriculture Ministry. It would not have occurred to any of us then to think that within a few years they would both be abroad and that I would be able to speak to them on the phone from thousands of miles away.

There was only one telephone in the village then. It had never worked, as far as anyone knew. It was not meant to — it was really a badge of office, a scepter. It belonged to the government, and it resided in the house of the village headman. When a headman was voted out in the local elections, the telephone was ritually removed from his house and taken to the victor's. It was carried at the head of a procession, accompanied by drums and gunshots, as though it were a saint's relics. "We carried the telephone that year," people would say, meaning "We swept the elections."

Nabeel's family was one of the poorest in the village — and the village was not by any means prosperous. Few families in the village had more than five *feddans* of land, but most had one or two. Nabeel's family had none at all. That was one of the reasons that he and his brothers had all got an education: schools and colleges were free, and they had no land to claim their time.

Nabeel lived with his parents in a three-room adobe hut, along with Aly and Fawzia and their three other brothers. Aly worked in the fields for a daily wage when there was work to be had; their father carried a tiny salary as a village watchman. He was a small, frail man with sunken cheeks and watery gray eyes. As a watchman he had the possession of a gun, an ancient Enfield, that was kept in a locked chest under his bed. He said that he'd last had occasion to use it some fifteen years ago, when somebody spotted a gang of thieves running through Hassan Bassiuni's cornfields. The thieves had escaped, but the gun had mowed down half the field — it was really very much like a blunderbuss. He was very proud of it. Once when a fire broke out in Shahata Hammoudah's house and everyone was busy doing what they could, I noticed Nabeel's father running in the opposite direction. When I next looked around, he was standing at attention in front of the burning house, holding his gun, smiling benignly.

Nabeel's mother, a dark, fine-boned woman, secretly despaired of her husband. "He's been defeated by the world," she would say sometimes. "There's no one to stand beside Nabeel and his brothers except themselves."

Now, eight years later, Nabeel's father and mother were both dead. "And the saddest thing," Fawzia said to me, "is that they didn't live to see how things have changed for us."

The three mud-walled rooms were gone now. In their place was a bungalow, or at least its skeleton — four or five rooms, in a largely unfinished state but built of brick and cement and entirely habitable. There was provision for a bathroom, a kitchen, a living room, as well as another entire apartment upstairs, exactly like the one below. That was where Nabeel would live once he was married, Fawzia said to me. She, for her part, was content; in her house she now had a television set, a cassette recorder, and a washing machine.

It wasn't just her life that had changed. When I first came to the village, in 1980, there were only three or four television sets there, and they belonged to the handful of men who owned fifteen to twenty *feddans* of land, the richest men in the village. Those men still had their fifteen to twenty *feddans* of land and their black-and-white television sets. It was the families who had once been thought of as the poor folk of the village whose homes were now full of all the best-known brand names in Japan — television sets, washing machines, kitchen appliances, cameras . . . I could not have begun to imagine a change on this scale when I left the village in 1981. If I had not witnessed it with my own eyes, I would not have believed it possible.

It was a kind of revolution, but it had happened a long way away. It had been created entirely by the young men who had gone to work in Iraq, once that country began to experience severe labor shortages because of its war with Iran. They were carried along by a great wave of migration. In the late 1980s there were estimated to be between two and three million Egyptians in Iraq. Nobody knew for sure: the wave had surged out of the country too quickly to be measured. All of Nabeel's contemporaries were gone now — all the young men with high school educations and no jobs and no land and nothing to do but play football and lounge around the water taps when the girls went to fetch water in the evenings. Some of the old men used to say that they would all go to the bad. But in the end it was they who had transformed the village.

"It's we who've been the real gainers in the war," one of the village schoolteachers said to me while I was walking down the lanes, gaping at all the newly built houses and buildings. "The Iraqis are doing all the fighting, it's they who're dying. The Arab countries are paying them to break the back of Khomeini's Islamic revolution. For them it's a matter of survival. But in the meantime, while Iraqis are dying, others are making money. But it won't last — that money's tainted, and the price is going to be paid later, someday."

The young men who'd left were paying a price already. "Life is really hard there," their families said. "You never know what's going to happen from day to day." And they would tell stories about fights, about lone Egyptians being attacked on the streets, about men being forced to work inhuman hours, about how the Iraqi women would look at Egyptian men from their windows, because so many of their own men were dead, and how it always led to trouble, because the Iraqis would find out and kill both the woman and the Egyptian.

"How does Nabeel like it in Iraq?" I asked his brother Aly.

"He's fine," said Aly. "He's all right."

"How do you know?"

"That's what he says on the cassettes," he said. "I'm sure he's all right."

"I hope so," I said.

He was frowning now. "God knows," he said. "People say life is hard out there."

Nabeel could not tell me as much over the telephone, with his boss listening. But he was well, he said, and so was his cousin Ismail, and they were managing fine, living with their relatives and friends from back home. In turn he asked me about India, my job, my family. Then I heard a noise down the line; it sounded like another voice in the same room. Nabeel broke off to say, "Coming, just a moment."

I said quickly, "I'm going back to India soon. I'll try and visit you on the way."

"We'll be expecting you," he said. In the background I could hear the voice again, louder now.

"You'd better go now," I said.

"I'll tell Ismail you're coming," he said hurriedly. "We'll wait for you."

But the year passed and the visit eluded me.

2

It was exactly three weeks since Saddam Hussein had invaded Kuwait, and miraculously, Abu-Ali, the old shopkeeper, was on his feet. That was how he happened to see me as I walked down the road past his window.

Nabeel's village was just a mile and a half away, and I was on my way there when Abu-Ali sent a child running after me. Abu-Ali's house was where the asphalt road ended and the dirt track began. Taxi drivers would not go any farther.

Abu-Ali was standing by the window again cradling a radio, twiddling the knob. He had always behaved as though all the village's worries had fallen on his shoulders. Now it looked as though he had taken on all of Egypt's.

The radio was a big one, with a built-in cassette recorder, but in Abu-Ali's huge, swollen hands it seemed as slim and fragile as an advanced model of a calculator. It spat out a medley of electronic sounds as the pointer flashed across its face. But the sounds were lost; the noise in the room was already deafening. Abu-Ali's cousin's daughter was getting married next door. A crowd of women and children had gathered in the lane outside their house. A boy was beating a tin washbasin with a spoon, and the women and children were clapping in time and chanting, *"Ya rumman, ya rumman,"* singing of the bride as the bloom of a pomegranate.

At intervals Abu-Ali rose from his bed, went to the window, glared at the women and children outside, shuffled back, and collapsed onto his bed again. This was an astonishing feat. When I first knew him years ago, he was already so fat that he found it nearly impossible to leave his bed. Now he was fatter still. Every time he stood up, his belly surged away from him like backwash leaving a beach. It was pure greed, his neighbors had always said; he ate the way other people force-fed geese — he could eat two chickens and a pot of rice at one sitting. And now that there was all this Iraqi money in his house, that was exactly what he did sometimes — ate two whole chickens and a pot of rice, right after the midday prayers.

"Ate it," muttered Abu-Ali, shuffling across the room yet again. "The son of a bitch just ate it like it was a chicken's liver. Saw a tasty little morsel and just swallowed it."

He sounded envious: an appetite was something he could understand.

"So what do you expect?" someone said. The room was quite full now: several men had stopped by to see Abu-Ali on their way to the wedding. "What was Kuwait but a tasty little morsel cooked up by the British and sucked dry by the Americans?"

"Just ate it!" Abu-Ali twirled the knob of the radio, sending the pointer screeching through a succession of stations. "BBC, BBC," he muttered, "where's that son-of-a-bitch BBC?"

A distant, haranguing voice suddenly burst out of the radio, screaming shrilly. Abu-Ali started back in surprise, almost dropping the radio. "Who's this son of a bitch now?"

"That's Damascus," said someone.

"No, it's those son-of-a-bitch Americans broadcasting in Arabic," said someone else.

"No, it's Riyadh," said Abu-Ali. "It sounds like a Saudi."

"Riyadh is where he should have gone," said another man. "But he didn't — stopped too soon. It's those Saudi sons of bitches who should have been fixed."

I jogged the elbow of the man sitting next to me. I knew him well once; he used to teach in a nearby school. Now he was teaching in the Yemen; he'd come home on a visit, intending to leave once the summer holidays ended. But his wife wouldn't let him go; she had four children to bring up, and she was not going to let him vanish into a war zone.

"Do you know if Nabeel Badawy is back from Iraq yet?" I asked him.

"Nabeel?" he said. He'd been looking distracted, anxious, ever since he came into the room. Now he looked as though he'd been dazed by the noise and the cigarette smoke. The man next to him had his arm firmly in his grasp; he was shouting into his other ear, his voice hoarse.

"The worst sons of bitches, the most ungrateful, do you know who they are?" he shouted.

"Nabeel Idris Badawy," I said insistently. "You remember him?"

"The Palestinians," shouted the man hoarsely. "The worst sons of bitches."

"Nabeel Idris Badawy," I repeated. "From Nashawy?"

"From Nashawy?" said the schoolteacher. "How many wars have we fought for them, you tell me? Haven't I lost my own brother?"

"Nabeel Idris Mustafa Badawy," said the schoolteacher jubilantly, his voice rising to a shout. "He was in Iraq — my nephew told me."

"Them and the Israelis, God forsake them, the sons of bitches. In the end they're always at the bottom of everything."

"I know Nabeel's in Iraq," I shouted back. "But do you know if he's back yet?"

He thought for a moment and then shook his head. "No," he said, "I can't tell you. There are so many boys over there, you know, it's impossible to keep track. Mabrouk Hussein is still there, you know, my own nephew. You remember him? And there are others from this village — there's Fahmy and Abusa and . . ."

He began to repeat the names, as everyone else who had come into the room had done. The village was a very small one, no more than 350 souls, just a hamlet really. I knew it well when I lived in the area. At that time only one man from the village was abroad; he taught Arabic in a school in Zaire. But over the past few years more than a dozen of its young men had left. Most had gone to Iraq, a couple to Jordan (it was almost the same thing). Several had returned since the beginning of the year, but five still remained, trapped in Iraq. People said their names over and over again, as though to conjure them out of Iraq, back to the village: Mabrouk, who used to keep goal; Abusa — "the Frown" — who never smiled; Fahmy, who used to ride out to the fields on a sheep. I remembered them coming to visit me in the evenings, full of questions: "What do you grow in India? Do you have schools? Do you have weddings? Rain? An army?" They were very young. None of them had ever been farther than the local town. The machines with which they were most familiar were their *kababis* — the Persian wheels their cattle drove, round and round for hours every day, to water their fields. Mabrouk had once come running to my room, hugely excited, and dragged me away to his house to see the brand-new water pump his family had bought. It was very important for him and his family that I take a look at it, for like all the pumps in the area, it was from India (the generic name for water pump was *makana hindi,* "the Indian machine"). No matter that I had said, time after time, that I knew nothing about water pumps, I was always asked for an opinion when somebody bought one.

This one was exactly like the others: a big green machine with a spout and an exhaust pipe. They had hung an old shoe on the spout and stuck an incense stick in the exhaust pipe to protect it from the evil eye. I knocked on the spout with my knuckles and patted its diesel tank in a well-informed kind of way. "What do you think?" Mabrouk's father said. "Is it all right?"

I knocked a little harder, frowning.

He was anxious now: "So, what do you think?"

I smiled. "It's a very good one — excellent."

There was a sigh of relief. "Get the Indian doctor some tea."

Mabrouk had shaken my hand. "I knew you would be able to tell . . ."

And now Mabrouk was in the immediate vicinity of chemical and nuclear weapons, within a few minutes' striking distance of the world's most advanced machinery. It would be he who would have to pay the price of the violence that was invented in quiet, pastoral laboratories in Heidelberg and Berkeley.

"Do you think the Americans are ever going to leave the sacred land?" a young man said at the top of his voice. People fell silent, listening. Outside, the clapping seemed suddenly louder, the girls' voices more insistent.

"Never," he shouted. "Never — they're never going to leave the

sacred places. Now that they're there, they're going to stay till
the end of time. They've finally achieved what they'd never managed in a thousand years of history. And who's responsible? The
Saudis — the sons of bitches."

"*Ya rumman, ya rumman!*" The beat was growing faster; the
spoons were drumming out a crescendo on the washbasins. Glancing out of the window, I saw three young men walking down the
lane. They had all recently returned from Iraq. Abu-Ali's youngest
son was among them. The girls stole looks at them as they walked
past, singing at the tops of their voices. They were hoping perhaps
that they'd stop and join in the singing and dancing, as young men
used to. But these three youths walked straight past them. They
had small, derisory smiles under their clipped mustaches. They
were embarrassed at the sight of their sisters and cousins drumming out a beat on washbasins while waiting for a groom who
was going to arrive in a pickup truck. They had grown accustomed
to seeing weddings with big bands and hired BMWs. They were
savvy, street-smart in some ways — some of them could recite the
prices of the best brand-name goods as though they'd memorized
a catalogue. They could tell you what counted as a good price for
anything ranging from a pair of Nike shoes to a video camera. If
you'd paid a piaster more, you'd been had, someone had "laughed
at you." The girls were going to be disappointed. These young
men were not going to tie up their jallabeyyas and dance to the
rhythm of dented washbasins.

"Why'd you think the Americans and the British have always
supported those son-of-a-bitch sheiks?" my friend the schoolteacher said. "Why do you think? Because it was the easiest way to
get back all the money they spent on oil — it all went straight back
to their casinos and hotels. And they knew someday they would be
able to get back here through those sheiks, the sons of bitches."

The girls were beginning to irritate Abu-Ali. He shuffled up to
the window and yelled, "Will you stop that noise? Can't you see
we're trying to listen to the news on the radio?"

His voice was legendary: it shook the mud floor. The girls
stopped their singing for a moment, taken by surprise. But soon

they started again, softly at first and then louder, gradually. The wedding had been planned a year ago, long before the invasion. They'd been looking forward to it for a long time; they had no wish whatever to forgo one of their few diversions.

"Didn't I tell you to stop that noise?" Abu-Ali ran out of breath, mopped his forehead.

"He's been like this ever since the invasion," the schoolteacher whispered to me. "Taken it personally."

In fact Abu-Ali had been lucky. His three sons, who'd all spent long periods of time in Iraq, were back in Egypt now. The youngest had returned just a month before the invasion. "People say that God was watching over him," his mother had said to me when I went into the house to see her. "They say, 'You should praise God for bringing him back in time' — as though I didn't know it."

Abu-Ali had bought a Datsun pickup truck with his sons' earnings. It was making good money now, ferrying goods between the nearby towns and villages. He had also built apartments for his sons, all of them expensively furnished with the heavy, gilded furniture that was favored in rural Egypt. Still, there was one more thing he wanted: a car. He had been just about ready to send two of his sons back to Iraq when the war broke out. He'd even bought the tickets.

"That Saddam Hussein," he said. "How could anyone know he'd do this?"

I could have told him of a conversation I'd recorded in my diary on September 30, 1980, when I was living down the road in Nashawy. It was a conversation with one of Nabeel's cousins, a bright young medical student, about the Iran-Iraq war:

I asked him whether he thought that after the war Saddam Hussein was going to emerge as the strong man of the Middle East. He said no, he never would, because Egypt's army was the strongest in the Middle East, and perhaps in the world; because Egypt's soldiers were the best in the world!

I could still remember thinking about that exclamation mark. "That Saddam Hussein," snarled Abu-Ali. "I want to kill him."

His youngest son came into the room and was amazed to see me. After the greetings were over, he said, "Do you know, I used to work for Indians in Iraq? But they were a different kind of Indian—Shia Muslims, Bohras. I used to work in a hotel they ran in Karbala. It's a great pilgrimage center, you know."

I was startled: I had only very recently met a group of Bohra Muslims. On my way to Cairo from Calcutta, I'd had to stop at Amman airport to catch a connecting flight. I'd met them at the airport. They'd been stranded in Karbala for several days after the invasion. They'd been very worried, because some members of their party had American and British passports. But when they got to the border, it had been all right; the guards had let them through without a word. "We're Muslims," they said, "so it didn't matter." In Karbala they'd stayed in a Bohra hotel, they'd said—very well run, clean, comfortable. It was an odd coincidence.

"Why did you come through Jordan at a time like this?" he asked. I explained that the trip had been arranged a long time back.

"I traveled through Jordan too once," he said. "It was a nice place then. But look at it now. Have you seen the pictures on the TV news? They're frightening. That man . . ."

"I want to kill that Saddam Hussein," bellowed his father. "He's spoiled everything." The thought of that lost car was sawing into his flesh.

"This war's going to be a disaster," said his son, shaking his head. But he had a look of relief on his face: at least his father wouldn't be able to send him back there now.

"Did you ever come across Nabeel in Iraq?" I asked.

"Nabeel?" he repeated after me. "Nabeel who?"

"Nabeel Idris Mustafa Badawy," I said. "From Nashawy."

He thought for a moment and shook his head. "No. I didn't even know he was there. It's a big country, and there are so many Egyptians there . . ."

A pickup truck drew up outside in a flurry of horns. The washbasins began to crash together, the women began to ululate. The groom had arrived. Abu-Ali paid no notice. He was shouting: ". . . he doesn't know how much harm he's doing to his country . . ."

Many of the men in the room went rushing out to receive the groom. I slipped out with them, unnoticed. Abu-Ali was still shouting: "He has to be killed, as soon as possible."

Everywhere in Egypt people seemed to be talking of killing. In the taxi out from Cairo, the six passengers had all agreed that Saddam had to be killed. But then somebody had added, "And what about the Man here? Hasn't he got to go first?" This met with a chorus of approval: "He's going to die, the Man"; ". . . and if someone wants to kill him, he can count on me for help."

Never before in Egypt had I heard ordinary people so much as criticize their president in public, among strangers, far less talk of killing him, even if only metaphorically. I looked out the window, half expecting the driver to stop the taxi. But soon enough he too was talking of killing—the Iraqis, the Americans, Palestinians, Israelis, Saudis . . .

It was as though the whole country had been startled suddenly out of sleep and fallen out of bed, fists clenched, swinging wildly at everything in sight.

The fact is that it has been a long sleep, and on the whole the dreams have been good. So good that in the dreamtime Egypt has floated away from earth into the upper atmosphere.

For the past few years the principal sources of Egypt's national income have been these: the repatriated earnings of its workers abroad, Western aid, and tourism. Oil and fees from the Suez Canal follow, but not close behind. Life aboveground—where most countries have their economies—has contributed increasingly little. A few decades ago Egypt used to grow enough food to feed itself and export some too. Since then, in exactly the period in which India and China have gone from dependency to self-sufficiency in food, Egypt has reached a point where it has to import as much as 70 percent of its grain. To pay for its food, it needs foreign exchange. And so tourism has become a desperately serious business, a matter of economic survival.

Minds are hard at work thinking of ways to make Egypt ever more attractive to tourists, ever more fantastic. A year or so ago they hit upon the idea of turning a town into an opera set. Luxor, they decided — the ancient Thebes — would be just the right setting for Verdi's *Aïda*. It needed a fair bit of work to turn a real town and some real ancient Egyptian ruins into an Italian's fantasy of ancient Egypt, but they did a thorough job. Luxor got new roads, new hotels, and miles of brand-new wharfs along the east bank of the Nile. The wharfs are now lined with steamers, often two or three deep: great floating hotels, several stories high, with many decks of cabins as well as restaurants, bars, saunas, gyms, swimming pools. They bring ever-increasing numbers of tourists to Luxor. Last year Egypt had about two million tourists. Almost every single one of them passed through Luxor.

A very large proportion of the tourists come in the steamers. They are taken to the ruins and back again in air-conditioned coaches. The adventurous few take horse-drawn carriages. All the petty difficulties and irritations of traveling in Egypt have been done away with; the only Egyptians the tourists ever encounter are tour guides and waiters (the number is not negligible).

Outside the temple in Karnak is a large notice, prominently displayed. It catches the eye because it is entirely in Arabic. The notices at the monuments are usually in several languages — Arabic, English, French, and sometimes even German. But in more ways than one, this notice is not like the others. It contains a list of do's and don'ts for Egyptian visitors — don't make a noise, don't climb the monuments. It ends by exhorting them to behave in a manner "appropriate to Egyptian culture." I read it carefully. It makes me think of my aunt in Calcutta, who wanted her money back after visiting the lion sanctuary at the Gir forest in Gujarat. "Why," she yelled at the travel agent, "they were just sleeping, lying in the dust like lizards. Shouldn't someone tell them that they've got to behave like lions?"

I think of stealing the notice, but the tourist police are watching. It seems to me like an icon of the contemporary Middle East: something inestimably precious is found under the earth, and immediately everybody on top is expected to adjust their behavior accordingly. In this case the pipeline doesn't take anything away — it brings people in and whisks them through, hermetically sealed.

In the evenings, when the cool breeze blows in from the Nile, the people of Luxor gather on the promenade along the riverfront. The steamers are brilliantly lit. They are a bit like glass cases at an aquarium: they seem to display entire cross-sections of an ecological niche. The strollers lean over the railings and watch: there's a honeymooning couple, peering nervously from behind the curtains of their cabin, people sitting at the bar, a trim old lady pumping away at a cycling machine, the waiters watching television. The best time to watch the steamers is dinnertime. The tourists file up the stairs, out of the bars, and into the dining room. They sit at their tables, and then the lights are dimmed. Suddenly "folkloristic troupes" appear, dressed in embroidered *fustans,* and break into dance. The tourists put down their silverware and watch the dancers. The strollers lean forward and watch the tourists. Egyptians watching foreigners watching Egyptians dance.

What if the strollers burst into dance? I ask myself. What then?

In the meanwhile the steamers help to keep Egypt's economy afloat. But it would take only one well-aimed blow to push it under — something that would at one stroke send large numbers of Egyptian workers back from the Gulf, put a stop to tourism, and halt the flow of ships through the Suez Canal: something just like the invasion of Kuwait, for example.

Of course, then there would be an increase in Western aid. The $7 billion debt for armaments might be canceled (as it has been). There would be no need for an economy anymore. The fantasies of military strength would become real. The whole country would be a weapon, supported by the world outside. Just like Iraq was, for so many years.

3

Fawzia was standing at the door of the new house; she saw me as I turned the corner. "Nabeel's not back yet, *ya* Amitab," she said the moment she saw me. "He's still over there, in Iraq, and here we are sitting here and waiting."

"Have you had any news from him? A letter?"

"No, nothing," she said, leading me into their house. "Nothing at all. The last time we had news of him was when Ismail came back two months ago."

"Ismail's back?"

"Praise be to God." She smiled. "He's back in good health and everything."

"Where is he?" I said, looking around. "Can you send for him?"

"Of course," she said. "He's just around the corner, sitting at home. He hasn't found a job yet — does odd jobs here and there, but most of the time he has nothing to do. I'll send for him right now."

I looked around while I waited. Something seemed to have interrupted the work on their house. When I'd last seen it, I had had the impression that it would be completed in a matter of months. But now, a year and a half later, the floor was still just a platform of packed earth and gravel. The tiles had not been laid yet, and nor had the walls been plastered or painted.

"*Hamdulillah al-salama.*" Ismail was at the door, laughing, his hand extended. "Why didn't you come?" he said as soon as the greetings were over. "You remember that day you telephoned from America? Nabeel telephoned me soon after he'd spoken to you. He just picked up the phone and called me where I was working. He told me that you'd said that you were going to visit us. We expected you for a long time. We made space in our room and thought of all the places we'd show you. But you know, Nabeel's boss, the shop owner? He got really upset — he didn't like it a bit that Nabeel had got a long-distance call from America."

"Why didn't Nabeel come back with you? What news of him?"

"He wanted to come back. In fact, he had thought that he would. But then he decided to stay for a few more months, make a little more money, so that they could finish building this house. You see how it's still half finished — all the money was used up. Prices have gone up this last year, everything costs more."

"And besides," said Fawzia, "what would Nabeel do back here? Look at Ismail — just sitting at home, no job, nothing to do . . ."

Ismail shrugged. "But still, he wanted to come back. He's been there three years. It's more than most, and it's aged him. You'd see what I mean if you saw him. He looks much older. Life's not easy out there."

"What do you mean?"

"The Iraqis, you know." He pulled a face. "They're wild — all those years of war have made them a little like animals. They come back from the army for a few days at a time, and they go wild, fighting on the streets, drinking. Egyptians never go out on the streets there at night. If some drunken Iraqis came across you, they would kill you, just like that, and nobody would even know, for they'd throw away your papers. It's happened, happens all the time. They blame us, you see. They say, 'You've taken our jobs and our money and grown rich while we're fighting and dying.'"

"What about Saddam Hussein?"

"Saddam Hussein!" He rolled his eyes. "You have to be careful when you breathe that name out there — there are spies everywhere, at every corner, listening. One word about Saddam and you're gone, dead. In those ways it's terrible out there, though of course there's the money. But still, you can't live long out there, it's impossible. Did you hear what happened during the World Cup?"

Earlier in the year Egypt had played a soccer match with Algeria, to decide which team would play in the World Cup. Egypt had won, and Egyptians everywhere had gone wild with joy. In Iraq the hundreds of thousands of Egyptians who lived packed together, all of them young, all of them male, with no families, children, wives, nothing to do but stare at their newly bought television sets — they had exploded out of their rooms and into the streets in a delirium of joy. Their football team had restored to them that self-respect that their cassette recorders and television sets had somehow failed to bring. To the Iraqis, who have never had anything like a normal political life, probably never seen crowds except at pilgrimages, the massed ranks of Egyptians must have seemed like the coming of Armageddon. They responded by attacking them on the streets, often with firearms. Well trained in war, they fell upon the jubilant unarmed crowds of Egyptian workers.

"You can't imagine what it was like," said Ismail. He had tears in his eyes. "It was then that I decided to leave. Nabeel decided to leave as well, but of course he always needed to think a long time about everything. At the last minute he thought he'd stay just a little bit longer . . ."

A little later we went to his house to watch the news on the color television he had brought back with him. It sat perched on its packing case in the center of the room, gleaming new, with chickens roosting on a nest of straw beside it. Soon the news started and we saw footage from Jordan: thousands and thousands of men, some in trousers, some in jallabeyyas, some carrying their television sets on their backs, some crying out for a drink of water, stretching all the way from the horizon to the Red Sea, standing on the beach as though waiting for the water to part.

There were more than a dozen of us in the room now. We were crowded around the television set, watching carefully, minutely, looking at every face we could see. But there was nothing to be seen except crowds. Nabeel had vanished into the pages of the epic exodus.

DANCING IN CAMBODIA

1993

O<small>N MAY 10</small>, 1906, at two in the afternoon, a French liner called the *Amiral-Kersaint* set sail from Saigon carrying a troupe of nearly a hundred classical dancers and musicians from the royal palace at Phnom Penh. The ship was bound for Marseille, where the dancers were to perform at a great colonial exhibition. It would be the first time Cambodian classical dance was performed in Europe.

Also traveling on the *Amiral-Kersaint* was the sixty-six-year-old ruler of Cambodia, King Sisowath, along with his entourage of several dozen princes, courtiers, and officials. The king, who had been crowned two years before, had often spoken of his desire to visit France, and for him the voyage was the fulfillment of a lifelong dream.

The *Amiral-Kersaint* docked in Marseille on the morning of June 11. The port was packed with curious onlookers; the city's trams had been busy since seven, transporting people to the vast, covered quay where the king and his entourage were to be received. Two brigades of gendarmes and a detachment of mounted police were deployed to keep the crowd from bursting in.

The crowd had its first brief glimpse of the dancers when the *Amiral-Kersaint* loomed out of the fog shortly after nine and drew alongside the quay. A number of young women were spotted on the bridge and on the upper decks, flitting between portholes and clutching each other in what appeared to be surprise and astonishment.

Within minutes a gangplank decorated with tricolored bunting had been thrown up to the ship. Soon the king himself appeared on deck, a good-humored, smiling man dressed in a tailcoat, a jewel-encrusted felt hat, and a dhotilike Cambodian sampot made of black silk. The king seemed alert, even jaunty, to those privileged to observe him at close range: a man of medium height, he had large, expressive eyes and a heavy-lipped mouth topped by a thin mustache.

King Sisowath walked down the gangplank with three pages following close behind him; one bore a ceremonial gold cigarette case, another a gold lamp with a lighted wick, and a third a gold spittoon in the shape of an open lotus. The king was an instant favorite with the Marseillais crowd. The port resounded with claps and cheers as he was driven away in a ceremonial landau, and he was applauded all the way to his specially appointed apartments at the city's Préfecture.

In the meanwhile, within minutes of the king's departure from the port, a section of the crowd rushed up the gangplank of the *Amiral-Kersaint* to see the dancers at first hand. For weeks now the Marseille newspapers had been full of tantalizing snippets of information: it was said that the dancers entered the palace as children and spent their lives in seclusion ever afterward; that their lives revolved entirely around the royal family; that several were the king's mistresses and had even borne him children; that some of them had never stepped out of the palace grounds until this trip to France. European travelers went to great lengths to procure invitations to see these fabulous recluses performing in the palace at Phnom Penh; now here they were in Marseille, visiting Europe for the very first time.

The dancers were on the ship's first-class deck; they seemed to be everywhere, running about, hopping, skipping, playing excitedly, feet skimming across the polished wood. The whole deck was a blur of legs, girls' legs, women's legs, "fine, elegant legs," for all the dancers were dressed in colorful sampots which ended shortly below the knee.

The onlookers were taken by surprise. They had expected perhaps a troupe of heavily veiled, voluptuous Salomes; they were not quite prepared for the lithe, athletic women they encountered on the *Amiral-Kersaint*. Nor indeed was the rest of Europe. An observer wrote later: "With their hard and close-cropped hair, their figures like those of striplings, their thin, muscular legs like those of young boys, their arms and hands like those of little girls, they seem to belong to no definite sex. They have something of the child about them, something of the young warrior of antiquity, and something of the woman."

Sitting regally among the dancers, alternately stern and indulgent, affectionate and severe, was the slight, fine-boned figure of the king's eldest daughter, Princess Soumphady. Dressed in a gold-brown sampot and a tunic of mauve silk, this redoubtable woman had an electrifying effect on the Marseillais crowd. They drank in every aspect of her appearance: her betel-stained teeth, her chestful of medals, her close-cropped hair, her gold-embroidered shoes, her diamond brooches, and her black silk stockings. Her manner, remarked one journalist, was at once haughty and childlike, her gaze direct and good-natured; she was amused by everything and nothing; she crossed her legs and clasped her shins just like a man. Indeed, except for her dress she was very much like one man in particular — the romantic and whimsical Duke of Reichstadt, *l'Aiglon,* Napoleon's tubercular son.

Suddenly, to the crowd's delight, the princess's composure dissolved. A group of local women appeared on deck, accompanied by a ten-year-old boy, and the princess and all the other dancers rushed over and crowded around them, admiring their clothes and exclaiming over the little boy.

The journalists were quick to seize this opportunity. "Do you like French women?" they asked the princess.

"Oh! Pretty, so pretty . . ." she replied.

"And their clothes, their hats?"

"Just as pretty as they are themselves."

"Would Your Highness like to wear clothes like those?"

"No!" the princess said after a moment's reflection. "No! I am not used to them and perhaps would not know how to wear them. But they are still pretty . . . oh yes . . ."

And with that she sank into what seemed to be an attitude of somber and melancholy longing.

2

I only once ever met someone who had known both Princess Soumphady and King Sisowath. Her name was Chea Samy, and she was said to be one of the greatest dancers in Cambodia, a national treasure. She was also Pol Pot's sister-in-law.

She was first pointed out to me at the School of Fine Arts in Phnom Penh, a rambling complex of buildings not far from the Wat Phnom, where the UN's twenty-thousand-strong peacekeeping force has its headquarters. It was January, only four months before countrywide elections were to be held under the auspices of UNTAC, as the UN's Transitional Authority in Cambodia is universally known. Phnom Penh had temporarily become one of the most cosmopolitan towns in the world, its streets a traffic nightmare, with UNTAC's white Land Cruisers cutting through shoals of careering scooters, mopeds, and *cyclo-pousses* like whales cruising through drifting plankton.

The School of Fine Arts was hidden from this multinational traffic by piles of uncleared refuse and a string of shacks and shanties. Its cavernous halls and half-finished classrooms were oddly self-contained, their atmosphere the self-sustaining, honeycomb bustle of a huge television studio.

I had only recently arrived in Phnom Penh when I first met Chea Samy. She was sitting on a bench in the school's vast training hall — a small woman with the kind of poise that goes with the confidence of great beauty. She was dressed in an ankle-length skirt, and her gray hair was cut short. She was presiding over a class of about forty boys and girls, watching them go through their exercises, her gentle, rounded face tense with concentration. Occasionally she would spring off the bench and bend back a dancer's arm or push in a waist, working as a sculptor does, by touch, molding their limbs like clay.

At the time I had no idea whether Chea Samy had known Princess Soumphady or not. I had become curious about the princess and her father, King Sisowath, after learning of their journey to Europe in 1906, and I wanted to know more about them.

Chea Samy's eyes widened when I asked her about Princess Soumphady at the end of her class. She looked from me to the student who was interpreting for us as though she couldn't quite believe she had heard the name right. I reassured her: yes, I really did mean Princess Soumphady, Princess Sisowath Soumphady.

She smiled in the indulgent, misty way in which people recall a favorite aunt. Yes, of course she had known Princess Soumphady, she said. As a little girl, when she first went into the palace to learn dance, it was Princess Soumphady who had been in charge of the dancers: for a while the princess had brought her up . . .

The second time I met Chea Samy was at her house. She lives a few miles from Pochentong airport, on Phnom Penh's rapidly expanding frontier, in an area that is largely farmland, with a few houses strung along a dirt road. The friend whom I had persuaded to come along with me to translate took an immediate dislike to the place. It was already late afternoon, and she did not relish the thought of driving back on those roads in the dark.

My friend, Molyka, was a midlevel civil servant, a poised, attractive woman in her early thirties, painfully soft-spoken, in the Khmer way. She had spent a short while studying in Australia on a government scholarship, and spoke English with a better feeling for nuance and idiom than any of the professional interpreters I had met. If I was to visit Chea Samy, I had decided, it would be with her. But Molyka proved hard to persuade: she had become frightened of venturing out of the center of the city.

Not long before she had been driving with a friend of hers, the wife of an UNTAC official, when her car was stopped at a busy roundabout by a couple of soldiers. They were wearing the uniform of the "State of Cambodia," the faction that currently governs most of the country. "I work for the government too," she told them, "in an important ministry." They ignored her; they wanted money. She didn't have much, only a couple of thousand riels. They asked for cigarettes; she didn't have any. They told her to get out of the car and accompany them into a building. They were about to take her away when her friend interceded. They let her go eventually: they left UN people alone on the whole. But as she drove away they shouted after her, "We're going to be looking out for you — you won't always have an Untác in the car."

Molyka was scared, and she had reason to be. The government's underpaid (often unpaid) soldiers and policemen were increasingly prone to banditry and bouts of inexplicable violence. Not long before, I had gone to visit a hospital in an area where there were frequent hostilities between State troops and the Khmer Rouge. I had expected that the patients in the casualty ward would be principally victims of mines and Khmer Rouge shellfire. Instead I found a group of half a dozen women, some with children, lying on grimy mats, their faces and bodies pitted and torn with black shrapnel wounds. They had been traveling in a pickup truck to sell vegetables at a nearby market when they were stopped by a couple of State soldiers. The soldiers asked for money; the women handed out some, but the soldiers wanted more. The women had no more to give and told them so. The soldiers let the truck pass but stopped it again that evening, on its way back. They didn't ask for anything this time; they simply detonated a fragmentation mine.

Soon afterward I was traveling in a taxi with four Cambodians along a dusty, potholed road in a sparsely inhabited region in the northwest of the country. I had dozed off in the front seat when I was woken by the rattle of gunfire. I looked up and saw a State soldier standing in the middle of the dirt road, directly ahead. He was in his teens, like most uniformed Cambodians; he was wearing round, wire-rimmed sunglasses, and his pelvis was thrust out MTV-style. But instead of a guitar he had an AK-47 in his hands, and he was spraying the ground in front of us with bullets, creating a delicate tracery of dust.

The taxi jolted to a halt; the driver thrust an arm out of the window and waved his wallet. The soldier did not seem to notice; he was grinning and swaying, probably drunk. But when I sat up in the front seat, the barrel of his gun rose slowly until it was pointing directly at my forehead. Looking into the unblinking eye of that AK-47, unaccountably, two slogans flashed through my mind; they were scrawled all over the walls of Calcutta when I was the same age as that soldier. One was "Power comes from the barrel of a gun," and the other "You can't make an omelet without breaking eggs." It turned out he had only the first in mind.

Molyka had heard stories like these, but living in Phnom Penh, working as a civil servant, she had been relatively sheltered until that day when her car was stopped. The incident frightened her in ways she couldn't quite articulate; it reawakened a host of long-dormant fears. Molyka was only thirteen in 1975, when the Khmer Rouge took Phnom Penh. She was evacuated with her whole extended family, fourteen people in all, to a labor camp in the province of Kompong Thom. A few months later she was separated from the others and sent to work in a fishing village on Cambodia's immense freshwater lake, the Tonlé Sap. For the next three years she worked as a servant and nursemaid for a family of fisherfolk.

She saw her parents only once in that time. One day she was sent to a village near Kompong Thom with a group of girls. While sitting by the roadside, quite by chance, she happened to look up from her basket of fish and saw her mother walking toward her. Her first instinct was to turn away; she thought it was a dream. Every detail matched those of her most frequently recurring dream: the parched countryside, the ragged palms, her mother coming out of the red dust of the road, walking straight toward her . . .

She didn't see her mother again until 1979, when she came back to Phnom Penh after the Vietnamese invasion. She managed to locate her as well as two of her brothers after months of searching. Of the fourteen people who had walked out of her house three and a half years before, ten were dead, including her father, two brothers, and a sister. Her mother had become an abject, terrified creature after her father was called away into the fields one night, never to return. One of her brothers was too young to work; the other had willed himself into a state of guilt-stricken paralysis after revealing their father's identity to the Khmer Rouge in a moment of inattention — he now held himself responsible for his father's death.

Their family was from the social group that was hardest hit by the revolution, the urban middle classes. City people by definition, they were herded into rural work camps. The institutions and forms of knowledge that sustained them were destroyed — the judicial system was dismantled, the practice of formal medicine was discontinued, schools and colleges were shut down, banks and credit were done away with; indeed, the very institution of money was abolished. Cambodia's was not a civil war in the same sense as Somalia's or the former Yugoslavia's, fought over the fetishism of small differences: it was a war on history itself, an experiment in the reinvention of society. No regime in history had ever before made so systematic and sustained an attack on the middle class. Yet if the experiment was proof of anything at all, it was ultimately of the indestructibility of the middle class, of its extraordinary tenacity and resilience, its capacity to preserve its forms of knowledge and expression through the most extreme kinds of adversity.

Molyka was only seventeen then, but she was the one who had to cope, because no one else in the family could. She took a job in the army and put herself and her brothers through school and college; later she acquired a house and a car; she adopted a child, and, like so many people in Phnom Penh, she took in and supported about half a dozen complete strangers. In one way or another she was responsible for supporting a dozen lives.

Yet now Molyka, who at the age of thirty-one had already lived through several lifetimes, was afraid of driving into the outskirts of the city. Over the past year the outlines of the life she had put together were beginning to look frayed. Paradoxically, at precisely the moment when the world had ordained peace and democracy for Cambodia, uncertainty had reached its peak within the country. Nobody knew what was going to happen after the UN-sponsored elections were held, who would come to power and what they would do once they did. Molyka's colleagues had all become desperate to make some provision for the future — by buying, stealing, selling whatever was at hand. Those two soldiers who had stopped her car were no exception. Everyone she knew was a little like that now — ministers, bureaucrats, policemen, they were all people who saw themselves faced with yet another beginning.

Now Molyka was driving out to meet Pol Pot's brother and sister-in-law, relatives of a man whose name was indelibly associated with the deaths of her own father and nine other members of her family. She had gasped in disbelief when I first asked her to accompany me. To her, as to most people in Cambodia, the name Pol Pot was an abstraction; it referred to a time, an epoch, an organization, a form of terror — it was almost impossible to associate it with a mere human being, one who had brothers, relatives, sisters-in-law. But she was curious too, and in the end, overcoming her fear of the neighborhood, she drove me out in her own car, into the newly colonized farmland near Pochentong airport.

The house, when we found it, proved to be a comfortable wooden structure built in the traditional Khmer style, with its details picked out in bright blue. Like all such houses it was supported on stilts, and as we walked in, a figure detached itself from the shadows beneath the house and came toward us: a tall, vigorous-looking man dressed in a sarong. He had a broad, pleasant face and short, spiky gray hair. The resemblance to Pol Pot was startling.

I glanced at Molyka; she bowed, joining her hands, as he welcomed us in, and they exchanged a few friendly words of greeting. His wife was waiting upstairs, he said, and led us up a wooden staircase to a large, airy room with a few photographs on the bare walls: portraits of relatives and ancestors, of the kind that hang in every Khmer house. Chea Samy was sitting on a couch at the far end of the room. She waved us in and her husband took his leave of us, smiling, hands folded.

"I wanted to attack him when I first saw him," Molyka told me later. "But then I thought, it's not his fault. What has he ever done to me?"

3

Chea Samy was taken into the palace in Phnom Penh in 1925, as a child of six, to begin her training in classical dance. She was chosen after an audition in which thousands of children participated. Her parents were delighted: dance was one of the few means by which a commoner could gain entry to the palace in those days, and to have a child accepted often meant preferment for the whole family.

King Sisowath was in his eighties when she went into the palace. He had spent most of his life waiting in the wings, wearing the pinched footwear of a crown prince while his half-brother Norodom ruled center stage. The two princes held dramatically opposed political views: Norodom was bitterly opposed to the French, while Sisowath was a passionate Francophile. It was because of French support that Sisowath was eventually able to succeed to the throne, in preference to his half-brother's innumerable sons.

Something of an eccentric all his life, King Sisowath kept no fixed hours and spent a good deal of his time smoking opium with his sons and advisers. During his visit to France, the authorities even improvised a small opium den in his apartments at the Préfecture in Marseille. "Voilà!" cried the newspapers. "An opium den in the Préfecture! There's no justice left!" But it was the French who kept the king supplied with opium in Cambodia, and they could hardly do otherwise when he was a state guest in France.

By the time Chea Samy entered the palace in 1925, King Sisowath's behavior had become erratic in the extreme. He would wander nearly naked around the grounds of the palace, wearing nothing but a *kramar*, a length of checkered cloth, knotted loosely around his waist. It was Princess Soumphady who was the central figure in the lives of the children of the dance troupe: she was a surrogate mother who tempered the rigors of their training with a good deal of kindly indulgence, making sure they were well fed and clothed.

On King Sisowath's death in 1927, his son Monivong succeeded to the throne, and soon the regime in the palace underwent a change. The new king's favorite mistress was a talented dancer called Luk Khun Meak, and she now gradually took over Princess Soumphady's role as "the lady in charge of the women." Meak made use of her influence to introduce several members of her family into the palace. Among them were some relatives from a small village in the province of Kompong Thom. One of them — later to become Chea Samy's husband — took a job as a clerk at the palace. He in turn brought two of his brothers to Phnom Penh. The youngest was a boy of six called Saloth Sar, who was later to take the *nom de guerre* Pol Pot.

Chea Samy made a respectful gesture at a picture on the wall behind her, and I looked up to find myself transfixed by Luk Khun Meak's stern, frowning gaze. "She was killed by Pol Pot," said Chea Samy, using the generic phrase with which Cambodians refer to the deaths of that time. The distinguished old dancer, mistress of King Monivong, died of starvation after the revolution. One of her daughters was apprehended by the Khmer Rouge while trying to buy rice with a little bit of gold. Her breasts were sliced off and she was left to bleed to death.

"What was Pol Pot like as a boy?" I asked, inevitably.

Chea Samy hesitated for a moment. It was easy to see that she had often been asked the question before and had thought about it at some length. "He was a very good boy," she said at last, emphatically. "In all the years he lived with me, he never gave me any trouble at all."

Then, with a despairing gesture, she said, "I have been married to his brother for fifty years now, and I can tell you that my husband is a good man, a kind man. He doesn't drink, doesn't smoke, has never made trouble between friends, never hit his nephews, never made difficulties for his children . . ."

She gave up; her hands flipped over in a flutter of bewilderment and fell limp into her lap.

The young Saloth Sar's palace connections ensured places for him at some of the country's better-known schools. Then, in 1949, he was awarded a scholarship to study electronics in Paris. When he returned to Cambodia three years later, he began working in secret for the Indochina Communist Party. Neither Chea Samy nor her husband saw much of him, and he told them very little of what he was doing. Then, in 1963, he disappeared; they learned later that he had fled into the jungle along with several well-known leftists and Communists. That was the last they heard of Saloth Sar.

In 1975, when the Khmer Rouge seized power, Chea Samy and her husband were evacuated like everyone else. They were sent off to a village of "old people," longtime Khmer Rouge sympathizers, and along with all the other "new people" were made to work in the rice fields. For the next couple of years there was a complete news blackout and they knew nothing of what had happened and who had come to power: it was a part of the Khmer Rouge's mechanics of terror to deprive the population of knowledge. They first began to hear the words "Pol Pot" in 1978, when the regime tried to create a personality cult around its leader in an attempt to stave off imminent collapse.

Chea Samy was working in a communal kitchen at the time, cooking and washing dishes. Late that year some party workers stuck a poster on the walls of the kitchen: they said it was a picture of their leader, Pol Pot. She knew who it was the moment she set eyes on the picture.

That was how she discovered that the leader of Angkar, the terrifying, inscrutable "Organization" that ruled over their lives, was none other than little Saloth Sar.

4

A few months later, in January 1979, the Vietnamese "broke" Cambodia, as the Khmer phrase has it, and the regime collapsed. Shortly afterward Chea Samy and her husband, like all the other evacuees, began to drift out of the villages they had been imprisoned in. Carrying nothing but a few cupfuls of dry rice, barefoot, half starved, and dressed in rags, they began to find their way back toward the places they had once known, where they had once had friends and relatives.

Walking down the dusty country roads, encountering others like themselves, the bands of "new people" slowly began to rediscover the exhilaration of speech. For more than three years now they had not been able to say a word to anyone with confidence, not even their own children. Many of them had reinvented their lives in order to protect themselves from the obsessive biographical curiosity of Angkar's cadres. Now, talking on the roads, they slowly began to shed their assumed personae; they began to mine their memories for information about the people they had met and heard of over the past few years, the names of the living and the dead.

It was the strangest of times.

The American Quaker Eva Mysliwiec arrived in the country in 1981; she was one of the first foreign relief workers to come to Cambodia and is now a legend in Phnom Penh. Some of her most vivid memories of that period are of the volcanic outbursts of speech that erupted everywhere at unexpected moments. Friends and acquaintances would suddenly begin to describe what they had lived through and seen, what had happened to them and their families and how they had managed to survive. Often people would wake up in the morning looking worse than they had the night before: they would see things in their dreams, all those things they had tried to put out of their minds when they were happening because they would have gone mad if they'd stopped to think about them — a brother called away in the dark, an infant battered against a tree, children starving to death. When you saw them in the morning and asked what had happened at night, what was the matter, they would make a circular gesture, as though the past had been unfolding before them like a turning reel, and they would say simply, "Camera."

Eventually, after weeks of wandering, Chea Samy and her husband reached the western outskirts of Phnom Penh. There, one day, entirely by accident, she ran into a girl who had studied dance with her before the revolution. The girl cried, "Teacher! Where have you been? They've been looking for you everywhere."

There was no real administration in those days. Many of the resistance leaders who had come back to Cambodia with the Vietnamese had never held administrative positions before; for the most part they were breakaway members of the Khmer Rouge who had been opposed to the policies of Pol Pot and his group. They had to learn on the job when they returned, and for a long time there was nothing like a real government in Cambodia. The country was like a shattered slate: before you could think of drawing lines on it, you had to find the pieces and fit them together.

But already the fledgling Ministry of Culture had launched an effort to locate the classical dancers and teachers who had survived. Its officials were overjoyed to find Chea Samy. They quickly arranged for her to travel through the country to look for other teachers and for young people with talent and potential.

"It was very difficult," said Chea Samy. "I did not know where to go, where to start. Most of the teachers had been killed or maimed, and the others were in no state to begin teaching again. Anyway, there was no one to teach. So many of the children were orphans, half starved. They had no idea of dance — they had never seen Khmer dance. It seemed impossible; there was no place to begin."

Her voice was quiet and matter-of-fact, but there was a quality of muted exhilaration in it too. I recognized that note at once, for I had heard it before: in Molyka's voice, for example, when she spoke of the first years after the Pol Pot time, when slowly, patiently, she had picked through the rubble around her, building a life for herself and her family. I was to hear it again and again in Cambodia, most often in the voices of women. They had lived through an experience very nearly unique in human history: they had found themselves adrift in the ruins of a society that had collapsed into a formless heap, with its scaffolding systematically dismantled, picked apart with the tools of a murderously rational form of social science. At a time when there was widespread fear and uncertainty about the intentions of the Vietnamese, they had had to start from the beginning, literally, like rag pickers, piecing their families, their homes, their lives together from the little that was left.

Like everyone around her, Chea Samy too had started all over again — at the age of sixty, with her health shattered by the years of famine and hard labor. Working with quiet, dogged persistence, she and a handful of other dancers and musicians slowly brought together a ragged, half-starved bunch of orphans and castaways, and with the discipline of their long, rigorous years of training they began to resurrect the art that Princess Soumphady and Luk Khun Meak had passed on to them in that long-ago world when King Sisowath reigned. Out of the ruins around them they began to forge the means of denying Pol Pot his victory.

5

Everywhere he went on his tour of France, King Sisowath was accompanied by his palace minister, an official who bore the simple name of Thiounn (pronounced *Chunn*). For all his Francophilia, King Sisowath spoke no French, and it was Minister Thiounn who served as his interpreter.

Minister Thiounn was widely acknowledged to be one of the most remarkable men in Cambodia; his career was without precedent in the aristocratic, rigidly hierarchical world of Cambodian officialdom. Starting as an interpreter for the French, at the age of nineteen, he had overcome the twin disadvantages of modest birth and a mixed Khmer-Vietnamese ancestry to become the most powerful official at the court of Phnom Penh: the minister simultaneously of finance, fine arts, and palace affairs.

This spectacular rise owed a great deal to the French, to whom he had been of considerable assistance in their decades-long struggle with Cambodia's ruling family. His role had earned him the bitter contempt of certain members of the royal family, and a famous prince had even denounced the "boy interpreter" as a French collaborator. But with French dominance in Cambodia already assured, there was little that any Cambodian prince could do to check the growing influence of Minister Thiounn. Norodom Sihanouk, King Sisowath's great-nephew, spent several of his early years on the throne smarting under Minister Thiounn's tutelage: he was to describe him later as a "veritable little king," "as powerful as the French résidents-supérieurs of the period."

The trip to France was to become something of a personal triumph for Minister Thiounn, earning him compliments from a number of French ministers and politicians. But it also served a more practical function, for traveling on the *Amiral-Kersaint,* along with the dancers and the rest of the royal entourage, was the minister's son, Thiounn Hol. In the course of his stay in France, the minister succeeded in entering him as a student in the École Coloniale. He was the only Cambodian commoner to be accepted; the other three were all princes of the royal family.

Not unpredictably, the minister's son proved to be a far better student than the princelings and went on to become the first Cambodian to earn university qualifications in France. Later, the minister's grandsons too, scions of what was by then the second most powerful family in Cambodia, were to make the journey to France.

One of those grandsons, Thiounn Mumm, earned considerable distinction as a student in Paris, acquiring a doctorate in applied science and becoming the first Cambodian to graduate from the exalted École Polytechnique. In the process he also became a central figure within the small circle of Cambodians in France. The story goes that he made a point of befriending every student from his country and even went to the airport to receive new-comers.

Thiounn Mumm was, in other words, part mentor, part older brother, and part leader, a figure immediately recognizable to any-one who has ever inhabited the turbulent limbo of the Asian or African student in Europe — that curious circumstance of social dislocation and emotional turmoil that for more than a century now has provided the site for some of the globe's most explosive political encounters. The peculiar conditions of that situation, part exile and part a process of accession to power, have allowed many strong and gifted personalities to have a powerful impact on their countries through their influence on their student contempo-raries. Thiounn Mumm's was thus a role with a long colonial ge-nealogy. And he brought to it an authority beyond that of his own talents and forceful personality, for he was also a member of a po-litical dynasty — the Cambodian equivalent of the Nehrus or the Bhuttos.

Among Thiounn Mumm's many protégés was the young Pol Pot, then still known as Saloth Sar. It is generally believed that it was Thiounn Mumm who was responsible for his induction into the French Communist Party in 1952. Those Parisian loyalties have proved unshakeable: Thiounn Mumm and two of his brothers have been members of Pol Pot's innermost clique ever since.

That this ultraradical clique should be so intimately linked with the palace and with colonial officialdom is not particularly a mat-ter of surprise in Cambodia. "Revolutions and coups d'état always start in the courtyards of the palace," a well-known political figure in Phnom Penh told me. "It's the people within who realize that the king is ordinary, while everyone else takes him for a god."

I heard the matter stated even more bluntly by someone whose family had once known the Thiounns well. "Ever since their grand-father's time," he said, "they wanted to be king."

Be that as it may, it is certainly possible that the Thiounns, with their peculiarly ambiguous relationship with the Cambodian mon-archy, were responsible, as the historian Ben Kiernan has suggested, for the powerful strain of "national and racial grandiosity" in the ideology of Pol Pot's clique. That strain has eventually proved dominant: the Khmer Rouge's program now consists largely of an undisguisedly racist nationalism whose principal targets, for the time being, are Vietnam and Cambodia's own Vietnamese minority.

A recent defector, describing his political training with the Khmer Rouge, told UN officials that "as far as the Vietnamese are concerned, whenever we meet them we must kill them, whether they are militaries or civilians, because they are not ordinary civilians but soldiers disguised as civilians. We must kill them, whether they are men, women, or children, there is no distinction, they are enemies. Children are not militaries but if they are born or grow up in Cambodia, when they will be adult, they will consider Cambodian land as theirs. So we make no distinction. As to women, they give birth to Vietnamese children."

Later, shortly before the elections, there was a sudden enlargement of the Khmer Rouge's racist vocabulary. No matter that its own guerrillas had been trained by British military units in the not-so-distant past, it began inciting violence against "white-skinned, point-nosed UNTAC soldiers."

6

The more I learned of Pol Pot's journey to France, and of the other journeys that had preceded it, the more curious I became about his origins. One day, late in January, I decided to go looking for his ancestral village in the province of Kompong Thom.

Kompong Thom has great military importance, for it straddles the vital middle section of Cambodia; the town of the same name lies at the strategic heart of the country. It is very small: a string of houses that grows suddenly into a bullet-riddled marketplace, a school, a hospital, a few roads that extend all of a hundred yards, a bridge across the Sen River, a tall, freshly painted wat, a few outcrops of blue-signposted UNTAC land, and then the countryside again, flat and dusty, clumps of palms leaning raggedly over the earth, fading into the horizon in a dull gray-green patina, like mold upon a copper tray.

Two of the country's most important roadways intersect to the north of the little town. One of them leads directly to Thailand and has long been one of the most hotly contested highways in Cambodia, for the Khmer Rouge controls large chunks of territory on either side of it. The State troops who are posted along the road are under constant pressure, and there are daily exchanges of shells and gunfire.

The point where the two roads meet is guarded by an old army encampment, now controlled by the State. A tract of heavily mined ground runs along its outer perimeter; the minefield is reputed to have been laid by the State itself, partly to keep the Khmer Rouge out, but also to keep its own none-too-willing soldiers in.

Here, in this strategic hub, this center of centers, looking for Pol Pot's ancestral home, inevitably I came across someone from mine. He was a Bangladeshi sergeant, a large, friendly man with a bushy mustache. We had an ancestral district in common in Bangladesh, and the unexpectedness of this discovery — at the edge of a Cambodian minefield — linked us immediately in a ridiculously intimate kind of bonhomie.

The sergeant and his colleagues were teaching a group of Cambodian soldiers professional de-mining techniques. They were themselves trained sappers and engineers, but as it happened, none of them had ever seen or worked in a minefield that had been laid with intent to kill, so to speak. For their Cambodian charges, on the other hand, mines were a commonplace hazard of everyday life, like snakes or spiders.

This irony was not lost on the Bangladeshi sergeant. "They think nothing of laying mines," he said in trenchant Bengali. "They scatter them about like popped rice. Often they mine their own doorstep before going to bed, to keep thieves out. They mine their cars, their television sets, even their vegetable patches. They don't care who gets killed. Life really has no value here."

He shook his head in perplexity, looking at his young Cambodian charges. They were working in teams of two on the mine-field, an expanse of scrub and grass that had been divided into narrow strips with tape. The teams were inching along their strips, one man scanning the ground ahead with a mine detector, the other lying flat, armed with a probe and trowel, ready to dig for mines. By this slow, painstaking method, the team had cleared a couple of acres in a month's time. This was considered good progress, and the sergeant had reason to be pleased. Generally speaking, Bangladeshi military units have an enviable reputation in Cambodia and are said to do thoughtful developmental work wherever they are posted, in addition to their duties.

In the course of their work, the sergeant and his colleagues had become friends with several Cambodian members of their team. But the better they got to know them and the better they liked them, the more feckless they seemed, the more hopeless the country's situation appeared. This despite the fact that Cambodians in general have a standard of living that would be considered envi-able by most people in Bangladesh or India; despite the fact that Kompong Thom, for all that it has been on the battlefront for decades, is neater and better ordered than any provincial town in the subcontinent. Despite the fact that the sergeant was himself from a country that had suffered the ravages of a bloody civil war in the early seventies.

"They're working hard here because they're getting paid in dollars," the sergeant said. "For them it's all dollars, dollars, dollars. Sometimes, at the end of the day, we have to hand out a cou-ple of dollars from our own pockets to get them to finish the day's work." He laughed. "It's their own country, and we have to pay them to make it safe. What I wonder is, what will they do when we're gone?"

I told him what a longtime foreign resident of Phnom Penh had said to me: that Cambodia was actually only fifteen years old; that it had managed remarkably well, considering it had been built up almost from scratch after the fall of the Pol Pot regime in 1979, and that in a situation of near-complete international isolation.

Europe and Japan had received massive amounts of aid after the Second World War, but Cambodia, which had been subjected to one of the heaviest bombings in the history of war, had got virtually nothing. Yet Cambodians had made do with what they had.

But the sergeant was looking for large-scale proofs of progress — roads, a functioning postal system, Projects, Schemes, Plans — and their lack rendered meaningless those tiny, cumulative efforts by which individuals and families reclaim their lives — a shutter repaired, a class taught, a palm tree tended — which are no longer noticeable once they are done, since they sink into the order of normalcy, where they belong, and cease to be acts of affirmation and hope. He was the smallest of cogs in the vast machinery of the UN, but his vision of the country, no less than that of the international bureaucrats and experts in Phnom Penh, was organized around his part in saving it from itself.

"What Cambodians are good at is destruction," he said. "They know nothing about building — about putting things up and carrying on."

He waved good-naturedly at the Cambodians, and they waved back, bobbing their heads, smiling, and bowing. Both sides were working hard at their jobs, the expert and the amateur, the feckless and the responsible: doughty rescuer and hapless rescued were taking their jobs equally seriously.

Later I got a ride with an Austrian colonel in an UNTAC car, a white, air-conditioned Land Cruiser. He was a small, dapper, extremely loquacious man. He'd spent most of his working life on UN missions; he rated the Cambodia operation well above Lebanon, a little below Cyprus. But he was still planning to get out of Kompong Thom — too much tension, too many shells overhead.

We stopped to pick up a Russian colonel, a huge man, pearshaped, like a belly dancer gone to seed. His khaki shorts looked like bikini briefs on his gigantic legs.

The Russian reached for the radio, which was tuned to the UNTAC radio station, and turned it off. "Yap, yap, yap, yap," he said, glaring at the Austrian.

The Austrian shrank back, but plunged into battle a couple of minutes later, mustache bristling. "I like that station," he cried. His voice was high, terrier-like. "I like it, I want to listen to it."

The Russian jammed a tree stump of a knee across the radio and looked casually out the window. The Austrian snatched his hand back, but his defeat was only temporary. He turned to look out the window and sighed. "Such a beautiful country," he said, "such wonderful people — always smiling. But why are they always at war? Why can't they get on with building their country?"

He grinned at the Russian. "I suppose we'll be going to Russia next — eh, my friend?"

The Russian sprang bolt upright, sputtering. The veins on his temples bulged. "No," he barked, "no, not Russia, never, maybe Ukraine . . . But not Russia, never."

Then a truck appeared on the road ahead of us, gradually taking shape within a cloud of dust. It was packed with people, many of whom seemed to be wearing olive-green fatigues. A man was leaning over the driver's cabin, looking directly at us: he had an unusual-looking cap on his head. It was green and looked Chinese, like something a Khmer Rouge guerrilla might wear. The Russian and the Austrian were suddenly on the edge of their seats, straining forward.

The truck went past in a flurry of dust, the people in it waved, and we got a good look at the cap. There was lettering on it; it said "Windy City Motel."

7

I got blank stares when I asked where Pol Pot's village was. Pol Pot had villages on either side of Route 12, people said, dozens of them; nobody could get to them, they were in the forest, surrounded by minefields. I might as well have asked where the State of Cambodia was. Nor did it help to ask about Saloth Sar; nobody seemed ever to have heard of that name.

One of the people I asked, a young Cambodian called Sros,

offered to help, although he was just as puzzled by the question as everybody else. He worked for a relief agency and had spent a lot of time in Kompong Thom. He had never heard anybody mention Pol Pot's village and would have been skeptical if he had. But I persuaded him that Pol Pot was really called Saloth Sar and had been born near the town; I'd forgotten the name of the village, but I had seen it mentioned in books and knew it was close by.

He was intrigued. He borrowed a scooter and we drove down the main street in Kompong Thom, stopping passersby and asking respectfully, "Bong, do you know where Pol Pot's village is?"

They looked at us in disbelief and hurried away: either they didn't know or they weren't saying. Then Sros stopped to ask a local district official, a bowed, earnest-looking man with a twitch that ran all the way down the right side of his face. The moment I saw him, I was sure he would know. He did. He lowered his voice and whispered quickly into Sros's ear. The village was called Sbauv, and to get to it we had to go past the hospital and follow the dirt road along the River Sen. He stopped to look over his shoulder and pointed down the road.

There was perhaps an hour of sunlight left, and it wasn't safe to be out after dark. But Sros was undeterred; the thought that we were near Pol Pot's birthplace had a galvanic effect on him. He was determined to get there as soon as possible.

He had spent almost his entire adult life behind barbed wire, one and a half miles of it, in a refugee camp on the Thai border. He had entered it at the age of thirteen and had come to manhood circling around and around the perimeter, month after month, year after year, waiting to see who got out, who got a visa, who went mad, who got raped, who got shot by the Thai guards. He was twenty-five now, diminutive but wiry, very slight of build. He had converted to Christianity at the camp, and there was an earnestness behind his ready smile and easygoing manners that hinted at a deeply felt piety.

Sros was too young to recall much of the "Pol Pot time," but he remembered vividly his journey to the Thai border with his parents. They left in 1982, three years after the Vietnamese invasion. Things were hard where they were, and they'd heard from Western radio broadcasts that there were camps on the border where they would be looked after and fed.

Things hadn't turned out quite as they had imagined. They ended up in a camp run by a conservative Cambodian political faction, a kind of living hell. But they bribed a "guide" to get them across to a UN-run camp, Khao I Dang, where the conditions were better. Sros went to school and learned English, and after years of waiting, fruitlessly, for a visa to the West, he took the plunge and crossed over into Cambodia. That was a year ago. With his education and his knowledge of English he had found a job without difficulty, but he was still keeping his name on the rosters of the UN High Commission for Refugees.

"My father says to me, there will be peace in your lifetime and you will be happy," he told me. "My grandfather used to tell my father the same thing, and now I say the same thing to my nephews and nieces. It's always the same."

We left Kompong Thom behind almost before we knew it. A dirt road snaked away from the edge of the city, shaded by trees and clumps of bamboo. The road was an estuary of deep red dust: the wheels of the ox carts that came rumbling toward us churned up crimson waves that billowed outward and up into the sky. The dust hung above the road far into the distance, like spray above a rocky coastline, glowing red in the sunset.

Flanking the road on one side were shanties and small dwellings, the poorest I had yet seen in Cambodia, some of them no more than frames stuck into the ground and covered with plaited palm leaves. Even the larger houses seemed little more than shanties on stilts. On the other side of the road the ground dropped away sharply to the River Sen: a shrunken stream now, in the dry season, flowing sluggishly along at the bottom of its steep-sided channel.

It was impossible to tell where one village ended and another began. We stopped to ask a couple of times, the last time at a stall where a woman was selling cigarettes and fruit. She pointed over her shoulder: one of Pol Pot's brothers lived in the house behind the stall, she said, and another in a palm-thatch shanty in the adjacent yard.

We drove into the yard and looked up at the house. It was large compared to those around it, a typical wooden Khmer house, on stilts, with chickens roosting underneath and clothes drying between the pillars. It had clearly seen much better days and was badly in need of repairs.

The decaying house and the dilapidated, palm-thatched shanty in the yard took me by surprise. I remembered having read that Pol Pot's father was a well-to-do farmer, and I had expected something less humble. Sros was even more surprised; perhaps he had assumed that the relatives of politicians always got rich, one way or another. There was an augury of something unfamiliar here — a man of power who had done nothing to help his own kin. It was a reminder that we were confronting a phenomenon that was completely at odds with quotidian expectation.

Then an elderly woman with close-cropped white hair appeared on the veranda of the house. Sros said a few words to her, and she immediately invited us up. Greeting us with folded hands, she asked us to seat ourselves on a mat while she went inside to find her husband. Like many Khmer dwellings, the house was sparsely furnished, the walls bare except for a few religious pictures and images of the Buddha.

The woman returned followed by a tall, gaunt man dressed in a faded sarong. He did not look as much like Pol Pot as the brother I had met briefly in Phnom Penh, but the resemblance was still unmistakable.

His name was Loth Sieri, he said, seating himself beside us, and he was the second oldest of the brothers. Saloth Sar had gone away to Phnom Penh while he was still quite young, and after that they had not seen very much of him. He had gone from school to college in Phnom Penh, and then finally to Paris. He smiled ruefully. "It was the knowledge he got in Paris that made him what he is," he said.

Saloth Sar had visited them a few times after returning to Cambodia, but then he had disappeared and they had never seen him again. It was more than twenty years now since he, Loth Sieri, had set eyes on him. They had been treated no differently from anyone else during the Pol Pot time; they had not had the remotest idea that Pol Pot was their brother Sar, born in their house. They found out only afterward.

Was Saloth Sar born in that very house? I asked. Yes, they said, in the room beside us, right next to the veranda.

When he came back from France, I asked, had he ever talked about his life in Paris? What he'd done, who his friends were, what the city was like?

At that moment, with cows lowing in the gathering darkness, the journey to Paris from that village on the Sen River seemed an extraordinary odyssey. I found myself very curious to know how Loth Sieri and his brothers had imagined Paris, and their own brother in it. But no. The old man shook his head: Saloth Sar had never talked about France after he came back. Maybe he had shown them some pictures — he couldn't recall.

I remembered from David Chandler's biography that Pol Pot was very well read as a young man and knew large tracts of Rimbaud and Verlaine by heart. But I was not surprised, somehow, to discover that he had never allowed his family the privilege of imagining.

Just before getting up, I asked if Loth Sieri remembered his relative the dancer Luk Khun Meak, who had first introduced his family into the royal palace. He nodded, and I asked, "Did you ever see her dance?"

He smiled and shook his head; no, he had never seen any royal dancing, except in pictures.

It was almost dark now; somewhere in the north, near the minefield, there was the sound of gunfire. We got up to go, and the whole family walked down with us. After I had said goodbye and was about to climb onto the scooter, Sros whispered in my ear that it might be a good idea to give the old man some money. I had not thought of it; I took some money out of my pocket and put it in his hands.

He made a gesture of acknowledgment, and as we were about to leave he said a few words to Sros.

"What did he say?" I asked Sros when we were back on the road.

Shouting above the wind, Sros said, "He asked me, 'Do you think there will be peace now?'"

"And what did you tell him?" I said.

"I told him, 'I wish I could say yes.'"

8

On July 10, 1906, one month after their arrival in France, the dancers performed at a reception given by the minister of colonies in the Bois du Boulogne in Paris. "Never has there been a more brilliant Parisian fête," said Le Figaro, "nor one with such novel charm." Invitations were much sought after, and on the night of the performance cars and illuminated carriages invaded the park like an "army of fireflies."

While the performance was in progress, a correspondent spotted the most celebrated Parisian of all in the audience, the bearded, Mosaic figure of "the great Rodin . . . [going] into ecstasies over the little virgins of Phnom Penh, whose immaterial silhouettes he drew with infinite love."

Rodin, now, at the age of sixty-six, France's acknowledged apostle of the arts, fell immediately captive: in Princess Soumphady's young charges he discovered the infancy of Europe. "These Cambodians have shown us everything that antiquity could have contained," he wrote soon afterward. "It is impossible to think of anyone wearing human nature to such perfection; except them and the Greeks."

Two days after the performance Rodin presented himself at the dancers' Paris lodgings, at the Avenue Malakoff, with a sketchbook under his arm. The dancers were packing their belongings in preparation for their return to Marseille, but Rodin was admitted to the grounds of the mansion and given leave to do what he pleased. He executed several celebrated sketches that day, including a few of King Sisowath.

By the end of the day the artist was so smitten with the dancers that he accompanied them to the station, bought a ticket, and traveled to Marseille on the same train. He had packed neither clothes nor materials, and according to one account, upon arriving in Marseille he found that he was out of paper and had to buy brown paper bags from a grocery store.

Over the next few days, sketching feverishly in the gardens of the villa where the dancers were now lodged, Rodin seemed to lose thirty years. The effort involved in sketching his favorite models, three restless fourteen-year-olds called Sap, Soun, and Yem, appeared to rejuvenate the artist. A French official saw him placing a sheet of white paper on his knee one morning; he "said to the little Sap: 'Put your foot on this,' and then drew the outline of her foot with a pencil, saying 'Tomorrow you'll have your shoes, but now pose a little more for me!' Sap, having tired of atomizer bottles and cardboard cats, had asked her 'papa' for a pair of pumps. Every evening—ardent, happy, but exhausted—Rodin would return to his hotel with his hands full of sketches and collect his thoughts."

Photographs from the time show Rodin seated on a garden bench, sketching under the watchful eyes of the policemen who had been posted at the dancers' villa to ensure their safety. Rodin was oblivious: "The friezes of Angkor were coming to life before my very eyes. I loved these Cambodian girls so much that I didn't know how to express my gratitude for the royal honor they had shown me in dancing and posing for me. I went to the Nouvelles Galeries to buy a basket of toys for them, and these divine children who dance for the gods hardly knew how to repay me for the happiness I had given them. They even talked about taking me with them."

On their last day in France, hours before they boarded the ship that was to take them back to Cambodia, the dancers were taken to the celebrated photographer Baudouin. On the way, passing through a muddy alley, Princess Soumphady happened to step on a pat of cow dung. Horrified, she raised her arms to the heavens and flung herself, wailing, upon the dust, oblivious of her splendid costume. The rest of the troupe immediately followed suit: within moments the alley was full of prostrate Cambodian dancers, dressed in full performance regalia.

"What an emptiness they left for me!" wrote Rodin. "When they left . . . I thought they had taken away the beauty of the world . . . I followed them to Marseille; I would have followed them as far as Cairo."

His sentiments were exactly mirrored by King Sisowath. "I am deeply saddened to be leaving France," the king said on the eve of his departure. "In this beautiful country I shall leave behind a piece of my heart."

9

The trip to France evidently cast King Sisowath's mind into the same kind of turmoil, the same tumult, that has provoked generations of displaced students — the Gandhis, the Kenyattas, the Chou en Lais, among thousands of their less illustrious countrymen — to reflect upon the unfamiliar, wintry worlds beyond the doors of their rented lodgings.

On September 12, 1906, shortly after their return to Cambodia, the king and his ministers published their reflections in a short but poignant document. Cast in the guise of a royal proclamation, it was in fact a venture into a kind of travel writing. It began: "The visits that His Majesty made to the great cities of France, his rapid examination of the institutions of that country, the organization of the different services that are to be found there, astonished him and led him to think of France as a paradise." Emulation, they concluded, was "the only means of turning resolutely to the path of progress."

Over the brief space of a couple of thousand words the king and his ministers summed up their views on the lessons that France had to offer Cambodia. Most of these had to do with what later came to be called "development": communications had to be improved, new land cleared for agriculture; peasants had to increase their production, raise more animals, exploit their forests and fisheries more systematically, familiarize themselves with modern machinery, and so on. A generation later, Cambodian political luminaries such as Khieu Samphan, writing their theses in Paris, were to arrive at oddly similar conclusions, although by an entirely different route.

But it was on the subject of the ideal relationship between the state and its people that the king and his ministers were at their most prescient. It was here, they thought, that Europe's most important lessons lay. "None should hesitate to sacrifice his life," they wrote, "when it is a matter of the divinity of the king or of the country. The obligation to serve the country should be accepted without a murmur by the inhabitants of the kingdom; it is glorious to defend one's country. Are Europeans not constrained by the same obligation, without distinction either of rank or of family?"

Alas for poor King Sisowath, he was soon to learn that travel writing was an expensive indulgence for those who fell on his side of the colonial divide. In 1910 the Colonial Ministry in Paris wrote asking the king to reimburse the French government for certain expenses incurred during his trip to France. As it happened, Cambodia's budget had paid for the entire trip, including the dancers' performance at the Bois du Boulogne. In addition, the king, who was ruinously generous by nature, had personally handed out tips and gifts worth several thousands of francs. In return he and his entourage had received a few presents from French officials. Among these were a set of uniforms given by the minister of colonies and some rosebushes that had been presented to the king personally at the Elysée Palace by none other than the president of the republic, Armand Fallières. The French government now wanted to reclaim the price of the uniforms and the rosebushes from the Cambodians.

For once the obsequious Minister Thiounn took the king's side. He wrote back indignantly, refusing to pay for gifts that had been accepted in good faith.

The royal voyage to France found its most celebrated memorial in Rodin's sketches. The sketches were received with acclaim when they went on exhibition in 1907. After seeing them, the German poet Rilke wrote to the master to say, "For me, these sketches were among the most profound of revelations."

The revelation Rilke had in mind was of "the mystery of Cambodian dance." But it was probably the sculptor rather than the poet who sensed the real revelation of the encounter: the power of Cambodia's involvement in the culture and politics of modernism, in all its promise and horror.

10

As for King Sisowath, the most significant thing he ever did was to authorize the founding of a high school where Cambodians could be educated on the French pattern. Known initially as the Collège du Protectorat, the school was renamed the Lycée Sisowath some years after the king's death.

The Lycée Sisowath was to become the crucible for Cambodia's remaking. A large number of the students who were radicalized in Paris in the fifties were graduates of the lycée. Pol Pot himself was never a student there, but he was closely linked with it, and several of his nearest associates were Sisowath alumni, including his first wife, Khieu Ponnary, and his brother-in-law and longtime deputy, Ieng Sary.

Among the most prominent members of that group was Khieu Samphan, one-time president of Pol Pot's Democratic Kampuchea and now the best known of the Khmer Rouge's spokesmen. Through the 1960s and early 1970s, Khieu Samphan was one of the preeminent political figures in Cambodia. He was renowned throughout the country as an incorruptible idealist: stories about his refusal to take bribes, even when begged by his impoverished mother, have passed into popular mythology. He was also an important economic thinker and theorist; his doctoral thesis on Cambodia's economy, written at the Sorbonne in the 1950s, is still highly regarded. He vanished in 1967, and through the next eight years he lived in the jungle, through the long years of the Khmer Rouge's grim struggle, first against Prince Sihanouk, then against the rightist regime of General Lon Nol, when American planes subjected the countryside to saturation bombing.

Khieu Samphan surfaced again after the 1975 revolution, as president of Pol Pot's Democratic Kampuchea. When the regime was driven out of power by the Vietnamese invasion of 1979, he fled with the rest of the ruling group to a stronghold on the Thai border. As the Khmer Rouge's chief public spokesman and emissary, he played a prominent part in the UN-sponsored peace negotiations. Later, in the months before the elections, it was he who was the Khmer Rouge's mouthpiece as it reneged on the peace agreements while launching ever more vituperative attacks on the UN. The Khmer Rouge's maneuvers did not come as a surprise to anyone who had ever dealt with its leadership; the surprise lay rather in the extent to which UNTAC was willing to go in appeasing them. Effectively, the Khmer Rouge succeeded in taking advantage of the UN's presence to augment its own military position while sabotaging the peace process.

In 1991 and 1992, when Khieu Samphan was traveling around the world making headlines, there was perhaps only a single soul in Phnom Penh who followed his doings with an interest that was not wholly political: his forty-nine-year-old younger brother, Khieu Seng Kim, who lives very close to the school of classical dance.

The school's ability to surprise being what it is, I took it in my stride when I met Khieu Seng Kim one morning, standing by the entrance to the compound. A tall man with a cast in one eye and untidy grizzled hair, he was immediately friendly, eager both to talk about his family and to speak French. Within minutes of our meeting we were sitting in his small apartment, on opposite sides of a desk, surrounded by neat piles of French textbooks and dog-eared copies of *Paris-Match*.

The brick wall behind Khieu Seng Kim was papered over with

pictures of relatives and dead ancestors. The largest was a glossy magazine picture of his brother Khieu Samphan, taken soon after the signing of the peace accords, in 1991. The photograph shows the assembled leaders of all the major Cambodian factions: Prince Sihanouk; Son Sann, of the centrist Khmer People's National Liberation Front; Hun Sen, of the "State of Cambodia"; and of course Khieu Samphan himself, representing the Khmer Rouge. In the picture everybody exudes a sense of relief, bonhomie, and optimism; everyone is smiling, but no one more than Khieu Samphan.

Khieu Seng Kim was a child in 1950, when his brother, recently graduated from the Lycée Sisowath, left for Paris on a scholarship. By the time he returned with his doctorate from the Sorbonne, eight years later, Khieu Seng Kim was fourteen, and the memory of going to Pochentong airport to receive his older brother stayed fresh in his mind. "We were very poor then," he said, "and we couldn't afford to greet him with garlands and a crown of flowers, like well-off people do. We just embraced and hugged and all of us had tears flowing down our cheeks."

In those days, in Cambodia, a doctorate from France was a guarantee of a high-level job in the government, a sure means of ensuring entry into the country's privileged classes. Khieu Samphan's mother wanted nothing less for herself and her family. She had struggled against poverty most of her life; her husband, a magistrate, had died early, leaving her with five children to bring up on her own. But when her son refused to accept any of the lucrative offers that came his way despite her entreaties, once again she had to start selling vegetables to keep the family going. Khieu Seng Kim remembers seeing his adored brother, the brilliant economist with his degree from the Sorbonne, sitting beside his mother, helping her with her roadside stall.

In the meanwhile, Khieu Samphan taught in a school, founded an influential left-wing journal, and gradually rose to political prominence. He even served in Sihanouk's cabinet for a while, and with his success the family's situation eased a little.

And then came the day in 1967 when he melted into the jungle.

Khieu Seng Kim remembers the day well: it was Monday, April 24, 1967. His mother served dinner at seven-thirty, and the two of them sat at the dining table and waited for Khieu Samphan to arrive; he always came home at about that time. They stayed there till eleven, without eating, listening to every footstep and every sound; then his mother broke down and began to cry. She cried all night, "like a child who has lost its mother."

At first they thought that Khieu Samphan had been arrested. They had good reason to, for Prince Sihanouk had made a speech two days before, denouncing Khieu Samphan and two close friends of his, the brothers Hu Nim and Hou Yuon. But no arrest was announced, and nor was there any other news the next day.

Khieu Seng Kim became a man possessed. He could not believe that the brother he worshipped would abandon his family; at that time he was their only means of support. He traveled all over the country, visiting friends and relatives, asking if they had any news of his brother. Nobody could tell him anything. It was only much later that he learned that Khieu Samphan had been smuggled out of the city in a farmer's cart the evening he failed to show up for dinner.

He never saw him again.

Eight years later, in 1975, when the first Khmer Rouge cadres marched into Phnom Penh, Khieu Seng Kim went rushing out into the streets and threw himself upon them, crying, "My brother is Khieu Samphan, my brother is your leader." They looked at him as though he were insane. "The revolution doesn't recognize families," they said, brushing him off. He was driven out of the city with his wife and children and made to march to a work site just like everybody else.

Like most other evacuees, Khieu Seng Kim drifted back toward Phnom Penh in 1979, after the Pol Pot regime had been overthrown by the Vietnamese invasion. He began working in a factory, but within a few months it came to be known that he knew French and had worked as a journalist before the revolution. The new government contacted him and invited him to take up a job as a journalist. He refused; he didn't want to be compromised or associate himself with the government in any way. Instead, he worked with the Department of Archaeology for a while as a restorer and then took a teaching job at the School of Fine Arts.

"For that they're still suspicious of me," he said with a wry smile. "Even now. That's why I live in a place like this, while everyone in the country is getting rich."

He smiled and lit a cigarette; he seemed obscurely pleased at the thought of being excluded and pushed onto the edges of the wilderness that had claimed his brother decades ago. It never seemed to have occurred to him to reflect that there was probably no other country on earth where the brother of a man who had headed a genocidal regime would actually be invited to accept a job by the government that followed.

I liked Khieu Seng Kim; I liked his quirky younger-brotherishness. For his sake I wished his mother were still alive — that indomitable old woman who had spread out her mat and started selling vegetables on the street when she realized that her eldest son would have no qualms about sacrificing his entire family on the altar of his idealism. She would have reminded Khieu Seng Kim of a few home truths.

II

According to his brother, Khieu Samphan talked very little about his student days upon his return from France. He did, however, tell one story that imprinted itself vividly on the fourteen-year-old boy's mind. It had to do with an old friend, Hou Yuon. Khieu Seng Kim remembers Hou Yuon well; he was always in and out of the house, a part of the family.

Hou Yuon and his brother Hu Nim played pivotal roles in the Communist movement in Cambodia: along with Khieu Samphan, they were the most popular figures on the left through the sixties and early seventies. Then as now, Pol Pot preferred to be a faceless puppeteer, pulling strings behind a screen of organizational anonymity.

The two brothers were initiated into radical politics at about the same time as Khieu Samphan and Pol Pot; they attended the same study groups in Paris; they did party work together in Phnom Penh in the sixties, and all through the desperate years of the early seventies they fought together, shoulder by shoulder, in conditions of the most extreme hardship, with thousands of tons of bombs crashing down around them. So closely linked were the fortunes of Khieu Samphan and the two brothers that they became a collective legend, known together as the Three Ghosts.

Khieu Samphan's acquaintance with Hou Yuon dated back to their schooldays at the Lycée Sisowath in Phnom Penh. Their friendship was sealed in Paris in the fifties and was the subject of the story Khieu Samphan told his brother on his return.

Once, at a Cambodian gathering in Paris, Hou Yuon made a speech in which he criticized the corruption and venality of Prince Sihanouk's regime. He was overheard by an official, and soon afterward his government scholarship was suspended for a year. Since Khieu Samphan was known to be a particular friend of his, his scholarship was suspended too.

To support themselves, the two men began to sell bread. They would study during the day, and at night they would walk around the city hawking long loaves of French bread. With the money they earned, they paid for their upkeep and bought books; the loaves they couldn't sell they ate. It was a hard way to earn money, Khieu Samphan told his brother, but at the same time it was also oddly exhilarating. Walking down those lamp-lit streets late at night, talking to each other, it was as though he and Hou Yuon somehow managed to leave behind the nighttime of the spirit that had befallen them in Paris. They would walk all night long, with the fragrant, crusty loaves over their shoulders, looking into the windows of cafés and restaurants, talking about their lives and about the future . . .

Hou Yuon was one of the first to die when the revolution began to devour itself: his moderate views were sharply at odds with the ultraradical, collectivist ideology of the ruling group. In August 1975, a few months after the Khmer Rouge took power, he addressed a crowd and vehemently criticized the policy of evacuating the cities. He is said to have been assassinated as he left the meeting, on the orders of the party's leadership. His brother Hu Nim served for a while as minister of information. Then, on April 10, 1977, he and his wife were taken into Interrogation Center S-21 — the torture chambers at Tuol Sleng in Phnom Penh. He was executed several months later, after confessing to being everything from a CIA agent to a Vietnamese spy.

Khieu Samphan was then head of state. He is believed to have played an important role in planning the mass purges of that period.

For Khieu Samphan and Pol Pot, the deaths of Hou Yuon, Hu Nim, and the thousands of others who were executed in torture chambers and execution grounds were not a contradiction but rather a proof of their own idealism and ideological purity. Terror was essential to their exercise of power. It was an integral part not merely of their coercive machinery but of the moral order on which they built their regime, a part whose best description still lies in the line that Brückner, most prescient of playwrights, gave to Robespierre (a particular hero of Pol Pot's): "Virtue is terror, and terror virtue" — words that might well serve as an epitaph for the twentieth century.

12

Those who were there then say there was a moment of epiphany in Phnom Penh in 1981. It occurred at a quiet, relatively obscure event: a festival at which classical Cambodian music and dance were performed for the first time since the revolution.

Dancers and musicians from all over the country traveled to Phnom Penh for the festival. Proeung Chhieng, one of the best-known dancers and choreographers in the country, was among those who made the journey; he came to Phnom Penh from Kompong Thom, where he had helped assemble a small troupe of dancers after the fall of Democratic Kampuchea. He himself had trained at the palace since his childhood, specializing in the role of Hanuman, the monkey god of the Ramayana epic, a part that is one of the glories of Khmer dance. This training proved instrumental in Proeung Chhieng's survival: his expertise in clowning and mime helped him persuade the interrogators at his labor camp that he was an illiterate lunatic.

At the festival he met many fellow students and teachers for the first time after the revolution: "We cried and laughed while we looked around to see who were the others who had survived. We would shout with joy: 'You are still alive!' and then we would cry thinking of someone who had died."

The performers were dismayed when they began preparing for the performance: large quantities of musical instruments, costumes, and masks had been destroyed over the past few years. They had to improvise new costumes to perform in; instead of rich silks and brocades, they used thin calico, produced by a government textile factory. The theater they were to perform in, the Bassac, was in relatively good shape, but there was a crisis of electricity at the time, and the lighting was dim and unreliable.

But people flocked to the theater the day the festival began. Onesta Carpene, a Catholic relief worker from Italy, was one of the handful of foreigners then living in Phnom Penh. She was astonished at the response. The city was in a shambles: there was debris everywhere, spilling out of the houses onto the pavements, the streets were jammed with pillaged cars, there was no money and very little food. "I could not believe that in a situation like that people would be thinking of music and dance," she said. But still they came pouring in, and the theater was filled far beyond its capacity. It was very hot inside.

Eva Mysliwiec, who had arrived recently to set up a Quaker relief mission, was one of the one of the few foreigners present at that first performance. When the musicians came onstage, she heard sobs all around her. Then, when the dancers appeared, in their shabby, hastily made costumes, suddenly everyone was crying, old people, young people, soldiers, children — "You could have sailed out of there in a boat."

The people who were sitting next to her said, "We thought everything was lost, that we would never hear our music again, never see our dance." They could not stop crying; people wept through the entire performance.

It was a kind of rebirth: a moment when the grief of survival became indistinguishable from the joy of living.

THE HUMAN COMEDY IN CAIRO

1990

I N EGYPT, the news that the writer Naguib Mahfouz was awarded the Nobel Prize in 1989 was greeted with the kind of jubilation that Egyptians usually reserve for soccer victories. Even though the fundamentalists sounded an ominous note, most people in Cairo were overjoyed. Months later everybody was still full of it. People would tell anecdotes about how the good news had reached Mahfouz. Swedish efficiency has met its match in Cairo's telephones: the news had broken over the wires before the committee (or whatever) could get through to Mahfouz. He was asleep, taking his afternoon siesta (no, it was early in the morning, and he just hadn't woken up yet), when his wife woke him and told him matter-of-factly that somebody wanted to congratulate him for winning the Nobel (no, it was she who wanted to congratulate him, didn't you see the story in . . .).

The stories were on everyone's lips: tales of national pride and collective hope. Mahfouz has a large following in Egypt and is personally popular: he is everybody's slightly eccentric but successful uncle, a modest, generous, kindly man who has spent over thirty years working as a civil servant. The rest of the Arab world was enthusiastic too, including the people of some countries who had their own favorite contestants (it had long been rumored that an Arab writer would soon win the prize). The award to Mahfouz was clearly a recognition of the achievements of Arabic literature, and even if it was several decades overdue, the Arab world in general responded to it with pride.

It would have been interesting, at that moment of elation, if some enterprising pollster had taken it into his head to put two questions to a representative sample of the reading public in the Arab world, the first question being "Do you think Naguib Mahfouz is the most interesting, innovative, or imaginative writer in Arabic today?" and the second, "Do you think that Naguib Mahfouz is the most appropriate candidate for the Nobel Prize for literature in the Arab world today?" It is my guess that the answer to the first question would have been largely no, and the answer to the second would have been generally yes.

In the gap between that no and that yes falls the award itself, and the extraordinary power it carries in countries like Egypt and India — old civilizations trying hard to undo their supersession in the modern world. Once, in my own city of Calcutta, in the gaudy heat of May, stuck in a crowded bus in a traffic jam, I overheard an unexpectedly literary conversation. A sweat-soaked commuter, on his way back from a hard day's work, missed his grip on the overhead rail and dropped his briefcase on his toe. A dam seemed to burst: he began to complain loudly about the traffic, the roads, the fumes, the uncollected garbage. One of his neighbors turned to him and said sharply, "What are you complaining about? Rabindranath Tagore won the Nobel Prize for literature in 1913, and wasn't he from Calcutta?" At this very moment someone stuck in a bus or a share-taxi in Tahrir or Shubra or some other traffic-clogged part of Cairo is almost certainly saying the same thing about Mahfouz. Thus does Stockholm regulate the traffic in Calcutta and Cairo.

In the United States, Mahfouz met with another kind of approval on the occasion of his triumph. The second paragraph of the *New York Times* story on Mahfouz's Nobel, carried on the front page, quoted Israelis declaring Mahfouz's politics to be perfectly acceptable. His work, his concerns, and his subjects came a poor second to this other aspect of his newsworthiness.

For a prize of such power, the ordinary standards of judgment that apply to books are held in suspension. What matters is that the writer's work be adequately canonical, which is to say massive, serious, and somehow a part of "world literature." If Mahfouz won on these counts, his was the victory of the decathlete, achieved by a slow accumulation of points rather than by a spectacular show of brilliance in a single event. To date, Mahfouz has written some thirty-five novels and twelve volumes of short stories, as well as several plays and screenplays; he is said to be widely read in philosophy and French literature; and he is credited with introducing absurdism and the stream-of-consciousness technique into Arabic literature. Whatever your opinion about any particular book of his, there can be no denying the weight of Mahfouz's contribution to modern Arabic literature. Thus the general popularity of the award.

2

Mahfouz was born in Cairo in 1911. His father was a minor functionary in the government, and he grew up in the heart of the old city, the crowded district that lies beyond the ancient university of Al-Azhar and the mausoleum of the Prophet's grandson, Sayidna Hussein. In the years of Mahfouz's childhood, it was an area where respectable families of modest means, struggling to put their children through school, lived above thriving little shops and businesses and looked out through their dusty windows at medieval mosques, hospitals, and religious schools. This is the world that Mahfouz has made peculiarly his own: a distinctively Cairene world of minor civil servants striving to make ends meet on their salaries, to push their children one rung higher on the civil service ladder while keeping up appearances against the pretensions of pushy grocers and arriviste café owners. No matter that this kind of person has moved out of the neighborhood (as did Mahfouz's family); their hopes and their anxieties remain much the same.

These are the people of Mahfouz's imaginative universes — a

small, distinctive group within the tumult of modern Egypt. Rural Egypt, which occupied so much of the imaginations of Mahfouz's most illustrious predecessors and contemporaries, never intrudes on his world. Indeed, it is almost artificially excluded. His characters never even have friends or relatives in the countryside, as they almost certainly would in the "real" world. This needs saying, if only because Mahfouz's world is sometimes said to be a microcosm of Egypt. If this is so, it is surely only in that special sense in which the sans-culottes of Paris were somehow a little more "the People" than the peasants of the Midi.

Much of the interest of Mahfouz lies in his avenue of entry into the world of his characters. He takes the most secret, the least accessible, route: the family. Of course, the family is one of the territories the novel has most successfully claimed for itself everywhere; all around the world there are novelists who, like Mahfouz, build their books on families and their histories, on the endless cycle of birth, marriage, and death. But in Mahfouz's hands, in the world of his People, this invitation into the family has an extra dimension of excitement.

In Egypt, and more generally in the Arab world, as in many conservative, traditional societies, the family is a secret, curtained world, protected from the gaze of outsiders by walls and courtyards, by veils and laws of silence. To be taken past those doors, into the forbidden space of failed marriages and secret desires, the areas that lie most heavily curtained under the genteel ethic of family propriety — and to be introduced into this by the most public of artifacts, a printed book — is to prepare oneself for the pleasurable tingle of the illicit. And once past that curtain, Mahfouz's reader discovers, with guilty delight, a quiet murmur of furtive gropings, dissatisfaction, and despair that confirms everything he has ever suspected about his neighbors. This is Mahfouz's particular talent: he has a fine instinct for discovering the fears, the prejudices, and the suspicions of his People and serving them back to them as fiction.

In his hands, the intricacies of family relationships become a kind of second language, with which he demonstrates to his readers the dangers that lurk at the margins of their world. These are predicaments that they can all too readily imagine, since they form the nightmare other-life that gives their respectability its meaning. This is a world in which sisters become prostitutes to help their brothers become "respectable employees," where fathers who drink encounter their sons in brothels, where ambition is always unscrupulous and young men who look above their station come to a sticky end, where boys who are allowed to stay out too late are plunged "deep into sin and addiction" and eventually end up in a region that can only be described as Mahfouz's Underworld.

That underworld is a landscape often encountered in his work, always sketched with portentous hints and suggestions, a region of pure fantasy, dank with the "odor of putrefaction," whose inhabitants always drink themselves into stupors, smoke hashish, fondle bosomy singers, and traffic vaguely in drugs. It is through devices such as these that Mahfouz invites his reader to marvel at the decay of the world as it should be. It is a sentiment that his People are only too willing to take to heart, oppressed as they are by the prospect of poverty and social decline on the one hand, and on the other by the images of wealth that they associate with those who control money and power in their societies.

The predicament is not peculiarly Egyptian. I can think of at least two eminent writers in Calcutta whose plots and material are uncannily similar to Mahfouz's (though Mahfouz is the more skillful practitioner of the craft). This is the kind of fiction that grows out of the sensibility of literate, urban "salaried employees" — who, caught between a vast sink of poverty and tiny, impenetrable enclaves of wealth, begin to look for some kind of meaning and authenticity in what they see as their own traditions of respectable gentility. That is their cruelest delusion, for their gentility has very little to do with the traditions of Egypt or India, Islam or Hinduism, and everything to do with Victorianism.

Much of Mahfouz's work seethes with the indignation that grows out of this particular sensibility, indignation at the corruption that allows the unscrupulous to grow rich while decent people labor to earn an honest wage. But indignation is about all it is. Its sources are not interesting enough to give it the fire of real rage or even the anger of outraged morality. Mahfouz has written some quasi-mystical parables, but he is not essentially a religious writer. Indeed, the Arab thinker whose name occurs most frequently in his work is Abu'l 'Ala al-Ma'arri, a medieval freethinker and rationalist. And although Mahfouz has written political satires, he is not essentially a political writer either. In his books politics and history generally serve as part of the background and mise en scène.

If there is something suspect, in the end, even about Mahfouz's indignation, it is probably because it never appears to be turned against his People's own ethic of respectability. His mother figures are impossibly good and forbearing, and girls who leave the sanctuary of the home and go out to work all too often fall prey to temptation. At its best, Mahfouz's work has some of the texture and the richness of detail of the nineteenth-century masters whose influence he acknowledges — Balzac, Tolstoy, Flaubert — but even at its bleakest and most melancholy (as in *The Beginning and the End*), his writing never approximates real tragedy. Its pathos seems to spring almost entirely from a sense of violated gentility. Even for a writer with Mahfouz's skill, it is hard to create tragedy out of the scramble for respectability.

It is in the observation of the small details on which the edifices of respectability are constructed that Mahfouz is really acute about his society. What the foreign reader needs explained is the real meaning of what it is to be a "salaried employee" in Egypt, the importance of the baccalaureate examinations, what it is to be an eighth-grade functionary. These are arcane and peculiarly Egyptian details, although they have nothing to do with the Egypt of the pharaohs or Mamelukes, or with anything particularly exotic. But it is those details that make up the fabric of respectable middle-class life in Egypt, and it is Mahfouz's singular gift that he is able to transform them into the stuff of fiction.

3

The American University in Cairo Press has long been doing a difficult and thankless job in making good writing in Arabic available in English translation. With Mahfouz's Nobel Prize and the sale of rights to their translations, their efforts have been richly rewarded. It is to be hoped that more and still better translations will be forthcoming soon, so that a wider spectrum of modern Arabic writing will receive the kind of attention it deserves. The four novels published by Doubleday are revised versions of the original American University in Cairo translations. Two of them were written in Mahfouz's early "realistic" period. *The Beginning and the End* is the melancholy but compelling story of a family pauperized by a sudden death. *Palace Walk* is the first book of Mahfouz's Cairene trilogy, written in 1956–1957, in which each book is named after a street in the old city. The trilogy, which charts the history of a Cairene family during the period between the wars, is a chronicle of the changes that occurred in Egyptian society over that period.

Palace Walk sets the stage for the later books; it is a depiction of what went before the changes, so to speak. The central figure in the book is a patriarch of rather extreme convictions: he has never once, in their decades-old marriage, allowed his wife to leave the house. This is a condition with which she is entirely satisfied, for she reveres her husband, except for one small thing — she longs to visit the mausoleum of Sayidna Hussein, which is down the road. One day one of her sons persuades her to venture out. She does, and for her pains she is struck by a motorcar. (Why do such terrible things happen, in Mahfouz's work, to women who leave their houses?) Worse still, the wrathful patriarch, upon discovering her dereliction, packs her off to her mother's, where she languishes, wringing her hands, until he summons her back. In the end, however, the turmoil of Egyptian politics — the last part of the book is set in the period of the 1919 riots against the British presence in Egypt — catches up with the apparently invincible patriarch and leaves him a broken man.

The novel has the feel of the sort of stories people tell about the old days, when they want their children to marvel at how much the world has come on since then. In a sense, of course, it is exactly that: Mahfouz was a very young child in the years in which his book is set, and his family had already moved out of the old part of the city. There are some perceptive observations about the psychology of patriarchy — there is a wonderful scene, for example, in which the patriarch's son, a brave and ardent nationalist, finds himself reduced to a quaking heap by the tone of his father's voice. But the reader would be better able to savor those moments, perhaps, if Mahfouz's sympathy with the patriarch were not so patent, if the book were not so pervaded by nostalgia for a time when men were men.

The other two novels, *The Thief and the Dogs* (1961) and *Wedding Song* (1981), date from Mahfouz's later period, which was less realistic and more experimental, and they are, frankly, awful. When the spirit moves Mahfouz to be technically adventurous, it also tends to push him away from his accustomed material, leaving him stranded in various exotic enclaves of society. *Wedding Song* is set among a group of raffish theater people who drink, gamble, take drugs, and have sex (the underworld again). A particularly disreputable couple has a son who is an idealistic young man; appalled by the lasciviousness and the immorality of his parents' circle, he exposes them in a play before staging his own death. *The Thief and the Dogs* is about . . . well, it's about an idealistic sort of fellow who becomes a thief because he is shocked by how rich some people are.

Unfortunately for Doubleday, and fortunately for English readers, the most delightful of Mahfouz's translated works, *Midaq Alley*, has long been available in a good translation by Trevor Le Gassick. It has recently been reissued by the Quality Paperback Book Club, and it is more worth reading than any of Doubleday's four. The novel is set in Mahfouz's familiar world — in a street in the old city — but it lacks the portentousness of some of his other work. It is written tongue-in-cheek, almost as self-parody, and it brims with moments of pure delight.

For instance: the homosexual café owner Kirsha — inevitably of dark and sullen aspect — is interrupted by his wife while entertaining a youth in his café. His wife marches up to the boy and screams, "Do you want to ruin my home, you rake and son of rakes . . . Who am I? Don't you know me? I am your fellow-wife . . ." The boy escapes, and she turns upon her protesting husband and shouts, in a "voice loud enough to crumble the walls of the café," "Shut your mouth! You are the . . . lavatory around here, you scarecrow, you disgrace, you rat-bag!" Among the awe-struck spectators is the baker's wife, who regularly beats her husband. She turns to him now and remarks, "You're always moaning about your bad luck and asking why you're the only husband who is beaten! Did you see how even your betters are beaten?" But eventually Kirsha has his say as well. "Oh you miserable pair, why on earth should the government punish anyone who kills off people like you?" His son declares that he wants to leave home and live in a place where houses have electricity. "Electricity?" retorts Kirsha. "Thanks be to God that your mother, for all her scandals, has at least kept our house safe from electricity!"

The inhabitants of this alley are a world away from the mythologized patriarch and his family on Palace Walk.

4

The Nobel Prize has had an unhappy consequence for Mahfouz. Soon after the announcement, possibly as a result of the Rushdie crisis, he began to receive death threats from Islamic fundamentalists. At issue was a book he wrote in 1959 called (in its English translation) *Children of Gebelawi*. It was an allegorical novel, in which three of the principal characters were said to represent the prophets Moses, Jesus, and Muhammad. The *'ulema*, the Muslim doctors of theology and religious law, declared Mahfouz's book to be offensive to Islam. The book was never published in Arabic in

Egypt, and for a while Mahfouz stopped writing altogether. But there were more books in time, and the controversy was largely forgotten — until the threats began.

An epoch passed in the Middle East between the late fifties and the late eighties. There is a world of difference between a group of learned scholars pronouncing an anathema and the death threats issued by bands of young men barely out of college. The evolution of the Mahfouz controversy is one very small indication of how dramatically the Middle East has changed within the lifetime of his own generation.

In Mahfouz's youth, Islam had been largely sidelined as a political ideology. In Turkey, Ataturk, with the power of the army behind him, appeared intent on pushing everything religious into the wings. During Mahfouz's college years in the late twenties and early thirties, the principal intellectual influence on him was a group of nationalists who had set themselves the task of creating a national culture for Egypt that would be distinctively Egyptian. The path they took lay in emphasizing Egypt's pharaonic and Hellenistic roots, to the point of disavowing all connections with the Arab and Islamic world. It was a time when everything was thinkable in Egypt and nothing was blasphemy.

If *Children of Gebelawi* had been written in those years, it would probably have passed without comment: every writer in Egypt, it would seem, was writing an allegory of some kind. But the book was written in the late fifties, when the political and religious climate in the Middle East had been profoundly altered by the establishment of Israel and then by the Nasserite revolution in Egypt. In Egypt, Islam acquired a new vitality and assertiveness, and the religious establishment was keen to remind everybody of that fact. But even then the *'ulema* followed procedure in condemning the book. There were no calls for bloodshed or retribution, just a clear message that those who persisted in the intellectual habits of the thirties would now have to contend with the doctors of religious law and their followers.

But now even the learned doctors are being slowly consumed by the fires that were kindled at that time. They have not the remotest connection with the bearded young men who now speak in the name of Islam in Egypt; they have themselves been declared unbelievers, pagans — even the most learned of the sheiks at Al-Azhar, for centuries the theological center of Sunni Islam. In 1977 one of their number, Mohammad al-Dhahabi, a religious scholar and a minister of the government department in the Ministry of Religious Endowments where Mahfouz worked for much of his life, was kidnapped and killed by a fundamentalist group called the Society of Muslims. At the subsequent trial, conducted by the army, the presiding general in so many words declared the 'ulema incompetent.

The scholars' only recourse now is to call the preachings of the fundamentalists un-Islamic, as indeed they are by scholastic standards. The Society of Muslims have effectively scorned Muslim history: they have rejected all of medieval Muslim scholarship, including the great jurists who set up the four major schools of Islamic law, and they have also claimed the right to interpret the Koran. A century ago it is they who would have been counted the blasphemers, and any one of their current claims would probably have cost them their lives. They have, in effect, vacated the whole concept of Islam as we know it, for Islam is a history as well as a doctrine and a practice. Yet today, for millions of Muslims in Egypt and elsewhere, it is they, and not the sheiks of Al-Azhar, who are the true Muslims.

The power of the fundamentalists has grown so phenomenally in Egypt over the past few years that they are now in a position to fight pitched battles with the police. Every so often they even claim to have "liberated" parts of Cairo and some other cities. Why, then, should these fundamentalists revive the charges brought against Mahfouz by their enemies, the learned doctors of religion? It must be the first matter on which they have been in agreement with them in several years. Mahfouz's book is evidently a pretext: their hostility almost certainly stems from his public support of the Camp David accords.

In responding to the threats against him, Mahfouz has shown an exemplary courage. Despite the ominous drift of the political life of his city, he has turned down the government's offer of bodyguards and has refused to change his life in any way. For the time being he appears to have faced down his enemies and shamed them into leaving him alone. In doing so, he has demonstrated the kind of heroism that is both the most necessary and the most rare in his volatile corner of the world: the quiet kind.

TIBETAN DINNER

1988

It was a while before the others at the table had finished pointing out the celebrities who had come to the restaurant for the gala benefit: the Broadway actresses, the Seventh Avenue designers, and the world's most famous rock star's most famous ex-wife, a woman to whom fame belonged like logic to a syllogism, axiomatically. Before the list was quite done, I caught a glimpse of something, a flash of saffron at the other end of the room, and I had to turn and look again.

Peering through a thicket of reed-necked women, I saw that I'd been right: yes, it was a monk in saffron robes, it really was a Buddhist monk—Tibetan, I was almost sure. He was sitting at the head of a table on the far side of the room, spectral in the glow of the restaurant's discreetly hidden lighting. But he was real. His robes were real robes, not drag, not a costume. He was in his early middle age, with clerically cropped hair and a pitted, wind-ravaged face. He happened to look up and noticed me staring at him. He looked surprised to see me: his chopsticks described a slow interrogative arc as they curled up to his mouth.

I was no less surprised to see him. He was probably a little less out of place among the dinner jackets and designer diamonds than I, in my desert boots and sweater, but only marginally so.

He glanced at me again, and I looked quickly down at my plate.

On it sat three dumplings decorated with slivers of vegetables. The
dumplings looked oddly familiar, but I couldn't quite place them.

"Who were you looking at?" said the friend who'd taken me
there, an American writer and actress who had spent a long time in
India and, in gratitude to the subcontinent, had undertaken to
show me the sights of New York.

I gestured foolishly with a lacquered chopstick.

She laughed. "Well, of course," she said. "It's his show — he
probably organized the whole thing. Didn't you know?"

I didn't know. All I'd been told was that this was the event of
the week in New York, very possibly even the month (it wasn't a
busy month): a benefit dinner at Indo-Chine, the in-est restaurant
in Manhattan — one that had in fact defied every canon of in-ism
by being in for almost a whole year, and that therefore had to be
seen now if at all, before the tourists from Alabama got to it. My
skepticism about the in-ness of the event had been dispelled by the
tide of paparazzi we'd had to breast on our way in.

Laughing at my astonishment, she said, "Didn't I tell you? It's a
benefit for the Tibetan cause."

More astonished still, I said, "Which Tibetan cause?"

"The Tibetan cause," someone said vaguely, picking at a curl of
something indeterminately vegetal that had been carved into a
flower shape. It was explained to me then that the benefit was
being hosted by a celebrated Hollywood star, a young actor who,
having risen to fame through his portrayal of the initiation rites
of an American officer, had afterward converted to Tibetan Buddhism and found so much fulfillment in it he was reported to have
sworn that he would put Tibet on the world map, make it a household word in the United States, like Maalox or Lysol.

"The odd thing is," said my friend, "that he really is very sincere
about this; he really isn't like those radical chic cynics of the sixties
and seventies. He's not an intellectual, and he probably doesn't
know much about Tibet, but he wants to do what little he can.
They have to raise money for their schools and so on, and the truth
is that no one in New York is going to reach into their pockets

unless they can sit at dinner with rock stars' ex-wives. It's not his fault. He's probably doing what they want him to do."

I looked at the Tibetan monk again. He was being talked to by an improbably distinguished man in a dinner jacket. He caught my eye and nodded, smiling, as he bit into a dumpling.

Suddenly I remembered what the dumpling was. It was a Tibetan *mo-mo,* but stuffed with salmon and asparagus and such-like instead of the usual bits of pork and fat. I sat back to marvel at the one dumpling left on my plate. It seemed a historic bit of food: one of the first genuine morsels of Tibetan *nouvelle cuisine.*

The last time I'd eaten a *mo-mo* was as an undergraduate, in Delhi.

A community of Tibetan refugees had built shacks along the Grand Trunk Road, not far from the university. The shacks were fragile but tenacious, built out of bits of wood, tin, and corrugated iron. During the monsoons they would cover the roofs with sheets of tarpaulin and plastic and weigh them down with bricks and stones. Often the bricks would be washed away and the sheets of plastic would be left flapping in the wind like gigantic prayer flags. Some of the refugees served *mo-mos,* noodles, and *chhang,* the milky Tibetan rice beer, on tables they had knocked together out of discarded crates. Their food was very popular among the drivers who frequented that part of the Grand Trunk Road.

In the university, it was something of a ritual to go to these shacks after an examination. We would drink huge quantities of *chhang*—it was very diluted, so you had to drink jugs of it—and eat noodle soup and *mo-mos.* The *mo-mos* were very simple there: bits of gristle and meat wrapped and boiled in thick skins of flour. They tasted of very little until you dipped them into the red sauce that came with them.

The food was cooked and served by elderly Tibetans; the young people were usually away, working. Communicating with them wasn't easy, for the older people rarely knew any but the most functional Hindi.

As we drank our jugs of *chhang,* a fog of mystery would descend on the windy, lamp-lit interiors of the shacks. We would look at the ruddy, weathered faces of the women as they filled our jugs out of the rusty oil drums in which they brewed the beer and try to imagine the journey they had made: from their chilly, thin-aired plateau 15,000 feet above sea level, across the passes of the high Himalayas, down into that steamy slum, floating on a bog of refuse and oil slicks on the outskirts of Delhi.

Everyone who went there got drunk. You couldn't help doing so — it was hard to be in the presence of so terrible a displacement.

It was an unlikely place, but Tibetans seem to have a talent for surviving on unlikely terrain. Ever since the Chinese invasion of Tibet, dozens of colonies of Tibetan refugees have sprung up all over India. Many of them run thriving businesses in woolen goods, often in the most unexpected places. In Trivandrum, near the southernmost tip of India, where the temperature rarely drops below eighty degrees Fahrenheit and people either wear the thinnest of cottons or go bare-bodied, there are a number of Tibetan stalls in the marketplace, all piled high with woolen scarves and sweaters. They always seem to have more customers than they can handle.

Once, going past the Jama Masjid in Delhi in a bus on a scorching June day, I noticed a Tibetan stall tucked in between the sugarcane juice vendors. Two middle-aged women dressed in heavy Tibetan *bakus* were sitting in it, knitting. The stall was stacked with the usual brightly colored woolen goods. The women were smiling cheerfully as they bargained with their customers in sign language and broken Hindi. A small crowd had gathered around them, as though in tribute to their courage and resilience.

I found myself looking around the restaurant, involuntarily, for another Indian face, someone who had been properly invited, unlike me. I suppose I was looking for some acknowledgment, not of a debt but of a shared history, a gesture toward those hundreds of sweaters in Trivandrum. I couldn't see any. (Later someone said they'd seen a woman in a sari, but they couldn't be sure; it might have been a Somali robe — this was, after all, New York.)

When I next caught the monk's eye, his smile seemed a little guilty: the hospitality of a poor nation must have seemed dispensable compared to the charity of a rich one. Or perhaps he was merely bewildered. It cannot be easy to celebrate the commodification of one's own suffering.

But I couldn't help feeling that if the lama, like the actor, really wanted to make Tibet a household word in the Western world, he wasn't setting about it the right way. He'd probably have done better if he'd turned it into an acronym, like TriBeCa or ComSubPac. And sold the rights to it to a line of detergents or even perhaps a breakfast cereal.

TiBet (where the Cause is): doesn't sound too bad — marketable, even.

FOUR CORNERS

1989

It BECOMES IMPOSSIBLE to ignore the Four Corners once Route 160 enters Colorado's Montezuma County: chevroned signposts spring regularly out of the sand and scrub, urging you toward it. Even if you had never heard of it before, did not know that it is the only point in the USA where four states meet, you are soon curious; it begins to seem like a major station, a Golgotha or Gethsemane, on this well-worn tourist pilgrimage.

The size and sleekness of the trailers and traveling homes heading toward it are eloquent of its significance. These are not the trailers you have grown accustomed to seeing in small towns in the South and Midwest — those shiny aluminum goldfish bowls that sit parked in back yards until the ballgame in the next town, when they get hitched onto pickup trucks and towed out to the ballpark to serve as adjuncts for tailgate parties. Not these; these are no ordinary trailers, they are recreational vehicles (RVs) — if not quite palaces, then certainly midtown condos, on wheels.

You get a real idea of how big they are only when you try to pass one on a two-lane road in a Honda Civic that lost its fifth gear 8000 miles ago. Before you are past the master bedroom, are barely abreast of the breakfast nook, that blind curve that seemed so far away when you decided to make a break for it is suddenly right upon you.

It teaches you respect.

Their owners' imaginations are the only limits on the luxuries those RVs may be made to contain.

Once, on a desolate stretch of road in the deserts of western Utah, I watched an RV pull into a sand-blown rest area right beside my battered Honda Civic. It was almost as long as a supermarket truck, and the air around it was sharp with the smell of its newness. A woman with white curly hair stuck her head out of a window, tried the air, and said something cheerful to someone inside, over the hum of the air conditioning. A moment later the door opened, a flight of stairs clicked magically into place under it, and she stepped out, throwing a wave and a cheery "How you doin'?" in my direction. She was carrying a couple of chairs and a rack of magazines. Her husband climbed out too, and in companionable silence they pulled an awning out of the side of the vehicle and unrolled a ten-foot length of artificial turf under it. She waved again, after the chair, the magazine rack, a pot of geraniums, and a vase with an ikebanaed orchid had been properly arranged on the patch of green. "I call this my bower," she said, smiling. "Join us for cakes and coffee?"

Never had a wilderness seemed so utterly vanquished.

Often those RVs have striking names: Winnebago, Itasca . . . The names of the dispossessed tribes of the Americas hold a peculiar allure for the marketing executives of automobile companies. Pontiac, Cherokee — so many tribes are commemorated in forms of transport. It is not a mere matter of fashion that so many of the cars that flash past on the highways carry those names, breathing them into the air like the inscriptions on prayer wheels. This tradition of naming has a long provenance: did not Kit Carson himself, the scourge of the Navajo, name his favorite horse Apache?

There are many of them on Route 160, those memorials to the first peoples of the Americas, bearing number plates from places thousands of miles away — New York, Georgia, Alaska, Ontario. Having come this far, everybody wants to see the only point where four states meet.

· · ·

There cannot be many places in the world quite as beautiful as the stretch of desert, mountain, and canyon that sprawls over the borders of the four states of Colorado, Utah, New Mexico, and Arizona. For the people who inhabited it at the time of the European conquest—the Diné, who came to be known as the Navajo—it was Diné Bikéyah, the country of the Diné, a land into which the First Beings climbed from the Underworlds through a female reed. To them it was the Fourth World, known as the Glittering.

Route 160 runs through some of the most spectacular parts of the Glittering World: around the caves and canyons of Mesa Verde and through the spectacular mesas that border on Monument Valley. Curiously, its one dull stretch comes when it dips south of the little town of Cortez and heads toward the Four Corners monument. The landscape turns scraggy and undecided, not quite desert and not quite prairie, knotted with dull gray-green scrub, and desert scarred by a few shallow ravines and low cliffs.

That is why it is impossible to miss the Four Corners monument.

It springs up out of nowhere, perched atop nothing, framed by the only stretch of dull country in the region. There is nothing remotely picturesque about its surroundings—no buttes, no mesas, not even a salience of rock or an undulation in the plain. With the greatest effort of the imagination it would not be possible to persuade oneself that this may once have been, like so many places in the Glittering World, a haunt of the Spider Woman or the Talking God or the Hero Twins. Legends of that kind need visible metaphors—wind-scarred buttes or lava fields—to attach themselves to the landscape. For the Four Corners monument the landscape does not exist; it sits squatly on the scrub like a thumbtack in a map, unbudging in its secular disenchantedness.

There is something majestic and yet uneasy about the absoluteness of its indifference to this landscape and its topography. It is simply a point where two notional straight lines intersect: a line of latitude, 37 degrees north, and a line of longitude, 109 degrees and 2 minutes west, the thirty-second degree of longitude west of Washington. These two straight lines form the boundaries between the four states. These lines have nothing whatever to do with the Glittering World; their very straightness is testimony to a belief in the unpeopledness of this land—they slice through the *tabula rasa* of the New World, leaving it crafted in their own image, enchanted with a new enchantment, the magic of Euclidean geometry.

The center of the Glittering World was Diné Tah, which lay around Largo Canyon, about eighty miles southeast of the Four Corners monument. To the Navajo it was the sacred heartland of their country. The first time they left it en masse was in the 1860s, after Colonel Kit Carson and the U.S. Army reduced them to starvation by scorching the earth of their Glittering World. Carson felt no personal animosity toward the Navajo. He is said to have commented once, "I've seen as much of 'em as any white man livin', and I can't help but pity 'em. They'll all soon be gone anyhow." He was an unlettered man, given to expressing himself plainly. Unlike him, his commanding officer, General James H. Carleton, had had the benefits of an education. He was therefore able to phrase the matter more dispassionately, clothed in the mellow light of current trends in science and theology: "In their appointed time He wills that one race of men—as in races of lower animals—shall disappear off the face of the earth and give place to another race . . . The races of the Mammoths and Mastodons, and great Sloths, came and passed away: the Red Man of America is passing away."

The Navajo were forced to march to an "experimental" camp at the Bosque Redondo. It was soon clear, however, that the experiment was not going to work, and in 1868 a commission headed by General William T. Sherman was sent to New Mexico to decide what was to be done with the Navajo. Addressing the commission, the Navajo leader, Barboncito, said, "When the Navajo were first created, four mountains and four rivers were pointed out to us, inside of which we should live, that was to be our country and was given to us by the first woman of the Navajo tribe." Later he said to the general, "I am speaking to you now as if I was speaking to a spirit and I wish you to tell me when you are going to take us to our country." They were permitted to return later the same year. Of their return, Manuelito, the most renowned of the Navajo war chiefs, said afterward, "We felt like talking to the ground, we loved it so." They were back in Diné Bikéyah, where every butte and mesa pointed to the sacred center of Diné Tah.

The Four Corners monument evokes a center too, in its own way. But that central point, the point from which its line of longitude takes its westerly orientation, that central zero degree from which its distance can be so exactly calculated, lies in another landscape, on another continent—far away in Greenwich, England. It is that distant place that the monument unwittingly celebrates.

The monument itself is modest by the standards of monuments in the United States. There is a wide, paved plaza, with plenty of parking space for cars and RVs. On the peripheries there are rows of stalls, manned by people from the neighboring Ute and Navajo reservations.

In the center of the plaza is a square cement platform fenced off by aluminum railings. There is a state flag on each side of the square and, towering above them, a flag of the United States of America, on an eagle-topped mast. Two straight lines are etched into the cement; they intersect neatly at the center of the platform. Somebody has thoughtfully provided a small observation post at one end of the square. There would be little point, after all, in taking pictures of the Four Corners if you couldn't see the two lines intersect. And to get them properly into your frame, you have to be above ground level.

You have to queue, both for your turn at the observation post and to get into the center of the platform. If there are two of you, you have to queue twice at each end, unless you can get somebody to oblige you by taking your picture (and that is easy enough, for there are no friendlier people in the world than American tourists). But queuing is no great trial anyway, even in the desert heat, for everyone is good-humored, and it is not long before you find your-self engaged in comparing notes on campgrounds and motels with everyone around you.

There is a good-natured spirit of competition among the people who walk into the center of the cement platform: everyone tries to be just a little original when posing for their photographs. A young couple kiss, their lips above the center and each of their feet in a different state. Another couple pose, more modestly, with one foot on each state and their arms around each other's shoulders. Six middle-aged women distribute themselves between the states, holding hands. An elderly gentleman in Bermuda shorts lets himself slowly down onto his hands and knees and poses with an extremity on each state and his belly button at the center. This sets something of a trend; a couple of middle-aged women follow suit. In the end a pretty teenage girl carries the day by striking a balletic pose on one leg, her toes dead center on the point where the lines intersect.

Men from the reservations lounge about in the shade of the stalls, around the edges of the plaza. Some rev their cars, huge, lumbering old Chevrolets and Buicks, startling the tourists. A boy, bored, drives into the scrub, sending whirlwinds of sand shooting into the sky. Others sit behind their stalls, selling "Indian" jewelry and blankets and Navajo fry bread. When evening comes and the flow of tourists dwindles, they will pack the contents of their stalls into their cars and go home to their reservations. No one stays the night here; there is nothing to stay for — the attractions of the place are wholly unworldly.

They will be back early next morning: the cars and RVs start ar-riving soon after dawn, their occupants eager to absorb what they can of the magic of the spectacle of two straight lines intersecting.

THE IMAM AND THE INDIAN

1986

I MET THE IMAM of the village and Khamees the Rat at about the same time. I don't exactly remember now — it happened more than six years ago — but I think I met the imam first.

But this is not quite accurate. I didn't really "meet" the imam: I inflicted myself upon him. Perhaps that explains what happened.

Still, there was nothing else I could have done. As the man who led the daily prayers in the mosque, he was a leading figure in the village, and since I, a foreigner, had come to live there, he may well, for all I knew, have been offended had I neglected to pay him a call. Besides, I wanted to meet him; I was intrigued by what I'd heard about him.

People didn't often talk about the imam in the village, but when they did, they usually spoke of him somewhat dismissively, but also a little wistfully, as they might of some old, half-forgotten thing, like the annual flooding of the Nile. Listening to my friends speak of him, I had an inkling, long before I actually met him, that he already belonged, in a way, to the village's past. I thought I knew this for certain when I heard that apart from being an imam, he was also, by profession, a barber and a healer. People said he knew a great deal about herbs and poultices and the old kind of medicine. This interested me. This was Tradition: I knew that in rural Egypt, imams and other religious figures are often by custom associated with those two professions.

The trouble was that these accomplishments bought the imam very little credit in the village. The villagers didn't any longer want an imam who was also a barber and a healer. The older people wanted someone who had studied at Al-Azhar and could quote from Jamal ad-Din Afghani and Mohammad Abduh as fluently as he could from the Hadith, and the younger men wanted a fierce, black-bearded orator, someone whose voice would thunder from the *mimbar* and reveal to them their destiny. No one had time for old-fashioned imams who made themselves ridiculous by boiling herbs and cutting hair.

Yet Ustad Ahmed, who taught in the village's secondary school and was as well read a man as I have ever met, often said — and this was not something he said of many people — that the old imam read a lot. A lot of what? Politics, theology, even popular science . . . that kind of thing.

This made me all the more determined to meet him, and one evening, a few months after I first came to the village, I found my way to his house. He lived in the center of the village, on the edge of the dusty open square that had the mosque in its middle. This was the oldest part of the village, a maze of low mud huts huddled together like confectionery on a tray, each hut crowned with a billowing, tousled head of straw.

When I knocked on the door, the imam opened it himself. He was a big man, with very bright brown eyes set deep in a wrinkled, weather-beaten face. Like the room behind him, he was distinctly untidy: his blue djellaba was mud-stained and unwashed, and his turban had been knotted anyhow around his head. But his beard, short and white and neatly trimmed, was everything a barber's beard should be. Age had been harsh on his face, but there was a certain energy in the way he arched his shoulders, in the clarity of his eyes, and in the way he fidgeted constantly, was never still: it was plain that he was a vigorous, restive kind of person.

"Welcome," he said, courteous but unsmiling, and stood aside and waved me in. It was a long dark room, with sloping walls and a very low ceiling. There was a bed in it and a couple of mats, but little else apart from a few scattered books. Everything bore that dull patina of grime that speaks of years of neglect. Later I learned that the imam had divorced his first wife and his second had left him, so that now he lived quite alone and had his meals with his son's family, who lived across the square.

"Welcome," he said again, formally.

"Welcome to you," I said, giving him the formal response, and then we began on the long, reassuring litany of Arabic phrases of greeting.

"How are you?"

"How are you?"

"You have brought blessings?"

"May God bless you."

"Welcome."

"Welcome to you."

"You have brought light."

"The light is yours."

"How are you?"

"How are you?"

He was very polite, very proper. In a moment he produced a kerosene stove and began to brew tea. But even in the performance of that little ritual there was something about him that was guarded, watchful.

"You're the *doktor al-Hindi*," he said to me at last, "aren't you? The Indian doctor?"

I nodded, for that was the name the village had given me. Then I told him that I wanted to talk to him about the methods of his system of medicine.

He looked very surprised, and for a while he was silent. Then he put his right hand to his heart and began again on the ritual of greetings and responses, but in a markedly different way this time, one that I had learned to recognize as a means of changing the subject.

"Welcome."

"Welcome to you."

"You have brought light."

"The light is yours."

And so on.

At the end of it I repeated what I had said.

"Why do you want to hear about *my* herbs?" he retorted. "Why don't you go back to your country and find out about your own?"

"I will," I said. "Soon. But right now . . ."

"No, no," he said restlessly. "Forget about all that; I'm trying to forget about it myself."

And then I knew that he would never talk to me about his craft, not just because he had taken a dislike to me for some reason of his own, but because his medicines were as discredited in his own eyes as they were in his clients'; because he knew as well as anybody else that the people who came to him now did so only because of old habits; because he bitterly regretted his inherited association with these relics of the past.

"Instead," he said, "let me tell you about what I have been learning over the last few years. Then you can go back to your country and tell them all about it."

He jumped up, his eyes shining, reached under his bed, and brought out a glistening new biscuit tin.

"Here!" he said, opening it. "Look!"

Inside the box was a hypodermic syringe and a couple of glass vials. This is what he had been learning, he told me: the art of mixing and giving injections. And there was a huge market for it too, in the village: everybody wanted injections, for coughs, colds, fevers, whatever. There was a good living in it. He wanted to demonstrate his skill to me right there, on my arm, and when I protested that I wasn't ill, that I didn't need an injection just then, he was offended. "All right," he said curtly, standing up. "I have to go to the mosque right now. Perhaps we can talk about this some other day."

That was the end of my interview. I walked with him to the mosque, and there, with an air of calculated finality, he took my hand in his, gave it a perfunctory shake, and vanished up the stairs.

·   ·   ·

Khamees the Rat I met one morning when I was walking through the rice fields that lay behind the village, watching people transplant their seedlings. Everybody I met was cheerful and busy, and the flooded rice fields were sparkling in the clear sunlight. If I shut my ears to the language, I thought, and stretch the date palms a bit and give them a few coconuts, I could easily be back somewhere in Bengal.

I was a long way from the village and not quite sure of my bearings when I spotted a group of people who had finished their work and were sitting on the path, passing around a hookah.

"*Ahlan!*" a man in a brown djellaba called out to me. "Hullo! Aren't you the Indian *doktor?*"

"Yes," I called back. "And who're you?"

"He's a rat," someone answered, raising a gale of laughter.

"Don't go anywhere near him."

"Tell me, *ya doktor,*" the Rat said, "if I get onto my donkey and ride steadily for thirty days, will I make it to India?"

"No," I said. "You wouldn't make it in thirty months."

"Thirty months!" he said. "You must have come a long way."

"Yes."

"As for me," he declared, "I've never even been as far as Alexandria, and if I can help it I never will."

I laughed; it did not occur to me to believe him.

When I first went to that quiet corner of the Nile Delta, I had expected to find on that most ancient and most settled of soils a settled and restful people. I couldn't have been more wrong.

The men of the village had all the busy restlessness of airline passengers in a transit lounge. Many of them had worked and traveled in the sheikdoms of the Persian Gulf, others had been in Libya and Jordan and Syria, some had been to the Yemen as soldiers, others to Saudi Arabia as pilgrims, a few had visited Europe: some of them had passports so thick they opened out like ink-blackened concertinas. And none of this was new; their grandparents and ancestors and relatives had traveled and migrated too, in much the same way as mine had in the Indian subcontinent—because of wars, or for money and jobs, or perhaps simply because they got tired of living always in one place. You could read the history of this restlessness in the villagers' surnames: they had names that derived from cities in the Levant, from Turkey, from faraway towns in Nubia; it was as though people had drifted here from every corner of the Middle East. The wanderlust of its founders had been plowed into the soil of the village; it seemed to me sometimes that every man in it was a traveler. Everyone, that is, except Khamees the Rat, and even his surname, as I discovered later, meant "of Sudan."

"Well, never mind, *ya doktor,*" Khamees said to me now. "Since you're not going to make it back to your country by sundown anyway, why don't you come and sit with us for a while?" He smiled and moved up to make room for me.

I liked him at once. He was about my age, in the early twenties, scrawny, with a thin, mobile face deeply scorched by the sun. He had that brightness of eye and the quick, slightly sardonic turn to his mouth that I associated with faces in the coffeehouses of universities in Delhi and Calcutta; he seemed to belong to a world of late-night rehearsals and black coffee and lecture rooms, even though, in fact, unlike most people in the village, he was completely illiterate. Later I learned that he was called the Rat — Khamees the Rat — because he was said to gnaw away at things with his tongue, like a rat did with its teeth. He laughed at everything, people said — at his father, the village's patron saint, the village elders, the imam, everything.

That day he decided to laugh at me.

"All right, *ya doktor,*" he said to me as soon as I had seated myself. "Tell me, is it true what they say, that in your country you burn your dead?"

No sooner had he said it than the women of the group clasped their hands to their hearts and muttered in breathless horror, "*Haram! Haram!*"

My heart sank. This was a conversation I usually went through at least once a day, and I was desperately tired of it. "Yes," I said, "it's true; some people in my country burn their dead."

"You mean," said Khamees in mock horror, "that you put them on heaps of wood and just light them up?"

"Yes," I said, hoping that he would tire of this sport if I humored him.

"Why?" he said. "Is there a shortage of kindling in your country?"

"No," I said helplessly, "you don't understand." Somewhere in the limitless riches of the Arabic language a word such as "cremate" must exist, but if it does, I never succeeded in finding it. Instead, for lack of any other, I had to use the word "burn." That was unfortunate, for "burn" was the word for what happened to wood and straw and the eternally damned.

Khamees the Rat turned to his spellbound listeners. "I'll tell you why they do it," he said. "They do it so that their bodies can't be punished after the Day of Judgment."

Everybody burst into wonderstruck laughter. "Why, how clever," cried one of the younger girls. "What a good idea! We ought to start doing it ourselves. That way we can do exactly what we like, and when we die and the Day of Judgment comes, there'll be nothing there to judge."

Khamees had got his laugh. Now he gestured to them to be quiet again.

"All right then, ya doktor," he said. "Tell me something else: is it true that you are a Magian? That in your country everybody worships cows? Is it true that the other day when you were walking through the fields you saw a man beating a cow and you were so upset that you burst into tears and ran back to your room?"

"No, it's not true," I said, but without much hope. I had heard this story before and knew that there was nothing I could say which would effectively give it the lie. "You're wrong. In my country people beat their cows all the time, I promise you."

I could see that no one believed me.

"Everything's upside-down in their country," said a dark, aquiline young woman, who, I was told later, was Khamees's wife.

"Tell us, *ya doktor,* in your country, do you have crops and fields and canals like we do?"

"Yes," I said, "we have crops and fields, but we don't always have canals. In some parts of my country they aren't needed because it rains all the year round."

"*Ya salám,*" she cried, striking her forehead with the heel of her palm. "Do you hear that, o you people? Oh, the Protector, oh, the Lord! It rains all the year round in his country."

She had gone pale with amazement. "So tell us then," she demanded, "do you have night and day like we do?"

"Shut up, woman," said Khamees. "Of course they don't. It's day all the time over there, didn't you know? They arranged it like that so that they wouldn't have to spend any money on lamps."

We all laughed, and then someone pointed to a baby lying in the shade of a tree, swaddled in a sheet of cloth. "That's Khamees's baby," I was told. "He was born last month."

"That's wonderful," I said. "Khamees must be very happy."

Khamees gave a cry of delight. "The Indian knows I'm happy because I've had a son," he said to the others. "He understands that people are happy when they have children. He's not as upside-down as we thought."

He slapped me on the knee and lit up the hookah, and from that moment we were friends.

One evening, perhaps a month or so after I first met Khamees, he and his brothers and I were walking back to the village from the fields when he spotted the old imam sitting on the steps that led to the mosque.

"Listen," he said to me, "you know the old imam, don't you? I saw you talking to him once."

"Yes," I said, "I talked to him once."

"My wife's ill," Khamees said. "I want the imam to come to my house to give her an injection. He won't come if I ask him, he doesn't like me. You go and ask."

"He doesn't like me either," I said.

"Never mind," Khamees insisted. "He'll come if you ask him — he knows you're a foreigner. He'll listen to you."

While Khamees waited on the edge of the square with his brothers, I went across to the imam. I could tell that he had seen me — and Khamees — from a long way off, that he knew I was crossing the square to talk to him. But he would not look in my direction. Instead, he pretended to be deep in conversation with a man who was sitting beside him, an elderly and pious shopkeeper whom I knew slightly.

When I reached them, I said "Good evening" very pointedly to the imam. He could not ignore me any longer then, but his response was short and curt, and he turned back at once to resume his conversation.

The old shopkeeper was embarrassed now, for he was a courteous, gracious man in the way that seemed to come so naturally to the elders of the village. "Please sit down," he said to me. "Do sit. Shall we get you a chair?"

Then he turned to the imam and said, slightly puzzled, "You know the Indian *doktor*, don't you? He's come all the way from India to be a student at the University of Alexandria."

"I know him," said the imam. "He came around to ask me questions. But as for this student business, I don't know. What's he going to study? He doesn't even write in Arabic."

"Well," said the shopkeeper judiciously, "that's true, but after all, he writes his own languages and he knows English."

"Oh, those," said the imam. "What's the use of *those* languages? They're the easiest languages in the world. Anyone can write those."

He turned to face me for the first time. His eyes were very bright, and his mouth was twitching with anger. "Tell me," he said, "why do you worship cows?"

I was so taken aback that I began to stammer. The imam ignored me. He turned to the old shopkeeper and said, "That's what they do in his country — did you know? They worship cows."

He shot me a glance from the corner of his eyes. "And shall I tell you what else they do?" he said to the shopkeeper.

He let the question hang for a moment. And then, very loudly, he hissed, "They burn their dead."

The shopkeeper recoiled as though he had been slapped. His hands flew to his mouth. "Oh God!" he muttered. *"Ya Allah."*

"That's what they do," said the imam. "They burn their dead."

Then suddenly he turned to me and said, very rapidly, "Why do you allow it? Can't you see that it's a primitive and backward custom? Are you savages that you permit something like that? Look at you — you've had some kind of education; you should know better. How will your country ever progress if you carry on doing these things? You've even been to the West; you've seen how advanced they are. Now tell me, have you ever seen them burning their dead?"

The imam was shouting now, and a circle of young men and boys had gathered around us. Under the pressure of their interested eyes my tongue began to trip, even on syllables I thought I had mastered. I found myself growing angry — as much with my own incompetence as with the imam.

"Yes, they do burn their dead in the West," I managed to say somehow. I raised my voice too now. "They have special electric furnaces meant just for that."

The imam could see that he had stung me. He turned away and laughed. "He's lying," he said to the crowd. "They don't burn their dead in the West. They're not an ignorant people. They're advanced, they're educated, they have science, they have guns and tanks and bombs."

"We have them too!" I shouted back at him. I was as confused now as I was angry. "In my country we have all those things too," I said to the crowd. "We have guns and tanks and bombs. And they're better than anything you have — we're way ahead of you."

The imam could no longer disguise his anger. "I tell you, he's lying," he said. "Our guns and bombs are much better than theirs. Ours are second only to the West's."

"It's you who's lying," I said. "You know nothing about this. Ours are much better. Why, in my country we've even had a nuclear explosion. You won't be able to match that in a hundred years."

So there we were, the imam and I, delegates from two superseded civilizations vying with each other to lay claim to the violence of the West.

At that moment, despite the vast gap that lay between us, we understood each other perfectly. We were both traveling, he and I: we were traveling in the West. The only difference was that I had actually been there, in person: I could have told him about the ancient English university I had won a scholarship to, about punk dons with safety pins in their mortarboards, about superhighways and sex shops and Picasso. But none of it would have mattered. We would have known, both of us, that all that was mere fluff: at the bottom, for him as for me and millions and millions of people on the landmasses around us, the West meant only this — science and tanks and guns and bombs.

And we recognized too the inescapability of these things, their strength, their power — evident in nothing so much as this: that even for him, a man of God, and for me, a student of the "humane" sciences, they had usurped the place of all other languages of argument. He knew, just as I did, that he could no longer say to me, as Ibn Battuta might have when he traveled to India in the fourteenth century, "You should do this or that because it is right or good, or because God wills it so." He could not have said it because that language is dead: those things are no longer sayable; they sound absurd. Instead he had had, of necessity, to use that other language, so universal that it extended equally to him, an old-fashioned village imam, and to great leaders at SALT conferences. He had had to say to me, "You ought not to do this because otherwise you will not have guns and tanks and bombs."

Since he was a man of God, his was the greater defeat.

For a moment then I was desperately envious. The imam would not have said any of those things to me had I been a Westerner. He would not have dared. Whether I wanted it or not, I would have had around me the protective aura of an inherited expertise in the technology of violence. That aura would have surrounded me, I thought, with a sheet of clear glass, like a bulletproof screen; or perhaps it would have worked as a talisman, like a press card, armed with which I could have gone off to what were said to be the most terrible places in the world that month, to gaze and wonder. And then perhaps I too would one day have had enough material for a book which would have had for its epigraph the line *The horror! The horror!*—for the virtue of a sheet of glass is that it does not require one to look within.

But that still leaves Khamees the Rat waiting on the edge of the square.

In the end it was he and his brothers who led me away from the imam. They took me home with them, and there, while Khamees's wife cooked dinner for us—she was not so ill after all—Khamees said to me, "Do not be upset, *ya doktor.* Forget about all those guns and things. I'll tell you what: *I'll* come to visit you in your country, even though I've never been anywhere. I'll come all the way."

He slipped a finger under his skullcap and scratched his head, thinking hard.

Then he added, "But if I die, you must bury me."

NOTES

THE GREATEST SORROW

36 *Nessun maggior dolore:* Dante Alighieri, *The Inferno,* trans R. & J. Hollander (New York: Doubleday, 2000), Canto V, lines 121–23.

38 The last Sinhala word: Michael Ondaatje, "Wells," in *Handwriting* (New York: Knopf, 1999), p. 50.

39 I will die, in autumn: Agha Shahid Ali, "The Last Saffron," in *The Country Without a Post Office* (New York: Norton, 1997), pp. 27–29.

43 We know: The lines of Dante's from which the title of this essay is taken are thought to be based on a passage from Boethius's *The Consolation of Philosophy:* "Among fortune's many adversities the most unhappy kind is once to have been happy" (Dante, *The Inferno,* p. 99).
At a certain point: Agha Shahid Ali, "Farewell," in *The Country Without a Post Office,* pp. 22–23.

46 At the heart of the book: I have described this event in detail in my book *In an Antique Land* (New York: Vintage, 1994), pp. 204–10.

48 Ranajit Guha: Ranajit Guha, *History at the Limit of World History* (New York: Columbia University Press, 2002), lecture III.

49 It is for this reason: It is not without interest that the corresponding administrative term — handed down from the Raj — is "civil disturbance."
"Everything is finished": "The Country Without a Post Office," in *The Country Without a Post Office,* pp. 49–50.
"For his first forty days": Ondaatje, "The Story," in *Handwriting.*

55 "With all the swerves": Ibid.

"THE GHAT OF THE ONLY WORLD"

61 At a certain point: Agha Shahid Ali, "Farewell," in *The Country Without a Post Office* (New York: Norton, 1997), pp. 22–23.

63 "Imagine me at a writer's conference": *Ravishing Disunities: Real Ghazals*

in English, ed. Agha Shahid Ali (Middletown, Conn.: Wesleyan University Press, 2000), pp. 1, 3, 13.

66   "A night of ghazals": Agha Shahid Ali, "I Dream I Am at the Ghat of the Only World," in *Rooms Are Never Finished* (New York: Norton, 2001), p. 97. It was Shahid's mother: Ibid., p. 99.

"I am not born": Agha Shahid Ali, "A Lost Memory of Delhi," in *The Half-Inch Himalayas* (Middletown, Conn.: Wesleyan University Press, 1987), p. 5. I would like to thank Daniel Hall for bringing this poem to my attention.

69   "I always move": "I Dream I Am at the Ghat," p. 101.

"It was '89": "Summers of Translation," in *Rooms Are Never Finished,* p. 30.

71   "and I, one festival": "Lenox Hill," in *Rooms Are Never Finished,* p. 17.

"Nothing will remain": "The Country Without a Post Office," in *The Country Without a Post Office,* p. 50.

"I will die, in autumn": "The Last Saffron," in *The Country Without a Post Office,* p. 27.

73   "Yes, I remember it": Ibid., p. 29.

74   "Mother, they asked me": "Lenox Hill," in *Rooms Are Never Finished,* pp. 18, 19.

COUNTDOWN

77   In the course of writing this piece I talked to many hundreds of people in India, Pakistan, and Nepal. The impossibility of severally listing these debts serves only to deepen my gratitude to those who took the time to meet me. The book would be incomplete, however, if I were not to acknowledge my gratitude to the following: Smt. Krishna Bose, M.P., Madiha Gauhur, Shahid Nadeem, Najam Sethi, Dr. Dursameem Ahmed, Eman Ahmed, Dr. Zia Miyan, Dr. M. V. Ramanna, Kunda Dixit, Kanak Dixit, Pritam and Meena Mansukhani, Radhika and Hari Sen, and my infinitely forbearing publisher, Ravi Dayal. Dr. Sunil Mukhi, Dr. Sumit Ranjan Das, Dr. Sourendu Gupta, and other scientists at the Tata Institute of Fundamental Research in Bombay were generous in giving of their time to discuss various aspects of the nuclear issue, from many different points of view: I owe them many thanks. I would also like to acknowledge the support of the *Ananda Bazaar Patrika, Himal,* and *The New Yorker.* I am particularly indebted to Nandi Rodrigo, who did an astonishingly thorough job of fact-checking my *New Yorker* piece, and to Bill Buford, who saw it to press. Madhumita Mazumdar contributed greatly to the background research and provided invaluable logistical support: I am deeply grateful to her.

"Countdown" owes its greatest debt to my wife, Deborah Baker. But for her urging, I would never have committed myself to the many months of labor that went into the writing of this piece; nor would I be in a position to publish it today, in this form, if it were not for her editing. I owe her many, many thanks.

THE MARCH OF THE NOVEL THROUGH HISTORY

106   "It has to be pointed out": Nirad Chaudhuri, *Thy Hand, Great Anarch!* (New York: Addison-Wesley, 1987), p. 155.

108   "To be up to date": Ibid., p. 156.

111   These stories left their mark: C. E. Dimock, in *The Literature of India, an Introduction,* ed. C. E. Dimock et al. (Chicago: University of Chicago Press, 1974).

114   "Those who are familiar": Bankim Chandra Chatterjee, *Essays and Letters,* in *Bankim Racha-navali* (Calcutta: Sahitya Samsad, n.d.).

115   "Notwithstanding all that has been written": Ibid., pp. 192–93.
      "obtain some knowledge": Ibid.

117   "The house of Mathur Ghose": *Rajmohun's Wife,* in *Bankim Rachanavali,* ed. Jogesh Chandra Bagal (Calcutta: Sahitya Samsad, n.d.), pp. 52–53.
      "Madhav therefore immediately hurried": Ibid., p. 17.

THE FUNDAMENTALIST CHALLENGE

126   "As far as the Vietnamese": This quotation is from an anonymously authored UNTAC document entitled "Interview with Khat Sali, Sihanoukville (9–10/1/1992)."

129   "at present several dozen people": Amnesty International, "Pakistan: Use and Abuse of Blasphemy Laws," July 24, 1994.
      "In a number of cases": Ibid.

132   "In a refugee camp": Internet report, n.d.

THE GHOSTS OF MRS. GANDHI

192   "began with the arrival": People's Union for Democratic Rights and People's Union for Civil Liberties, "Who Are the Guilty?: Report of a Joint Inquiry into the Causes and Impact of the Riots in Delhi from 31 October to 10 November 1984," New Delhi, 1984, p. 2.
      "Some people, the neighbors": Veena Das, "Our Work to Cry, Your Work

to Listen," in *Mirrors of Violence: Communities, Riots and Survivors in South-East Asia*, ed. Veena Das (Delhi: Oxford University Press, 1990).

200   "The decision to perceive": Dzevad Karahasan, "Literature and War," In *Sarajevo, Exodus of a City* (New York: Kodansha, 1994).

DANCING IN CAMBODIA

225   The account of the royal dance troupe's visit to France with King Sisowath is based on reports in *Le Petit Provençal, Le Petit Marseillais,* and *Le Figaro;* on the *Rapport-Général, Exposition Coloniale National de Marseille, 15 Avril–18 Novembre 1906* (1907), and its accompanying volume, *La Chambre de Commerce de Marseille et l'Exposition Coloniale de 1906* (1908), published by the Chamber of Commerce, Marseille; and on the following letters and documents in the Archives d'Outre-Mer at Aix-en-Provence: Résident-Supérieur in Phnom Penh to Hanoi, May 30, 1905 (re. princes' scholarships to study in France) (GGI 2576); Governor-General to the Minister of Colonies in Paris, April 5, 1906 (GGI 5822); report, F. Gautret, July 1906 (GGI 6643); Minister of Colonies to F. Gautret, Paris, July 18, 1906 (GGI 6643); *Fête du 5 Juillet, 1906, en l'honneur de SM le Roi du Cambodge* . . . (Ministry of Colonies, 1906); F. Gautret, to the Governor-General, Hanoi, August 20, 1906, Saigon (GGI 6643); itinerary, *Sejour de Sa Majesté Sisowath, Roi du Cambodge en France* (GGI 6643); Résident-Supérieur to Governor-General, January 18, 1907, containing a French translation of the royal proclamation on the king's voyage, issued under the signatures of King Sisowath and five ministers (GGI 5822); Minister Thiounn to Résident-Supérieur, July 9, 1907 (GGI 2576); correspondence between the Cour des Comptes, Paris, Saigon, and Phnom Penh on expenses of the royal entourage (1901–11), including Minister Thiounn's response (August 13, 1910) (GGI 15606). The quotations in section 8 are from *Rodin et l'Extrême Orient* (Musée Rodin, Paris, 1979), and from Frederic V. Grunefeld's *Rodin; A Biography* (New York: Holt, 1987). Biographical and other details on Cambodian politics and history are mainly from Milton E. Osborne's *The French Presence in Cochinchina and Cambodia: Rule and Response (1859–1950)* (Ithaca, N.Y.: Cornell University Press, 1969); David Chandler's *Brother Number One; A Political Biography of Pol Pot* (Westview, Conn.: Oxford University Press, 1992); Ben Kiernan's *How Pol Pot Came to Power: A History of Communism in Kampuchea, 1930–1975* (London: Verso, 1985), and Elizabeth Becker's *When the War Was Over: The Voices of Cambodia's Revolution and Its People* (New York: Simon & Schuster, 1986).

The author gratefully acknowledges the help of the staff of the

Archives d'Outre-Mer in Aix-en-Provence and of the following individuals: Christian Oppetit, conservator of the archives of the Département des Bouches-du-Rhône; Annie Terrier, Christianne Besse, Eva Mysliwiec, Chanthou Boua, Tan Sotho, Choup Sros, Kim Rath, Bill Lobban, Mr. T. P. Seetharam, Col. Suresh Nair, and Mrs. Pushpa Nair.